THREE CELL FLASHLIGHT

A LIFE OF SERVICE IN THE RCMP

AR Jay, Retired RCMP

◆ FriesenPress

One Printers Way
Altona, MB R0G 0B0
Canada

www.friesenpress.com

Copyright © 2023 by AR Jay
First Edition — 2023

All rights reserved.

No part of this publication may be reproduced in any form, or by any means, electronic or mechanical, including photocopying, recording, or any information browsing, storage, or retrieval system, without permission in writing from FriesenPress.

ISBN
978-1-03-916062-0 (Hardcover)
978-1-03-916061-3 (Paperback)
978-1-03-916063-7 (eBook)

Biography & Autobiography, Personal Memoirs

Distributed to the trade by The Ingram Book Company

TABLE OF CONTENTS

REGINA	1
GLACE BAY	22
INVERNESS	42
BADDECK	73
SYDNEY	113
SHELBURN	149
NEW GLASGOW	210
NEW GLASGOW TO HALIFAX	224

REGINA

TO R.C.M.P. DEPOT DIVISION

Hank found himself standing alone on the bow of the upper deck of the ice breaking car ferry, M.V. Abegweit on a bitterly cold and windy February morning with the knowledge that he had left behind everyone and everything he held near and dear. The whole ship shuddered and the black smoke poured out of the stack behind him as 'she' rode up on the solid pack of ice that stretched ahead as far as the eye could see towards the New Brunswick shore. He could hear the rumble of her powerful engines, but due to the heavy ice that morning, she was only moving at a snail's pace. As he glanced over the side of the bow, he could see as 'she' broke through, big, thick clampers of ice standing up on end, then squirting out from beneath the bow onto the surface of the pack, and go skittering along on a thin layer of water as though they were running from some intruding monster.

All morning his thoughts had been reflecting on his decision to go and the fact that he was leaving 'The Island' for good, to travel two thirds distance across this vast country to report to the recruit training Depot for the R.C.M.P. in Regina, Saskatchewan. Earlier that morning, his father and older sister had dropped him off at the train station in Charlottetown, a familiar place, as his Dad worked on the railroad. Once on the train, he travelled about an hour to the ferry terminal in Borden where the passenger train car in which he had been riding was shunted into the hold of the ferry from which all passengers disembarked and climbed the stairs to the lounge on the upper deck. The next two and a half hours were spent crossing the nine and a half mile wide Northumberland Strait that separated the island from the mainland. The same trip took only 45 minutes in summer.

Three Cell Flashlight

On arrival at the terminal in Cape Tormentine, New Brunswick, Hank returned with others to the passenger car in the hold of the ship. The car was shunted onto the mainland, hooked onto another train, which travelled another two hours to the railway junction in Moncton, New Brunswick. There, after a half hour wait, Hank boarded the train from Halifax headed for Montreal and beyond. This train had a sleeper car where he would spend the next four nights, enroute to Regina. It also had a dining car where he could satisfy his teenage appetite three times a day, be served by waiters, and eat with fine china and cutlery, even linen napkins. Some of this was familiar to him because for one week the previous month, he had used his father's railroad pass to make a one-week trip to Boston to visit his uncle Charlie's family. There, his two older male cousins toured him around the city and even took him to a Bruins hockey game in the old Boston Gardens. He also watched his very first show on a small black and white T.V. at his uncle's place.

Shortly after leaving Moncton on the train headed for Montreal, he met and became acquainted with three young men from Nova Scotia who were headed for the Air Force training camp in St. Jean, P.Q. This rang a bell with Hank because he had planned on applying for the Air Force if he had not been accepted by the R.C.M.P. He never mentioned that to them. They each talked about leaving home for the first time and their similar undertakings, but all agreed that their adventures paled in comparison to the destinations of their older brothers, fathers and uncles a little over a decade ago on the battle fields of Western Europe and elsewhere around the world. Some of them never returned and some of those that did were scarred for the rest of their lives.

Hank was born in a farmhouse in the small rural community of Brookville, the first son to Wilma and Andrew Jamison. He lived there until the age of six when his family moved into the nearby village of Spring Valley. He started school there and, as was the case at all other rural schools at the time, he could only go as far as Grade Ten. To take Grades Eleven and Twelve, his parents found two or three boarding houses in the city over the two years, so he could go to college and come home on weekends. When he got old enough he worked at seasonal jobs on vacation to make spending money, and when he got big enough, he worked on farms and highways as a labourer. There were no organized sports for young people in the village at that time, so the choices were do nothing or go to work. The latter was more logical if the goal was to make a living, which was much more popular with his parents who could use the financial help.

Hank had enquired about joining the R.C.M.P. before his eighteenth birthday at the large converted residence, which was then the P.E. I. Headquarters on Upper Prince Street in Charlottetown. He received the papers and applied shortly afterwards. At the time, young men between the ages of eighteen and twenty-five, five feet eight inches or taller, with Grade 10 education, able to pass a written and medical exam, were being accepted. Hank stood six feet tall, had his Grade Twelve certificate and readily passed both exams. He also had his Driver's License. Late the next January at the Douglas warehouse, Hank and his friend Willard had been loading 100-pound bags of seed potatoes into a boxcar destined for an ocean-going freighter, dockside at Souris, headed for Greece. The phone call came in that he was accepted by the R.C.M.P. and to report to Headquarters in Charlottetown the following morning to be sworn in. The day before, the ship's agent reported that two crewmembers of the freighter had jumped ship, and he was looking for replacements. He approached Willard and Hank who were tempted with the adventure, but when they checked with their parents, both vetoed the idea. Hank reported to the R.C.M.P. the following morning as instructed, and was sworn in by the Inspector in charge of staffing who, after the official ceremony with a Corporal as witness, he went to another room and returned with a 'forage cap' and put it on Hank's head to see how he'd look in uniform. Hank's head was larger than the cap so the others present had a chuckle as Hank was directed towards a mirror. The Inspector then handed Hank his train ticket to Regina, shook his hand, wished him well and Hank departed.

AT REGINA

Hank's troop mates were from Newfoundland to British Columbia and from all walks of life such as cooks, ranchers, linesmen, miners, fishermen, farmers, lumberjacks, Navy, postmen, labourers, students, pulp mill workers and truck drivers. Ahead of them were classes in P.T., Drill, Equitation, Swimming, Boxing, Driver Training, Identification, Typing and more. In the spring there was also a one- week survival course living in tents and fending for themselves in the Qu'appele Valley north of Regina. Most Sundays there was Church Parade to the Chapel at Depot, or one could go to the church of his choice in the city, if he had wheels. If the Troop was confined to barracks for some indiscretion or misdemeanour, they could not leave the base. At other times, those who wished and had wheels or taxi fare could request an evening pass to the city on weekends, but had to be signed in at the Guard House by 10:30 P.M. the same night. Near the end of training, the Troop boasted four private cars and one motorcycle; Hank didn't have any of them. But, if on weekends, the destination by private car was the Drake Hotel, Hank was usually invited to be a 'designated driver', even though the term had yet to be coined, because he didn't drink alcohol. Hank not only had to drive but had to enforce the 10:30 P.M. curfew and sometimes help to prop up one of the passengers who had a few too many ginger ales, while he signed in at the Guard House. During the week, in the evening after payday, a troop mate might phone in an order of burgers and milk shakes, to the Dutch Mill in the city. This would be delivered by cab to F Block, paid for with collected cash, hopefully enough to pay the bill and a tip for the driver. That seemed like a 'must' to accommodate the teenage-young adult appetites.

F Block consisted of three separate similar wings joined at the entry end by a common lavatory area with showers, toilets and urinals for up to ninety-six men when all wings were occupied. Speakers in the ceiling announced reveille at six A.M. each day, and the common area could best be described as mayhem as everyone scrambled to be ready for breakfast and the first assignment of the day. The mess hall was more than a city block from F block, which was a challenge on a cold, windy morning on the prairie. Hank soon learned he had to move his butt and walk fast if not run to all facilities on the base, but when he had all his kit, including jack boots, breeches, fur hat and Pea Jacket, he was prepared for the weather. He also learned to keep his feet at the side of his chair when he was wearing spurs, because if he got up in a hurry from the table and a spur caught in the front chair rung and tipped it over, everyone in the mess hall would applaud and some would even stand up. Talk about embarrassing!

The Troop remained in F Block for two months when E Block, a separate barrack block, closer to all facilities, became available, and through the astute negotiating by their Troop Leader Jim White, they acquired it. That was short-lived because two months later they moved again to D Block, the dorm above the Saddler and tailor's shops where a lot of fond memories were made by Hank and his mates who by now were becoming one big family of brothers. It was the last block they lived in until 'pass-out'. Because D Block was on the second floor, it had a fire escape made of one big round metal tube situated at the far end right next to Hank's bunk. On a hot, rainy weekend afternoon in the summer when they were confined to barracks, Hank and others donned their bathing suits, threw a bucket of water down the fire escape, jumped into the tube and slid down into the puddle waiting on the ground. Then run around the building and up the front stairs to try once again. Imagine the surprise of Mrs. Jones, the Sgt. Major's wife when these scantily clad young men came popping out of this big pipe and running around the building to the stairs. And imagine the surprise of Hank and his mates when Sgt. Major Jones confined them to barracks again for one week for their efforts. The Troop had at least two guitar players, a harmonica player and some fairly good singers, so in the evenings, the confinement was used as an opportunity to improve their musical talents and around that time adopted the 'Whiffenpoof' song as their Troop Anthem. The Troop had started out with the standard thirty-two men, and by this time had been whittled down to twenty-seven. Even though they were smaller in number, they were not all bosom pals. Hank was a red head with a temper and francophone mate Bordeleau from Quebec took pleasure from time to time teasing him about his red hair and the 'little Island' that he came from.

Hank would shout back,

"Shut up you frog, shut your f'n mouth".

One evening Hank had enough, walked the full length of the dorm, hauled him off his bunk, down onto the floor into his pit and before Hank could punch him in the mouth, Hank's mate and good friend Gary grabbed his right arm and with help from others, pulled Hank off. That was the end of the Bordeleau chatter. To everyone's credit, the Sgt. Major never heard about the 'scuffle'.

Each night a new schedule was posted on the wall outside the barrack room door. On one of his first days at Depot Hank and mates came from a foot drill class to a P.T., class and had to peel off all their winter clothing and change into shorts, T shirt and sneakers. Hank was late for gym class and the instructor, who never won a Mr. Congeniality contest, made Hank climb to the top of one of the four ropes suspended from the ceiling three times, and touch the ceiling each time, as punishment. He was never late for gym class again. Months later that same instructor had four pairs of boxing gloves for Hank and his troop mates to wear, stand in a circle, put the gloves on when ordered, and square off against a designated mate across the circle. Hank faced Bob Davidson and the two met in the centre of the circle, exchanged a few casual blows. That wasn't good enough for the instructor so at his bidding, the two mates increased their energy level. Earlier, all members of the troop had taken boxing lessons in a ring in the basement of the gym under the guidance of Sgt. Coughlin where occasionally Hank had been paired against Woody, a Gold Glove champion from Saskatchewan.

After a late Boxing class one afternoon during a couple of rounds in the ring against Woody, Hank's lips had been so badly swollen (no mouth guards) that he could only eat soup and crackers for supper. In the end he got so he could block and counterpunch with some authority. Hank was a bit taller than Bob and had a longer reach. They sparred for a minute, then Bob threw a haymaker which Hank blocked and countered with a right cross that caught Bob 'right on the beak'. Bob staggered back and collapsed flat on his back on the gym floor, out cold. Hank felt terrible, but a splash of cold water on Bob's face woke him up and he was none the worse for the wear. Some of the mates later teased Hank saying,

"Hey Rocky what's new, Boy I don't wanna mess with you."

SWIMMING

For Hank and most other troop mates, swimming classes were a major challenge. For one reason, Depot boasted an Olympic size pool with an eight-foot deep end, complete with lanes on floor and ceiling and a twelve foot diving tower. At age fifteen Hank acquired a Beginners License from a two week swimming course on the north shore of P.E.I., but that didn't (pardon the pun) hold much water with the Depot swimming instructors. Another obstacle for Hank was that he had no natural buoyancy. He couldn't float face-down or on his back without swimming. Also, he frequently became nauseated from the heavy dose of chlorine in the pool, presumably to combat those who didn't shower completely before entering. It was February and the drill for swimming was change out of your full uniform in the locker area between the gym and the pool, get into your bathing suit, pass through the showers, into the hallway enroute to the pool. There the condensation from the pool caused frost to accumulate on the single pane windows in the back doors, wait there and shiver, without a towel, for the previous troop to vacate the pool. Then step into a cold foot disinfectant in a concrete box before entering the pool. There was no thermometer in that hallway, but some days Hank estimated the temperature wasn't much above 40 F. Nobody complained because this was deemed to be all part of the conditioning process to 'make you a man' not 'a wimp'. In most boot camps that worked.

There were usually two instructors in the pool area, one named Clare who was tall and slim and could swim like a fish. At times he could be tough, but other times he showed compassion and was usually at the pool in the evenings when families of members came to swim, and was also there when Hank was ordered to take extra swimming practice. He was the one who taught Hank to relax, swim on his back and follow the lines on the ceiling. Hank has never forgotten him. Like all instructors in Depot, Clare was a regular member of the Force, but for reasons unknown to most recruits, had been transferred to Depot from the field. Maybe it was because of his prowess as a swimmer. The other swimming instructor was Butch, an overweight bully who revelled in verbally browbeating recruits and meting out various kinds of punishment such as extra laps around the pool and the ever-present push-ups. All recruits early on were ordered to jump off the ten foot high diving tower, head first or feet first, it didn't matter. Ben, one of the smaller troop mates was terrified of heights and could not jump. In several successive classes, Butch ordered him up onto the diving tower to jump, even threatened to throw him off, but thought better of it. Ben would stand there shaking but never did jump off that tower. Hank and the rest of his mates did jump, eventually. Near the end of swimming classes, each recruit had to pass several tests to win the Award of Merit and Bronze Star. The final test was to jump into the deep end of the pool fully clothed in 'fatigues' (work uniform), minus boots, and rescues a drowning victim. Butch usually volunteered to be the victim.

When the rescuer approached him, he took great pleasure in grabbing him, shoving him under water and holding him there for a few terrifying seconds, then relents, roll over and allow him to be towed to the side of the pool. Eventually, Hank and his mates passed their tests and lined up like tin soldiers in bathing suits only, on one side of the pool to receive their awards from their instructors.

EQUITATION

The first week in training, 'P' Troop was introduced to the stables and their Ride Master "Hollerin Harry" Armstrong (because of his loud voice and his desire to use it frequently). As Hank and his mates found out later, Harry's bark was 'bigger than his bite', but in those early days, he took great pleasure in setting the horses up on a pedestal so as to blast any trace of ego out of his recruits. He also liked to mispronounce their surnames to add a bit more salt to the wound. His dos and don'ts are too many for Hank to recall, but the most important one was "Don't ever hit a horse with anything" or the punishment would be "back-squadded", (removed from his troop to a junior troop behind) or worse". One horse was assigned to each recruit depending on Harry's assessment of his or her experience with horses. Some mates had never been close to a horse, so Harry assigned a quieter animal to them and, as all mates soon found out, the horses knew more than even the 'experienced' riders because they did the same drill every day, except Sunday. There were approximately eighty horses, forty on each side, of the large stable with a riding arena in the center. The horses were mostly home breeds from the Force farm at Fort Walsh, all colors, sizes and shapes for recruit training only. The best had been set-aside for the Musical Ride and were stabled in Ottawa. By the end of the first three months Hank had ridden a dozen or more different horses, because he didn't mind the change, and was born on a farm where horses were the main source of power. There were no tractors yet. Hank had learned to ride bareback before he was six. But he had never seen a saddle up close before Depot, an English saddle to be exact. No horn to grab onto likes the western model, in a case of horse and rider suddenly separating. This, and the regimental style required to be in the Musical Ride, was a source of constant turmoil between Hank and Harry. "Four feet from nose to croup" was the frequent command to all Harry's riding students as they trotted in circles around the arena. "Leg on there!", was another favourite command. The rider's hands also were to be held waist high in front of the saddle, six inches apart, each hand holding one rein at first, two reins later as the riders improved.

As a diversion, during winter, on a clear cold day, the troop would leave the shelter of the arena and ride out to the west on what Hank and his mates referred to as "the back forty". All for this occasion wore heavy buffalo coats, and the riders could enjoy the warmth of the animal beneath them.

The pace would be mostly a brisk walk except at one point Harry would allow a slow trot, but no galloping as each rider was to try to keep an orderly formation of sections with four horses abreast and eight rows deep. This was a real challenge with inexperienced riders, but an exercise toward the ultimate goal "the Musical Ride". When spring came there would be opportunities to 'take the show on the road' so to speak, in other words dress in red serge and ride down into the city and back when Harry believed the troop was ready for it. On Saturday mornings as another diversion, the troop was instructed to come in 'fatigues' and ankle boots for a bareback ride in the arena. After an orderly couple of laps, all riders stripped to the waist and on Harry's command, the game began with the object being that they would 'Indian wrestle' each other from their horse. Once on the ground, the 'looser' was to take his horse to one side of the arena and become an observer or cheerleader until the final two combatants wrestled one or the other from their horse and a winner was declared. Hank was frequently one of the last survivors but could never unseat his mate Woodie, a ranch kid who grew up in the saddle. What a wonderful fun way to end the week with rarely anyone hurt, just their pride, none seriously, and lots of laughs to go with it.

Each day in training consisted of mostly six one-hour classes, three in the morning and three in the afternoon. In addition some members, in teams of four might be assigned as Duty Troop, either at the Guard House, the stables, the Fire Hall or other locations throughout Depot. Occasionally in summer, one member might be assigned to be 'Orderly' at the museum during the day to host visitors. Hank enjoyed that assignment the most. Equitation, (working with, grooming, riding horses, and cleaning tack) usually lasted longer than one hour, sometimes three hours if the Training Officer so designated. Equitation was scheduled at least once a week during the 'first part' of training. Hank was born and raised on a farm where the only power was horses, became attached to them and to ride bareback at a young age. He had looked forward to learning to ride in a saddle on a 'Mountie' horse. In winter, most riding was done inside the arena in the centre of the stable complex. Before arriving in Depot, some troop mates had never even stood beside a horse let alone touch them. For this some of them were assigned to the quietest and best mannered horses in the stable.

Due to his familiarity with horses, Hank rode many different horses in the early days of training, until the ride instructor, "Hollerin Harry" decided Hank should stick with a nice little filly named Josie. Horses had been named alphabetically according to the year they were born, everything from Aaron to Wagg. They were not the uniform perfectly matched horses that you see in the Musical Ride, but a mixture of sizes and colours that were kept only for recruits to ride. Hank didn't enjoy the strict regimental way they were taught to ride, four feet between horses in single file, unless they were ordered into two or four-horse sections to practice training manoeuvres like the Musical Ride. This took timing and skill and a sense of satisfaction if done right. If not, do it over again, and again if necessary to get it right, not unlike other classes in the entire training syllabus. Most of the horses knew exactly what was required of them and the truth was they knew more than most 'green' riders. When Harry deemed Hank's Troop fit, he'd take them for a ride out onto the prairie and once for a ride into the city, even if it was -20 F and windy. But they were all dressed for it in buffalo coats and the horses were warm beneath them.

Later in ride training some Saturday mornings in the spring, Harry would tell Hank's Troop to come in 'fatigues' (work uniform), be prepared to ride bareback and strip down to the waist to participate in an" Indian Wrestle". In other words, try to knock other mates off their horse by whatever means. Once off, they were told to run to the side of the arena and stay clear. Josie was responsive and just loved this exercise and freedom to put her ears back and run at, or just compete against other horses. Hank early on tried facing another rider and physically grapple and try to pull him off his horse, but didn't have the upper body strength to do it. He decided a better way might be to ride up behind another rider closely and fast, stick his knee out and brush the other rider off. It worked, most times. Hank was frequently among the last two riders still mounted. Woody, who had been raised on a western ranch, was another survivor. Although Hank and his mates were reluctant to admit it, most horses in the stable knew more about the drills they were doing than the riders because they did it every day. Near the end of the ride, Hank was ordered to be a tour guide in the balcony above the arena for another Troop's 'ride passout' (Graduation), which consisted of all Musical Ride moves, except the 'Charge' at the end. He had learned that rule was because the charge involved the lowering of lances and horses at high speed, and the Inspectors didn't want any recruits speared or horses injured. Half way through the Troop Passout, a little horse named Joker threw his rider who gathered himself up off the dirt floor, ran to a side wall and watched while Joker completed the entire Passout with the reins hanging around his neck. Joker never made a mistake. Hank's Troop had its ride passout two weeks later and it went off without a hitch.

In those days, the broodmare operation was at a ranch near Fort Walsh, Alberta. Every few months, some two-year-old 'remounts' were shipped into Depot to be 'broken' to ride. Hank was one of the P Troop members chosen to help. For this exercise, the remount was harnessed with a saddle and a halter and a heavy rope lead- shank that was lashed close to the horn on the saddle of Walsh, or another big, experienced horse to ride. The remount and others were literally dragged around the arena, by bigger horses and riders until they were so tired, they would submit. Hank thought this exercise, and another practice of hanging an old pair of coveralls on the saddle of a remount and let it drag on the ground around the horse's feet, to be cruel. But it was the order of the day, and Hank kept his opinion to himself. Years later, Hank learned from friends 'on the ride' that these practices had been terminated, and within eight years of P troop's passout, equitation was removed from the recruit training syllabus altogether.

As with all operations involving animals, somebody has to feed and clean up after them. Depot was no exception. So every morning, some troop in Depot had to go to stables at six A.M., before breakfast, to clean the horses and the stables. Hank's Troop was no exception. Hank didn't mind this and enjoyed working around most of the eighty some horses. Mind you, the code from day one in the stable was "never strike or kick a horse or you'll be dismissed instantly". All contact with horses was designed to place them on a pedestal to erode any 'big feelings the recruit might have about himself'. The

Three Cell Flashlight

manure had to be shovelled into wheelbarrows, wheeled outside and up a ramp onto the one-ton flatbed 'stable' truck with sideboards.

On weekdays, this truck would be driven by hired hands out to a field and the manure spread on the ground. On weekends Hank and three troop mates might be assigned the job of 'stable orderly' which included near the end of their shift, driving the manure truck out to the pasture and unloading it. Not all mates had a driver's license, but Hank did, so he sometimes drove. One winter afternoon the running board on the truck was encrusted with ice. Hank got in all right, but when he stopped in the field, stepped out and tried to swing up onto the back, he slipped. He grabbed for the doorframe inside the cab and his cheap college ring on his left ring finger hooked on the metal above the door and for an instant Hank was left dangling by one arm. But the ring broke at the weld and Hank fell to the ground, picked himself up, checked his finger which bled a little, took the ring off and put it in his pocket, climbed up onto the back of the truck and never wore the ring again. Each section of the stable contained up to twenty horses in standing stalls tethered by their halter to the manger in front of them facing the outside wall and their rear over a shallow gutter along the shed row to collect the manure. To prevent being bored, Hank and his mates as 'stable orderlies' used to stand with shovel 'at the ready' and when they saw a horse raising its tail, they would run and catch the deposit before it hit the floor and yell "home run!"

One Sunday afternoon at the stable, when there was no one else around, Hank and his three mates dared each other to take the pride of the Ride Master's horse, 'Sandy' out of her stall, put a bridle and a rein on her, and ride her bare back as fast as she'd go around the empty arena. Hank accepted the challenge and was doing well until he was at the far end of the arena. Sandy decided she'd had enough and headed for the exit door at the other end of the arena. Hank hung on as best he could, but his mates closed the big metal sliding door at the last minute. Sandy put her head down, locked all fours and slid to a stop; Hank grabbed a handful of mane, did a front roll over her head and landed on his back on the concrete apron. It knocked the wind out of him, but he held onto the reins. After awhile he gathered himself up to the laughter of his mates now standing in the open doorway, brushed himself off, and took Sandy back to her stall. He brushed her down so there were no traces of her ride. Not a word was said by that four to any other troop mates or anyone else as far as Hank knew. He never did it again but that reminded him of "the chute". It was a narrow laneway outside the stable with a "jump" at the end of it where like the Indian Wrestle, for a break, Harry would take the Troop with some horses.

On a sunny spring day, one at a time, he'd send them down the lane and hopefully over the 'jump'. Not all horses were jumpers and not all recruits good riders, so more often than not the horse would do like Sandy did, stop suddenly before the jump. Usually the horse would lower its head, the rider would sail on over the jump alone, and hopefully not get hurt as the ground came up to meet him.

Some recruits for the R.C.M.P. arriving by train in Regina had the good fortune to be met by a 'duty driver' from Depot. No such luck for Hank, he had to take a cab. He reported to the Guard House at South Gate, Depot just before dusk and was directed to "F" Block, two city blocks west. He walked alone, carrying his brown cardboard suitcase containing all his belongings, against a cold prairie wind with the frost crunching under his overshoes, and found his destination. The majority of his Troop were already in barracks for the evening and Hank was greeted by some of them and shown to his "pit", (the area between his and the next bunk to the left.) The bunks were lined up on both sides of the room and were alphabetically assigned according to the surname of the recruit, Hart, Howell, Jans, Jamison, Jeffrey, Keck, etc. "F" block was a ground floor pre-fabricated military style barrack of plywood sections fastened to two-by-fours and bolted together to support the walls and ceiling. There were windows at intervals and an entry door at one end and an escape door at the other. There was no insulation but radiators with steam heat were more than welcome in those winter months. The beds were lined up with your feet against the outside wall. After a storm it was not uncommon for the bunks next to a window to have snow on the blanket at the foot. Each recruit was issued two blankets, one brown and one grey.

The brown had R.C.M.P. stamped across the middle, but no markings on the grey. There were also four cotton sheets, one pillow and two pillowslips for each bed. The beds had to be made meticulously each morning with the sheet and the brown blanket folded down part way, both tucked in so tight the inspector could bounce a quarter off them. The grey was stowed in the trunk at the foot of the bed. On day one Hank was directed to the basement of A

Block, the training division headquarters to be issued his full 'kit' (uniform}. There was so much kit, (clothing) he had to make two trips to carry it back to F Block.

FOOTNOTES RE: DEPOT

When Hank went to the Q.M. Stores in the basement of A Block to pick up his kit, for the first time, he was introduced to the indelible black marker with which he was obliged to print his initials on each item of kit, and his regimental number on some items. Such was the case with all his of troop mates. They were also obliged to order and pay for a steamer trunk from the canteen, which had to be inscribed on both ends with his initials and regimental number. This time with white paint applied from a tiny-shared can, with the butt end of a paper match, on both ends of the navy blue trunk. In addition to boots and items of uniform, there was also underwear, including long johns, along with the bedding.

Bed making was no great challenge to Hank at first, because he had made his own bed at home, but he soon found out on the Sgt. Major's first inspection that he didn't do it quite right. Both bed sheets had to be tight as a fiddle string with the corners folded under the mattress so a hurricane wouldn't blow them away. The brown blanket folded one-third down the bed had to be tight enough to bounce a quarter off it. Later on when that blanket was used for awhile, it had to withstand a 'whack' from a riding crop and not raise a particle of dust, or the owner would be C.B.'d (confined to barracks) for whatever number of the days the Inspector chose. Once a week, laundry and dry cleaning was picked up, and paid for by the recruit, on return.

Each Thursday night was 'fatigues' when the barrack room floor had to be 'scrubbed', dried and polished with paste wax using a ten pound, foot square concrete block with a long wooden handle on it, and a scrap piece of an old woollen blanket beneath it. For fun some mates found that sliding on the polished floor, wearing an old pair of woollen socks had the same effect. Although a labour-intensive task, it seemed also to be a time to strip down, all hands to pitch in and make the room sparkle as it should. It also instilled a pride of ownership, a sense of brotherhood and accomplishment.

During the first six months, one night a week, some troop mates would be detailed to attend the tack room in the stables to clean saddles, bridles and reins, so they too would sparkle especially for a parade or 'passout' (graduation). Similarly, in summer daylight, the whole troop, whether as punishment or not, would be assigned to sweep the parade square, prior to a special function or V.I.P. visit. At ninety degrees F, that was an event to forget. Likewise, so was being part of a snow shovel brigade on the footpath and bridge over the Waskana Creek to the city, in below zero temperatures F. with a northwest wind at fifty knots or more, freezing snowflakes to your face. On one such assignment, in spite of ear lugs down on his issue fur cap, Hank had frost bite on both cheeks, as did some other mates.

The Drill Instructor for P Troop was Cpl. Stevens small in stature, but mighty and in spite of his harsh front, seemed to take P Troop under his wing. He gave the impression that he wanted this troop to be the best damn troop that ever 'passed out' through the gates of Depot Division. He had the same big voice, which seemed to be a prerequisite for all drill instructors. One day early in their training, P troop was lined up in the drill hall for inspection. Cpl. Stevens stopped abruptly behind Hank, leaned in and said so all could hear;

"Am I hurting you?" "No Cpl. "came the reply. "Well I should be, because I'm standing on your hair!"

Hank had just a bit of 'peach fuzz' on the back of his neck. That was all part of the bravado that most instructors used to intimidate recruits and keep them on their toes. Every recruit was supposed to get a haircut at least twice a week. Although Depot had a barber on the base, Hank and some mates chipped in and bought new, recently available, electric clippers and cut each other's hair. It didn't have to be nice, but it was clean. The recruits were called 'skinheads' downtown anyway. P troop started out in the unheated drill hall in February, but by the time they completed one full hour of foot drill, nobody was cold. After a few drills together, Stevie tried several tall troop mates at the position of 'right marker' and finally settled on Don McLay who continued at that position all the way through to 'passout'. Hank was never considered for 'right marker'. He didn't want it anyway.

When spring came, P troop moved outside to the main parade square where the drills expanded to include .303 army rifles with slings. Handling them in quick precise display was not easy for Hank and others to master, but they eventually did after many repeated efforts under commands such as "order arms, present arms, slope arms" which had to be done by all in unison. If anyone goofed up on a drill, Cpl Stevens ordered him to march or run alone at top speed around the extended square by the officer's quarters, a distance of three to four hundred yards. If the punishment was more severe, the rifle was to be held over the head as the recruit ran. A rifle alone was not all that heavy, but held over the head for that distance was not an easy task, and if the rifle came down enroute, the recruit was invited to a do-over. This time when he returned, his arms felt like jelly.

"Do it right the first time or you go again!" blared Stevie.

Normal kit for all foot drill was Stetson hat, brown serge, breeches, jackboots with spurs and stripped sam-brown, sometimes leather gloves. All kit must be neat, clean and polished or more penalties would be added. As required by the syllabus, all troops graduating from training were expected to display to the 'brass' what they had learned. During the latter weeks of training it was apparent that Cpl. Stevens was on a mission to make P Troop the best damn Troop to ever walk out the gates of Depot Division, and he did!

TRAINING DEPOT REGINA - RIDING BAREBACK 'DOWN THE CHUTE'

The recruits in training, when thirty-two were finally together over the period of a month or more, when the Commanding Officer approved, were assembled into a 'troop' that was given in alphabetical letter, the initial 'P'. Some of his mates had been there since the first of January, so everyone now had to get used to what was left of a long, cold Prairie winter. Like every Canadian who spends their winters in Canada, the mates in 'P' Troop could hardly wait for spring to come so they might spend more time outdoors.

When spring came, like the Saturday morning Indian wrestling in the riding school, Hollerin Harry, to allow the mates of 'P' Troop a chance to 'let off some steam' would instruct Hank and his mates to assemble at the stables for a traditional ride "down the chute". This location consisted of a shabby fenced-in lane about sixty yards in length and twenty feet wide, out behind the stables, open at one end and closed on two sides and the other end.

Approximately thirty yards from the closed end was a one-rail 'jump' which could be adjusted up or down, like most jumps. Harry would instruct the height of the 'jump' on a given day, never higher than two feet. Mates were not allowed to choose their 'usual' mount for this event. Harry chose eight or ten horses according to size, disposition and jumping ability. He ordered them bridled with open bridles and well-worn lines that didn't have to be cleaned and polished after the exercise.

A mate who removed the designated horse from the stable was to be in charge of that animal except when Harry directed it to be released to the next mate to ride down the chute, when it was his 'turn'. Outside, on a sunny afternoon with only the 'P' Troop mates as observers, all assembled at the open end of "the chute". There were no benches to sit on while you waited your turn and no bleachers for a better vantage point. Just stand beside the "chute" anywhere from start to finish and wait your turn. Harry chose the riders in no particular order nor the horse they were to ride. The mates were free to cheer for, or boo each individual rider. Also laugh heartily when the horse galloped 'full tilt' down the "chute", at the last second brace all fours, slide into the jump with head and neck pointed to the ground and watch his rider sail over his head uttering a variety of helpless noises. Then to gather himself up, dust himself off, retrieve his horse and return it to its caretaker of the day. No known photos were taken and no real injuries were sustained, just a dent in the 'pride' of some riders. Believe it or not, some horses and riders made their trip "down the chute", cleared the jump, and circled back to the cheers of the assembled.

The brave or foolish ones after their first trip, especially if they didn't succeed the first time might choose the same horse or another horse and go again, but most chose the "once is enough" position and became a full time spectator. Back at the stables, brushing down the horses and putting gear away, there were lots of laughs which continued all the way back to the barracks, and sometimes on into the night, even after "lights out".

DEPOT DIVISION -MODEL DETACHMENT

Late in their training, the instructor Cpl Roberts assembled P troop in a separate building on the base, where they could get a glimpse of Detachment life. Inside there were bulletin boards, filing cabinets, desks, a typewriter, wanted posters, even a counter where the general public could come and lodge a complaint. Hank and his mates took turns role-playing as officer or the citizen while Cpl. Roberts dictated the script. The recruits were also introduced to the many RCMP forms to be typed, some in triplicate, completed and mailed to HQ. Some forms came with carbon paper already in them, but, for a single sheet that needed copies, detachments had boxes of carbon paper to insert between two plain sheets of paper. Hank soon found out that any of these forms were a nightmare when he made a typing error. Oh yes, Cpl. Roberts also reminded them that when the report was completed, the carbon paper was to be returned to the box for future use. WASTE NOT, WANT NOT!

TYPING CLASSES

Early in their training, Hank and his mates had been introduced to a room full of typewriters set up on small desks with chairs in front. Like many of his mates, Hank had never touched a typewriter. Cpl Peterson was their instructor and started them slowly memorizing the keyboard, where each number and letter was and which finger on which hand should type it. Over a period of weeks the troop improved their words –per- minute through exercises and tests. Hank's score went from 10 to 27 words with now only occasionally glancing at the keyboard. This skill stood him in good stead for the first 12 years of service in the field where he was obliged to type all his own reports. Some of his mates on detachment later could type with a lit cigarette stuck in their mouth. Hank had to wait until he was finished to have a smoke.

SURVIVAL COURSE

Half way through training Hank and his mates spent a week in tents in the Q'appelle Valley north of Regina. Included duties were some cooking, cleaning dishes, maintaining a neat clean sleeping area just like the barracks. Also physical training exercises, handling and shooting rifles, hiking, running, swimming, using a compass and all the activities the Troop Leader, Cst. White was required to cover, even a night of astronomy under the stars.

REGINA

DEPOT DIVISION PHYSICAL TRAINING

For this class, Hank and his mates had to be dressed in white boxer shorts and T shirts, washed and ironed by the recruit the night before, and white sneaker boots with white laces all cleaned and treated with white liquid shoe polish, bought in the canteen at the recruit's expense. The instructor, Cpl. Purdy, was a bit of a sadist, in Hank's eyes, but could be a pussycat at times. He drove his recruits hard as he whipped them into shape. Hank entered training at 171 pounds and left weighing 173 pounds but considerably tougher, with most muscles in the right places. One of the classic exercises by Purdy involved an arrest where the suspect didn't go quietly, and had to be forcibly placed in the back seat of a police car. He would first demonstrate on a 'volunteer' recruit and then have recruits pair up good guy/bad guy under his scrutiny. In the gym, there was no car to demonstrate on, so they had to apply imagination and energy, which ended in a lot of scuffles. Like other instructors, when he wished to give a break from routine he'd organize a pick-up game of basketball. Hank and some others had never played the game, so weren't very good at it. At one end of the gym, attached to the ceiling were four two-inch-diameter hemp ropes hanging down to within four feet of the floor. One of Cpl. Purdy's favourite punishments was to command the recruit to climb a rope to the top, touch the ceiling and propel back down, as many times as Purdy deemed necessary. Hank didn't make it the first time, but eventually did his share of climbs, and then some. It sure helped to build up his upper body strength.

Each class of gym training involved some manoeuvres similar to foot drill which, as P troop neared the end of training, included parallel bars, spring boards and box horses. These were to be a feature part of the troop's passout (graduation). During one of these practices Hank followed a single file of mates running and jumping onto the springboard, into a handstand on the box horse and a dismount over the far end, landing in a crouch position on the floor, at the far end of the box.

One time, near the last week of training, Hank didn't land correctly and his right ankle folded under him, tearing the ligaments so badly that he had to be helped off the floor and taken to the Post Hospital. There it was wrapped tightly in a tensor bandage and Hank was issued a pair of crutches by the attendant, for the first time ever. Learning to manoeuvre the crutches was a real challenge, but Hank prevailed. The result was at his P.T. passout two weeks later, Hank stood on the sidelines on crutches, with his parents, watching his troop mates go through their drills almost error free. Already rumours abounded that if he didn't graduate with his troop, Hank might be 'back-squadded' to a junior troop, and watch his mates being 'posted to the field' without him. That never happened, because Hank was determined to leave the crutches behind. He departed from Depot by train to Halifax, Nova Scotia with two of his mates, as scheduled. The ordered 'dress' for the trip was "review order", Stetson, Red Serge, including 'Jack boots' and breeches. In the mornings of the four-day trip, Hank could dress himself, including the boots and spurs. But in the evening, it took one mate to hold Hanks shoulders while the other pulled the boot off, due to swelling in the ankle.

The rest of the troop, were posted coast-to-coast, twelve to British Columbia, two to Newfoundland.

GLACE BAY

HELLO GLACE BAY

At Sydney Sub-Division H.Q. Hank was met by Donnie Goodwin from Glace Bay detachment driving a 1954 Meteor, into which Hank loaded everything he owned except his trunk. Donnie was a redhead like Hank, only a bit darker. He was shorter and older than Hank but in good shape. "Where'ya from? " he asked. "The Island" meaning P.E.I., said Hank, and the conversation continued across Sydney and on out towards Glace Bay. Halfway there, Donnie suddenly pulled over to the right shoulder, stopped and said, "Here, you drive" and opened the driver's door. Hank opened his door and almost stumbled getting out, as his head being swelled at the thought of getting to drive a real 'patrol car'. The rest of the way was uneventful as Donnie guided Hank through Glace Bay to the detachment on South Street. There he met three of the seven members stationed there. One was on leave and the Sgt. in charge was out.

One of them, George Timko was really happy to see Hank, because now he was no longer the junior man, filing index cards, cleaning floors, washing cars and running errands. Another said to Hank "By the way, you're in charge tonight". Hank said "What?" Another member announced that this was the annual Sub-Division Ball, at the Isle Royal Hotel in Sydney, and everybody was going. "But don't worry, if you get a call, Jones is on duty at New Waterford, he'll tell you what to do, and if he's not there, call the dispatcher on the radio in Sydney. If you're bored, there are always index cards to file, and a whole bunch of General Orders and instruction manuals to read". As good luck would have it, no calls came in, and by 10:30 P.M. Hank headed for his bunk in the single men's quarters, complete with telephone, above the garage.

Glace Bay detachment building was relatively new, with married quarters for the Sgt. and his family above the office, a three-car garage that had a wash bay in the one next to the office, with hot and cold running water. Hank was really 'wowed' by this. The next morning, Hank dressed in his best shirt, tie, boots and breeches, jackboots with spurs, ready to go at 8 o'clock, while the single revellers from the night before moaned and pushed themselves to get out of bed. When he got downstairs, Cst. Reid said "The Sgt. wants to see you in his office" and indicated the way. Hank's first thought was, 'What the Hell did I do now?' but gathered his courage together and marched smartly down the hall to the boss' office. There, sitting behind his desk was Sgt. House, a large middle- aged man, with the evidence of last night's party clearly visible on his face. "Cst. Jamison reporting, Sgt." said Hank, in as loud and firm a voice as he could muster.

"Sit down" ordered Sgt. House. Hank complied. "You gotta a gun?" asked the Sgt." "Yes Sgt." Came the reply. "Where is it?" "In my trunk" said Hank.

"Well, leave it there, because around here if you get into a scuffle making an arrest, and you're wearing the damn thing, they'll take it off you and shoot you. Or, you may get the shit kicked out of you, but you'll live to tell about it."

"Yes, Sgt." "Now go see Reid, and he'll have something for you. Uh, before you go, do you have a suit?" "Yes, Sgt." "Well, plan on wearing it the day after tomorrow. You'll be going on plain clothes with Palmer for two weeks while Craig, is away on leave."

Hank left the Sgt's office and thought; Wow, I'm in the field one day and already I'm in plainclothes.

GLACE BAY

That first full day of field duty was mostly getting acquainted with other members, reading manuals, taking phone calls, going to dinner at Noon with other single members at Mrs. McKay's in Town, and meeting her and her son Paul. She charged $10.00 a week for dinners whether you were there or not. On the way back from dinner they stopped in at Turner's Plumbing & Heating where Hank met Dave Rose who was roughly Hank's age, liked hunting and fishing and offered to show Hank around town on his next night off. That night, Hank went on night patrol with Larry, which consisted of driving through the gravel rural roads checking vehicles and fields for "deer jackers" (poachers who shoot deer at night, in season or out, by shining a light and catching the reflection in the deer's eyes).

They stopped and searched several vehicles but found no guns, no lights and no" jackers". The next morning when Hank and Larry went for breakfast at the Co-op, Hank met Jimmy Roberts who sold him his first ever Spin fishing rod and reel, on sale at the end of the season.

That day Hank went with Al Palmer in plain clothes in the unmarked car and Al showed him around town and some of the small villages outside the town, pointing out where some of the ex-cons and criminals lived. Suddenly they swung into a driveway and Al told Hank to stay in the car, got out and walked to a garage behind the house. He was gone less than five minutes, came back to the car, backed out and drove away. Al explained that the occupant operated a small engine repair shop and was one of Al's confidential informants. Al told Hank to keep that to himself, and tell no one, not even other members, because then the informant would no longer be confidential. He had learned that Rory McElroy from Reserve Mines had a 'still' in the woods out behind the airport, and that he'd probably be 'running off' a batch in the next day or two.

Al contacted the Sydney dog master Larry Ridgeway on the police radio from the car, and they made plans to go and check out the 'still' early Friday morning. Al picked up Hank at the detachment long before daylight. They met the dog wagon by an abandoned mine shaft, parked the police car, and went with Larry and his dog 'Hap' to a secluded spot beside a seldom used rail line. From there they walked a mile and half along the railway line, then into the woods to a site that Al knew Rory had used before, because there was a good water supply. It was still dark when they entered the woods, so they used their three-cell flashlights sparingly to keep from tripping over dead falls, bog holes and other debris in the forest. They held their breath that Rory wasn't there ahead of them.

When they located the 'still', they paused and waited several minutes for a sound of anyone else present. The coast was clear. They also watched for a trip wire that Rory may have set for intruders while Larry and Hap circled the area to find a hiding place/vantage point from where they could watch the 'still' site and hopefully not be seen. Larry chose a spot behind a recent deadfall that also had young bushes growing up around it, and the three men and the dog settled in and waited. Al had stepped into a water hole on the way in, and chose the opportunity to take his boot and sock off and hang the sock over a low dead branch to dry. By now it was beginning to 'get light' and Al debated whether he should put the wet sock back on, because it was still pretty cool and everyone got colder once they stopped.

Before long, there was a distant intermittent sound of men's voices that became clearer as they approached, but the sound came from different directions. Then suddenly Rory appeared, walking in a diminishing circle around the still site and Al and Larry knew he was checking for intruders. When Hap heard Larry whispering, he started to tremble and Larry had difficulty containing him.

MOONSHINER

Hap was a large Doberman, perhaps 80 pounds or more, and Hank jokingly wondered if the vibrations from Hap were shaking the ground at the 'still'. Al had told Hank before that Case Law required that the police wait until the 'still' produced at least a drop of moonshine as evidence, before they could legally arrest a suspect. That took almost an hour and when Al gave the signal to go, Larry cut Hap loose and the dog tore off straight for the helper, hit him high on the body with his front feet, knocked him to the ground and stood over him until his master got there. Meanwhile, Rory turned and ran hard into the woods with Hank hot on his trail, but Rory knew the woods and had a planned escape route that worked. Rory got away and Hank came back empty handed. Al knew the helper, who explained he was just there to get a free sample, so Al let him go. The trio collected a couple of ounces of moonshine; the worm and the 'still' parts needed as evidence, and destroyed the rest. That night Al and Hank dropped by Rory's house and arrested him. Later he was charged and convicted of making illicit spirits under the Excise Act. As this was his second offence Rory was later sentenced to six months in the County Jail.

The next weekend, after dark, Al and Hank staked out the home of a lady taxi driver on the outskirts of town who was known to sell 'bootleg liquor'. After an hour or more in the biting cold and no action, Al decided to pay

Annie a visit and search her house for any excessive quantity of liquor. Once inside the back door, Al told Hank to stay in the kitchen and watch Annie while he searched the upstairs. Hank stood with his arms folded and his back to the door facing Annie who had her back to the kitchen stove, hands on hips and thoroughly annoyed by her unexpected visitors. Hank, still a teenager bundled in warm clothes including a toque, with rosy cheeks shining under the kitchen ceiling light, made a feeble attempt at conversation to no avail.

In total disgust, after a long silence Annie asked "Just how old do you have to be to get into that f---'en outfit these days?" "Eighteen Ma'm", came the reply, just as Al appeared at the top of the stairs, made some parting comments to Annie, and for Hank, mercifully left the confines of Annie's kitchen. They never did catch Annie bootlegging.

On November 11th, Armistice Day, Hank was back in dress uniform, Stetson, red serge, breeches, jack boots, spurs and gloves, a drastic change, having been in plain clothes since fresh out of training. Hank wore a sweatshirt under his red serge. The two other constables, Larry and George, also were 'spit and polished', but Hank noticed their marching was perhaps a bit rusty.

The parade started downtown, and at the last minute, the VIP car was inserted at the lead, directly in front of Hank and his two companions marching three abreast. This was no limo, but an old unmarked black car from the town police force that burned oil, creating fumes that the three marching members were obliged to inhale, while they marched the mile and a half route to the Cenotaph. Once there, in No. 11, George and Hank were presented each with a .303 army rifle to stand 'at rest' (with the muzzle resting on the toe of the right boot and head bowed) for the hour-long ceremony, one on either side of the Cenotaph. By the time the ceremony was over, Hank was so cold, he could hardly feel his hands or feet, George and Larry were not much better, both regretting they hadn't worn warmer clothing under their tunics.

GLACE BAY

One night shortly before Christmas, Larry and Hank got called to attend the morgue in Glace Bay, at the request of Port Hastings detachment, as result of a fatal accident on the Canso Causeway earlier that evening. The information was, while a young couple were returning from the mainland, during a severe storm, the salt water spray was breaking over the causeway causing the windshield of their car to become so obscure, the wipers couldn't keep it clear. (There were no windshield washers in those days.) On the causeway, the young man who was driving didn't see a stalled truck ahead until the last second, swerved to the left to avoid it but the passenger side of the car went under the left rear corner of the truck box, striking his wife on the head killing her instantly. When Hank and Larry arrived at the morgue, the Coroner, funeral home personnel and others were gathered around a table in the brightly lit room. There, lying on her back completely naked, was this beautiful young woman, with no obvious scar on her body, but a small wound on the right side of her head partially evident by dried blood in her blond hair. It was the first time Hank had seen a completely naked woman, in such bright lights, that he struggled to hold back nausea. He never muttered a word, but all he could think of was 'so young, so vulnerable, such a waste, and the grief and guilt her husband must be suffering.' Because of this reaction, Hank was excused from attending the autopsy the next day. It was several days later before Hank could completely erase her image from his mind.

It wasn't all work and no play for Hank because on one of his first nights off, he walked the half-mile down to the beach at the end of North Street, sat on a large piece of driftwood and just listened to the waves from the Atlantic breaking on the shore. This was pure tonic for the boy from the 'Island' who had spent the last ten months on the Prairies. It was also an opportunity for Hank and his new friend Dave Rose to get acquainted by deer hunting in the fall, skating at the miner's forum, and dancing at St. Ann's Hall in Glace Bay. Also dancing at Venetian Gardens in Sydney and going fishing in the spring when they could hitch a ride. Larry extended their range when he sold Hank his '51 Dodge for $500.00, and helped him get financing at Household Finance at eighteen percent, to pay for it. Dave christened the car 'Maybelline' after a popular song they used to sing-along with, on the car radio.

On a Sunday summer afternoon Hank went with Al Palmer and his new wife Bev to Jimmy Robert's cottage on the Mira River. Al had previously invited Hank to his newly rented home in town for dinner, where they worked together and Hank helped him hang window blinds, drapes, clothes hangers and closet shelves, because Al wasn't very handy as a Mr. Fixit. This day at Jimmy's cottage, Al took Hank for a ride in a canoe away from the crowd, and gave Hank his first drink of rum, straight from the flask, with a swig of Pepsi as a 'chaser'. Hank barely was able to swallow a small taste, and it felt like it burned all the way down to his toes. Al laughed so hard he almost upset the canoe. Back on shore, Jimmy's eldest daughter Bess was there in her pink bikini, with ample bosom exposed, making eyes at Hank, much to his liking. They went for a walk along the river at dusk, stopped and sat on a piece of driftwood, hugged and kissed, but she wouldn't let Hank go any further.

VICIOUS GUARD DOG

During Hank's two weeks in plain clothes, one of the bootleggers that piqued Al's interest lived on an old residential street not far from the Number Two coal mine, named Otis (Buddy) McNeil. He had a small house with a big lot with no trees or shrubbery, only a large dog house for a vicious dog named Bruno set out by itself in the back of the yard. Bruno was strategically chained to the front of the dog house with just enough chain to allow him to patrol as far as both sides of the house, but not to the front, presumably so as to not scare away the 'clientele'. If you drove by, which Al and Hank did several times, the dog would just stand and watch, but if you walked by, he'd charge towards you, barking and frothing at the mouth until the chain fetched him up short. There didn't seem to be a woman or children living there so Al had concluded he was a bachelor.

Al and Hank had caught clients on two different nights coming away from the premises with a package, one on foot and one driving. Al let Hank show off his speed to catch the man on foot and they followed by car the man in an old pick up until he was clear away from the house. They each had a full, sealed quart of Black Diamond Demerara rum, which was seized, but neither would 'squeal' on McNeil. Instead they were charged with illegal possession of liquor, and one was arrested for obstruction and spent the night in Jail. In both cases, McNeil had gone to the back yard at night with a flashlight and returned shortly after carrying 'something' in the other hand into the house just before the client left with a 'package'. On a warm weekday afternoon Al and Hank drove by the McNeil premises. It looked like no one was home, and the dog was sleeping in his house. Al parked the car out of sight down the street and the officers walked back, sneaking into the back yard approaching the doghouse from behind. Al ran the last few steps, reached around to the front, slammed the door to the dog house and turned the lock button as the dog went berserk growling and thrashing around inside.

On close examination the men noticed that the piece of old conveyor belt under the dog house ran three or four feet out in front. Al picked up the outer end of belt and swung it to one side, the doghouse moving with it. They noticed that the earth under the belt was not packed down but loose and easy to move. They dug with their bare hands and few inches down they found the top of a copper hot water tank from an old kitchen stove. They lifted the lid and inside were six full quarts of Black Diamond rum the same kind as they had seized from the two clients previously.

As Hank dropped down to help take the bottles out of the tank, McNeil appeared from his afternoon nap demanding, "What the Hell do you guys think you're doin here? That's my Christmas booze!"

ç the doghouse. "Oh Yeah" said Al "Why don't you keep it inside the house?"

"The neighbours would only steal it," came the retort.

"Bruno watches it for me here."

"And what about the men we caught coming from here two nights in a row with the same brand of rum?" asked Al.

McNeil was at a loss for words. During the ensuing discussion, Al convinced McNeil he had been 'caught with the goods' that he was being charged with the illegal sale of Government Liquor, and the six bottles of rum were being seized as evidence. McNeil later appeared before a Justice of the Peace, where he plead guilty to the charge and was fined $100.00, plus costs or 30 days in jail. He paid the fine.

NEW FRIEND DAVE

One day while waiting to go to Court, Donnie and Hank stopped in at Turner's Plumbing and Heating to look at a hunting rifle. Donnie introduced Hank to the friendly young man behind the counter, Dave Rose who smiled and came out from behind the counter, vigorously shook Hank's hand and welcomed him to Glace Bay like he was the mayor.

"Where you from?" asked Dave. "P.E.I." Hank replied. "And what can I do for you fellas today?" asked Dave.

"I'm thinkin about trying my luck for a deer and I'm lookin for a nice, light easy- to- handle rifle." Said Donnie. Dave reached into the locked cabinet behind the counter, pulled the lever action to make sure there were no shells in the chamber and handed Donnie a new Remington 30-30 lever action. "How about this one?", Dave continued to relate how just earlier yesterday morning he was hunting out Tower Road way with a similar rifle, had shot a large doe and while he was gutting it, the buck wandered out to see what he was doing. Dave grabbed the rifle, racked a shell into the chamber and shot the second deer in less than twenty minutes. While he was telling this story, his eyes were dancing his face and his speech was unbridled with enthusiasm.

When he put his second tag on the last deer, it sunk in to his head that his deer season was over for this year because he had used both tags. After he finished gutting both deer, he left them there and walked to the nearest home, asked to use their phone and called his friend Jimmy who had an old half ton truck to come and get him and his deer before they both had to go to work.

Dave turned to Donnie, glanced at Hank and said, "I know that's hard to believe, but it's the gospel truth and I got the two deer hangin in my father's barn to prove it."

Then he offered to Donnie, "If you'd like me to go with you sometime, I'd be able to show you a few good places to try, but you'll have to do the shooting because I'm out of tags." "I'd liked to do that", Donnie continued.

"How much is the rifle?"

"Hundred and seventy-five dollars," Dave replied. "I'll take it, and a box of shells with it," said Donnie. When Donnie and Dave finished their business, Dave said, "Nice meeting you Hank, I'll talk to Mom, and maybe we'll have you over for supper some evening."

"Thanks, I'd like that very much," said Hank as he and Donnie left the store.

That, as they say, was the start of a beautiful friendship. Neither Dave nor Hank had a car, but Hank could easily walk to Dave's parent's place on Berkley Street to get a break from single men's quarters on his evenings off. His parents Fred and Rosa were simply two wonderful people formerly from Rose Blanche, Newfoundland who made Hank feel right at home in spite of

GLACE BAY

no T.V. and no family car. If Dave and Hank wanted to go out on the Town or go to a movie, they walked or got a lift with one of Dave's friends. If they had dates with a couple of pretty girls, Larry would lend Hank his 1951 Dodge two-door, which Hank later bought so they could go any time. After all, gas was only fifty cents a gallon, cigarettes were thirty-eight cents a pack, and a dozen bottles of beer cost two dollars and sixty-seven cents tax included. Both Dave and Hank smoked but didn't drink.

Before the car, during the winter, Dave and Hank walked to the Miner's Forum to watch the Glace Bay Miners play semi-pro games in the Maritime Major Hockey League against teams from five or six major centers in N.S., N.B. and P.E.I. The competition between the teams made for fierce and entertaining hockey during the season and come playoff time, rivalry was so serious between Sydney and Glace Bay, the fans from Glace Bay blocked the highway at Senator's Corner to prevent the fans from Sydney coming to the final games. An irate neighbour was heard to say "Somebody call the Mounties!" Hank and all available young able-bodied policemen were detailed to go and break down the barricades, arrest if necessary, but keep the highway open. This was for at least three nights during the playoffs in all kinds of weather with no extra lighting, just one-bulb streetlights and reliable three-cell flashlights with wands.

On nights for public skating at the forum Dave and Hank walked with their skates over their shoulders, when Hank was off duty. Dave was a better skater than Hank and was not satisfied to just 'skate around in circles' but experimented with his twirls and jumps in the center of the ice like a pro skater, sometimes falling on his ass to the delight of others watching. Hank was never sure if he was trying to expand his skating skills or simply trying to attract the attention of the young lady skaters.

One night he was successful and two pretty ladies joined Dave and Hank at center ice, they introduced each other as Dot and Ginnie. Dot went with Dave, Ginnie with Hank, and they skated a few rounds together until closing time. The girls said they lived in the same block on Victoria Street not far from the Forum and agreed to let the boys 'walk them home'. They came first to Ginnie's place where Hank escorted her up to the veranda, said goodnight, she gave him a peck on the cheek.

Then Dot and the boys walked to her home. The front door light was on and when Dave walked Dot to the front door, the door flew open. Her father reached out, pulled her in past him and proceeded to give Dave Hell for bringing her home so late. Dave tried to explain "But, but, but, we just came from skating, it's not even ten o'clock yet". His words fell on deaf ears. Dave never went back. Hank dated Ginnie after he bought the 1951 Dodge from Larry for five hundred dollars. They double-dated several times after that, Dave with other girls, travelling in Hank's first car, which Dave affectionately named 'Maybelline' after a popular song of the day. Ginnie was attractive, charming and funny, but she kept control of Hank so he was never able to 'get past first base'.

They went to movies and dances and had some memorable times together. Hank even came back to see Ginnie, after he was transferred to Inverness. They would pick up Dave and Bunny in Maybelline, and away they'd go, just like old times, but eventually they drifted apart, and Hank's interests moved in another direction. That's what happens to a young single Mountie, when frequent transfers occur during his first five years of service. Hank tried to stay in touch with Dave and Bunny in Glace Bay, but he made new friends wherever he went, and over time the old ones just seemed to drift away.

THE WAGON WHEEL

Every Friday night, between 9:00 PM and 1:00 AM, a character named Dougie 'Shakey' McNeil held dances in the upstairs of a large building, on the side of Maple Street in Reserve Mines, five miles outside of Glace Bay towards Sydney. 'Shakey' had no bouncers or security, but fully expected the R.C.M.P. to be available at his 'beck and call', should trouble break out, and the Sgt. in charge of the detachment complied. Most calls from the Wagon Wheel came in around Midnight, when most hands in single men's quarters were in bed, some fast asleep. There was an unwritten pecking order amongst the single men that, calls to the Wagon Wheel were to be taken by the two junior men, Hank and George. Yes, George had been jubilant when Hank arrived from training, because he no longer had to wash cars and other menial tasks as often as before, but he still had to answer the calls to the Wagon Wheel.

He and others had strategically placed the phone on Hank's bedside table, before Hank had arrived. Some Friday nights were quiet, but when they had to go, it was get up, get dressed in full uniform, get the car out of the garage, drive the ten minutes or more across town, emergency lights and siren when necessary, and in all kinds of weather. Some nights by the time they arrived, the fight would be over, and the offenders had scattered, either back into the hall or home. Sometimes they'd be still fighting in the middle of the street, with the crowd circled around them urging them on. George and Hank had no clubs or 'billy sticks', just three-cell flashlights and issue gloves.

They'd try to assess the situation by standing on the door sills of the police car, then, on signal, wade into the middle of the circle, grab one intoxicated fighter each, cuff them, if possible and drag them to the two- door car. Wrestle one into the back seat followed by one constable, and put the other in the passenger seat, while extracting promises that the fight would not continue inside the car, or they'd be left on the side of the road. None of this was unfamiliar to Hank because he had been involved in the odd dance hall fight in his later teen-age years at home. Looking back at the good things about the Wagon Wheel dances, there were no weapons, the bystanders didn't obstruct the police or help, the offenders were usually too drunk to hurt anyone, just flailing fists and boots, and there was a healthy respect for the law.

Neither George nor Hank at any time got a real 'punch in the mouth'. Then off to the Glace Bay jail in the basement of the Town Hall, perhaps wake a sleepy desk sergeant, who took great pleasure finding a resting place for the combatants. The officers usually had a few chuckles, followed by a "thanks til next time". Back home to bed, and hope the phone didn't ring again until morning. Then someone else in single men's quarters was obliged to take the two men out of jail, lay charges, take them before a Justice of the Peace and write the report.

RECENT FOLK LORE

A few years before Hank was posted to Glace Bay, Charles 'Dukie' McNeil and Frank Leudy broke into a 'Dairy' (convenience store) at Ryan River around Midnight. The owner, who lived upstairs, chased them out of the store with a shotgun, fired at them striking Dukie in the back. They jumped into Dukie's car and took off. He drove twenty some miles home, to Marconi Towers on the other side of Glace Bay. There, under the light of a kerosene lamp, it was rumoured he laid on his belly on the kitchen table, while his wife cut the shotgun pellets out of his back, with a razor blade, using illegal alcohol as both a sterilizer and sedative. Cst. Larry Reid had seen the scars a month or so later, when he arrested and strip-searched Dukie, on suspicion of another Break and Enter, in a small store in Donkin.

From time to time a dapper dude in shirt and tie, sports jacket and fedora would drop in to Glace Bay detachment to chat and sometimes meet with the Sgt. in charge in private, or to have a game of cards. He was introduced to Hank as simply 'Jimmy' and no other information was offered about him. Hank later learned he was hired by the town to keep an eye on some its policemen who themselves were suspected of crimes. One such suspect, Hank later learned, was the town motorcycle cop, Cst. Burns, who was small in stature but tough, comical, charming and seemed to work intermittent shifts. Word later was that 'Jimmy' caught Burns coming out the back window of a corner store on Victoria Rd. with an armload of cartons of cigarettes and other confections at three o'clock in the morning.

No official report was made of this, but before long Burns faded away like the Atlantic fog and was replaced on the motorcycle by a handsome young constable named Mark Gardner. Both 'rookies', Hank got to know him personally, and Mark somehow managed to acquire a used pair of R.C.M.P. issue jack boots, without spurs, which he wore proudly on his motorcycle. Mark worked his way up through the ranks and years later became the Chief of Glace Bay Town Police.

Sympathetic citizens were heard to remark that it was little wonder some Glace Bay policemen were forced to steal because their wages were so poor, but not all stole, 'by a long shot.'

Another loyal, dedicated, rugged Glace Bay town cop was a country boy from the Margarees named Jerome Gillis, who joined later in life with experience in farming, mining and logging and later was a friend of Hank and his wife Mary Ann. He stood over six feet tall, was afraid of nothing or no one, walked his beat alone at night with his three-cell flashlight and 'billy stick'.

They said "he put the fear of the Lord" into those coal miners who dared to challenge him and commanded great respect from citizens and peers alike.

Especially young constables fresh out of the Maritime Police Academy, some of whom feared going into dark alleys late at night. When two new, young constables came to Sgt. Gillis' sitting at his desk one-night complaining that they didn't like going into dark alleys in downtown Glace Bay.

Showing no compassion at all, Sgt. Gillis looked up and asked, "Did you lads pass all the courses at the Police College in Charlottetown?" To a combined "Yes Sgt.", the reply was "Well, you must have missed the one where they handed out 'guts' to policemen." That was the end of similar complaints to Sgt. Gillis from those two.

PETTY CRIMINALS

Two unemployed lads in the town of Glace Bay, Harry and Billy, home alone one evening while their ladies were at Bingo, the lads, drinking and playing cards and smoking cigarettes, ran out of booze and cigarettes at the same time. They tossed a coin and made a pact that one would walk a few blocks away and Break into a 'Dairy' (convenience store) to get some smokes and maybe some snacks while the other would walk a half a mile or more to the legion in No. 11 which was in an isolated, poorly- lit part of town and break in to get some beer. Harry drew the 'short straw' for that mission. At No. 11, under the cover of darkness, he snuck around the back or the legion, climbed a high board fence and jumped down on the other side. At that instant, the headlights of the Town Police paddy wagon, swung into the alleyway beside the legion. Harry buried his face in the tall grass, all the while thinking, "That rat Billy blew the whistle on me". As he lay there trembling on the ground, Harry was relieved that he didn't feel the long arm of the law touch his shoulder, and a deep voice saying "You are under arrest, come with me." When he summoned the courage to take a peek, Harry saw two of Glace Bay's finest, one with a tire iron, rip open the same side door of the Legion, which was to be his target. They entered, proceeded to quickly carry out several boxes of liquor, into the back of the paddy wagon, slam the back door, jump in, back out of the driveway, and disappear into the night. Even though the gaping side door of the legion, extended an invitation for Harry to 'help himself' to the leftovers, he was so relieved to go undetected, that he scurried back over the fence. He hurried home to tell Billy what he had seen, and try to explain why he returned empty handed. Billy had been much more successful, so they enjoyed some snacks and smokes, until their ladies returned home, when Harry amused them with the recount of his adventure.

ROOKIE HANK

In late winter/early spring, a call came in from Angus MacLaren of Catalone that the mainsail had been stolen off his boat. Up until now, Hank had been on patrol with Larry, Donnie or George and never, really on his own. Sgt. House decided this case might be a good one for Hank to attempt alone. On a sunny morning Hank drove the '54 Meteor out the shore road through Port Morien, Birch Grove and Mira Gut to Catalone at the end of one of the many bays from the Atlantic Ocean.

The MacLaren home was backed onto the bay with their twenty-five foot sailboat resting on skids at the outer edge of the backyard with no fence. Mr. MacLaren, a retired schoolteacher, put on his winter boots and jacket and accompanied Hank to the backyard, up onto the boat to the unlocked door of the cabin and opened it. "When I put her up for the winter, I took down the sail, folded it up and put it in here on the deck. When I came out to see how she wintered on Monday the sail was gone and there didn't seem to be anything else missing." Explained Mr. MacLaren.

"Can you describe it to me?" asked Hank as he pulled out his notebook.

"I don't know, I don't think it had any markings, it was just plain canvas, perhaps nine or ten feet high at the mast and maybe five or six feet along the boom. It was a special order to fit the boat, I suppose seven or eight years old." He replied.

Hank asked, "Have you any idea who stole it or when?"

"I've thought about that, I can't think of anybody around here and I have no idea when. Besides, there's not another boat like this in the harbour that the sail would fit." Mr. MacLaren continued, "I doubt if it went in the daylight, and Sheila and I usually spend our evenings in the front of the house. They could have walked across the ice or just came along the shore from the road out there. It wouldn't be hard to carry. Would you like a cup of tea?"

Hollow-leg Hank, at that time, couldn't turn down the offer of a tea and a biscuit with strawberry jam, so they went into the house together. There they talked about the weather, how long Hank had been in Glace Bay, how he liked it here, where Hank was from and how Mr. MacLaren was enjoying his retirement. After the break, Hank said he would check with the immediate neighbours if they saw anyone suspicious around the MacLaren sailboat and that he would "keep in touch" if he learned anything about the theft in future. Four or five neighbourhood calls later, Hank was unsuccessful learning anything about the missing sail.

Back at the office Larry listened attentively to Hank's account of his trip to Catalone and pointed to the drawer of similar 'theft files' that Hank could read and learn, not copy. Larry directed Hank to type a report about his 'theft of sail' investigation, to hopefully be approved by Sgt. House and sent to headquarters in Sydney. From training Hank already knew he needed a blank, triple-copy with carbon, Form C.237 to type his report on and hope that he didn't make too many mistakes that he couldn't erase and have to start all over again.

Over the next few weeks Hank returned to Catalone, checked in with Mr. MacLaren and found neither he nor Hank had anything to report. MacLaren had already ordered a replacement sail and was looking forward to "getting out on the water as soon as it was fit". Back at the office Hank made a 'note to file' and Sgt. House told Hank to keep the file open for another two months in case some new information came in. In this case, it never did.

TRUCK IN MIRA RIVER

One weekday morning in March, a call came in to Glace Bay detachment that a loaded gravel truck had punched the center span out of the Mira Ferry Bridge, and miraculously the driver had survived. On a clear, crisp winter morning Larry drove to Mira Ferry across country, almost an hour's drive and Hank went with him. Some of the roads were paved and some gravel, but they were all Ice- free with good traction. On arrival, they were pleased that some neighbours and the Department of Highways had already erected barricades that blocked both ends of the hundred-yard bridge to prevent further mishaps.

A bystander told the officers "he was some lucky, that driver. If it hadn't been for Ernie, he woulda drowned." Larry asked "Where is the driver now?"

"The ambulance took him to the hospital in Sydney awhile ago."

Three Cell Flashlight

"Does Ernie live around here?" Hank asked.

"Ya, that's his place, the second one up there on the Brickyard Road, the one with the boat out on the ice." Replied the bystander.

Larry and Hank drove up to Ernie Corrigan's, where they were invited in and offered a cup of tea and a biscuit by Mrs. Corrigan, both gratefully accepted as they sat at the kitchen table. After a few sips and a bite or two, Larry turned to Ernie and said, "Can you tell us what happened at the bridge?"

Hank took notes. "I was out in the shop around 9:30, and I heard this crash down towards the bridge. I went out and looked around the corner of the shop and the open water under the bridge was still sloshing around. All of a sudden this man's head popped up outta the water, and the current took him over to this side. He grabbed on to the edge of the ice and started hollering for help. I got my rowboat off the rack at the back of the shop and pushed it down the bank onto the ice stern first. I knew the ice would hold me because I was out on it yesterday. I ran straight for him, he was about sixty or seventy yards away. I slowed down as I got close, and eased the boat out towards him, all the time thinking, I hope this ice holds up under me here. I lifted the bow up so he could grab the stern and I tried to pull him out but he was too heavy, soaking clothes and all. Just then I heard Gordie coming, hollering "Hang on Ern, I'll give ya a hand" and he sure did. Between the two of us, we dragged him outta the water up onto the ice. He tried to make his feet, but it was too slippery and he was getting weak, so we rolled him into the boat and skidded it back up to my place. I called Verna and she called the ambulance and they were here in no time. Verna brought him a hot cuppa tea and a biscuit, and he hung in there till the ambulance got here." "Did you get his name?" Larry asked. "Boudreau, I think, Frank Boudreau." Larry and Hank thanked Mr. and Mrs. Corrigan profusely, went out to the police car, called dispatch in Sydney and asked them which hospital Boudreau had been taken to. In no time, dispatch came back with "St. Rita's."

At the hospital, the officers asked for Mr. Boudreau, were told the room number and that they could have a brief visit with him. They found him lying in bed in a semi-private room all cleaned up and in apparent good spirits. Larry introduced himself and Hank asked him if he could tell them what happened. This time Hank took a statement.

"It was the same as any other trip, when I started across the bridge I had a good load on, and I could feel each span sag a bit just like it always did. That was nothing new. I guess the load was too much for the center span this time, because it didn't only sag, it gave way and the whole works went to the bottom of the river and settled, Thank God, right side up. The engine stalled. In less than a minute, the water started coming in and I remembered my army boots had steel heels on them. I lay back on the seat and with a few good kicks, I got the windshield out and the cold water gushed in. Before the cab filled, I took a deep breath and crawled out onto the engine bonnet, shoved off from it, and was surprised how quick I could see daylight, and got to the surface. I took a big breath and was 'tickled pink' that I didn't come up under the ice. I'd of been a gonner. Thank God for those two guys and their boat."

Both Larry and Hank thanked Mr. Boudreau for his cooperation, congratulated him on his bravery, and wished him a speedy recovery. Two days later, Larry got word that Mr Boudreau had been released from hospital and was going back to his old job, driving gravel trucks. Days later Larry got word that the construction company that owned the gravel truck had hired Chester Hines and his 'monster' tow truck which, with the assistance of a diver, had retrieved the truck, without the load, from the bottom of the river.

THE DENTIST

During Hank's short time in Glace Bay he developed a toothache in one of his back molars. Due to his painful experiences with Dr. Redding in his home village he had developed an inherent fear of the dentist's chair, so he took aspirin and sleeping pills to combat the pain. Eventually with coaxing from his mentor Larry he gave in and went to see Dr. Tom Moffat on Main Street. Dr. Moffat was firm but precise and after a brief examination announced the tooth was ulcerated and needed to be extracted. Sensing Hank's trepidation, he and his assistant Maria proceeded to set up while assuring Hank that he would use plenty of Novocain, his anaesthetic of choice. Maria was average height, pretty, buxom, and friendly, but remained professional when Hank tried to befriend her. Hank was not surprised, as the boys at detachment had warned him about her and had named her 'Marie, the body' after a popular movie star of the day. At times while Hank was sedated and Maria was working closely around him, real or imagined or maybe it was only the rigidity of her starched uniform, Hank thought he could feel her breast brushing against his cheek.

After Dr. Moffat extracted the problem tooth where Hank had felt only the pain of the headlock he applied, he gave Hank some pills to clear up the infection and made an appointment for another visit to possibly replace a seven-year-old artificial crown on Hank's upper right front tooth. It had a gold back with a gold band at the gum line in front, which held the crown in place but was a constant food trap and difficult to maintain. As anyone who has had a crown installed on a tooth, there were several ensuing visits to have the crown replaced, and on one of them Hank 'got up the nerve' to invite Maria out on a date. She smiled and, following what seemed a long tantalizing pause said "OK" and gave Hank her parent's phone number.

His next evening off Hank picked Maria up at her home, met her parents, and went from there in Maybelline to the Drive-in theatre. Hank was proud and excited to be with her and she seemed happy with him. They had burgers and drinks from the canteen. During the movie they snuggled up, hugged and petted with a couple of quick kisses but not much else. Hank took her home early as suggested by her parents. By her body language and unspoken agreement, they never dated again.

After being transferred to Inverness, where the only available dentist in the next town was said to use whiskey as anaesthetic and not recommended for the new young Mountie in town, Hank returned to Glace Bay not only for dental appointments but to visit friends and once again to see Maria.

Later, when Dr. Moffat's name was mentioned in conversation, rumour had it that in the past, some female patients who had anaesthetic applied when Maria wasn't there, after they got home they found their upper under garments had been rearranged, but they had not pursued their complaint.

INVERNESS

TRANSFER TO INVERNESS DETATCHMENT

Next summer, Hank got one week's notice from his Sgt. House at Glace Bay detachment, that he had been transferred to Inverness detachment on the west coast of Cape Breton Island, one hundred and some miles away. Hank was exchanging places with Cst. Danch, and was to pack his kit into his trunk, load it into his car, and report to Inverness on Wednesday of next week. Hank finished up what few files he had, said his goodbyes. George helped him carry his trunk down the stairs, and load it into his '51 Dodge coupe that Larry had sold him for $500 dollars. Hank, on Larry's advice, had financed the car at HFC Finance at 18% interest. Enroute Hank stopped to confirm directions to Inverness, at Port Hastings Detachment, where he met Cpl. Al Ward and Cst. Bateman. It was a beautiful summer day as he drove along the shores of the Gulf of St. Lawrence like a tourist, feeling content with the adventure of it all. The members at Port Hastings couldn't resist jokingly warning Hank, that there'd be more than one tough coal miner waiting to try out the new Mountie in town. For emphasis they added a tale of the last young Mountie transferred into Inverness, being roughed up while making an arrest, and having his Brown Serge tunic ripped all the way up the back.

"You'd better keep your head up, those coal miners are tough!" Said another member with a grin. Hank bravely retorted, "It won't be the first miner I've arrested, and it probably won't be the last".

Hank arrived in Inverness late afternoon, found the detachment, met another Cpl. Ward and Cst Dave MacLean (John D.) who asked Hank to join him later for some supper at the Wonder Bar at the Corner. Dave described Inverness as a mining town that had seen better days and depended mostly on Government cheques and money "sent home from away" by relatives working in Boston, Toronto and Calgary and other locations around the world. In Glace Bay, Hank and other single men took their breakfast and evening meals on the road in cafeterias or restaurants and their Noon meals, if they were in town, at a private home owned by a widow Mrs. McKay, with her young son Jim. In spite of some home cooked meals, stomach problems were common amongst single members, at both locations. Hank, and most other members at the two detachments, smoked cigarettes or a pipe, the 'macho' thing to do. This also contributed to indigestion, but was not recognized as a problem by anyone at the time. In fact one single member at Inverness was known to grope around his bedside table, in the darkness of early morning, find cigarette and lighter, and light up while still in bed. When he went to the bathroom, he'd be shaving with the same cigarette still in his mouth, and the smoke swirling up into his eyes. Hank smoked but was never that badly hooked.

Inverness Detachment was a new building opened a month before Hank arrived, on a street that was paved like all the other streets in town, with 'coal slag'. Hank would later learn that on dry days, the wind blew the dust from the slag into doorways, and open car windows. On wet days, the dark grey mud splashed up on his car, and ruined his newly polished boots. Hank and other members there, found it difficult to keep their kit neat and clean, as they were taught in training. The detachment building was situated across the street from the side of the large Roman Catholic Church, both on a corner lot. It had one garage and one driveway, so other cars had to park on the street, or on the lawn beside the driveway. Up the street was a single family home to the North, before St. Mary's Hospital. Every morning, the first member on duty was required to sweep and polish the office floor and entryway. Inverness was a five-man detachment with a Corporal in charge, with two constables assigned to the town, and three to the County. All four constables lived and slept in single-men's quarters behind the detachment office, but rarely all four were there.

INVERNESS DETACHMENT

The two police cars at Inverness were Chevs, navy blue color, a '54 with a lot of rough miles on it and a '55 that appeared nearly new, partly because Cpl. Ward tended to keep it for himself as he had no private car. Both cars had six cylinder engines with a combined red light and siren on the roof and an RCMP crest on each door. Other equipment was a police radio with limited range, four tires, clutch, gearshift, brakes, gas pedal and a steering wheel. There was no structured schedule, no two men assigned to town, or three to the county. In fact, rarely were five men on duty at the same time what with days off, vacation, courses, sick days, medical appointments, court cases and other surprise duties.

In summer, the senior Constable was a popular candidate to relieve the boss at other nearby detachments while he went on vacation. Hank was too junior for this duty, but had to work extra shifts with others to take up the slack. Other than a spot check of vehicles at the entrance to town in spring and fall, there was little proactive duty. At the time, the men relied heavily on the local telephone operators to redirect calls to probable haunts of members when there was no one at the detachment office. Basically, the unwritten code was if there was an urgent call and you were in town, you go, in uniform or not. One summer afternoon Hank and his buddy, Cst. Brian Stevens were off duty swimming at the beach, and a call came in about a fight downtown near the liquor store. Both police cars were out of town, so Hank and Brian responded in Hank's car, swimsuits and sneakers, broke up the fight, took the two 'pugilists' to jail and returned to the beach.

Early the next year, Cpl Ward was replaced by Cpl. Cunning who ranked as one of the worst managers Hank knew in his entire career. He transferred in from the mainland 'under a cloud' amid a swirl of rumours with a chip on his shoulder. He was subject to mood swings and rarely delegated or discussed events of the previous or the coming day directly with his men. Rather, he came into the office from his quarters next door in the evening when the men were out on the road or off duty, signed or rejected the reports, and left notes in each member's basket indicating corrections from the past and instructions for the future. He was rarely there during the day, but gone somewhere with one of the two cars with no identified purpose and no estimated time of return. He too did not own a personal vehicle. He became a friend of the mine owner/operator in St. Rose who drove a new Cadillac and they spent a lot of time together. Occasionally in good weather his superiors in Sydney made surprise early-morning visits to try to catch him not on duty, but he thwarted them at every turn. Hank was on duty one such morning polishing the office floor, invited the Inspector and his Sgt. into the office and notified Cpl. Cunning next door of their presence. CpI. Cunning came to the door from his quarters partially dressed in uniform, excused himself, asked Hank to show them into his office and said "I'll be right with you gentlemen". Hank put the polisher in the closet and continued typing his reports from the night before. For some time there was a loud, heated discussion from his office but after the guests departed, Cpl. Cunning emerged with a smirk, seemingly unscathed.

BLOOD RELAYS

When Hank first arrived in Inverness through general discussion amongst the members, he learned that any day, on short notice, a call might come in requesting a police car meet the Port Hastings car at an appointed time and place on highway nineteen to pick up a delivery of urgently needed blood for a surgery at the Inverness Memorial hospital. It was apparent to Hank that other young constables relished the opportunity to drive a police car as fast as they dared in the name of saving someone's life. One fine late summer morning Hank got the nod to make a relay. He was to meet the Hastings car at Harbourview in front of the school with strict instructions from the Cpl in charge to drive smartly but carefully and to use the siren and red light when other traffic was present. Twenty–five minutes later Hank met Cst. Mel Bateman for the first time without incident, exchanged greetings, received the precious cargo, got back into his car and started towards Inverness with siren blaring, red light flashing and adrenalin pumping. Enroute he caught up to an old pickup with a load of hay hanging over the side and he surmised the driver could not see him in his rear view mirror and maybe couldn't hear the siren either. Hank slowed and waited for a break in oncoming traffic and a rare straight stretch where he could pass safely. After a few minutes near the top of a hill, the truck slowed, swung out to the left and bounced to the right over the shoulder and into a farm lane. Hank dropped his car into second gear, tramped on it and when the car got rolling, shifted into high and made it to the hospital in no time, stopped at the front door, grabbed the package off the front seat beside him, jumped out and met the nurse waiting for him at the front door. She was young and cute, said Thanks, smiled while she grabbed the package, turned quickly and headed inside. Hank later acquired her name and phone number, called and asked her for a date. She said, "Sorry but I'm already spoken for". Hank was disappointed but chalked it up to experience and carried on.

Hank made several similar relays that were uneventful except one. This time it was late winter just before dark with patches of black ice resulting from thawing during the day and freezing again before the salt truck got out. The traffic was light and Hank thought he was driving carefully but going downhill into a sharp left curve in the Glen he lost it and the car started drifting towards the guardrail. Hank steered to the left and braked gently, but to no avail. The front end of the car went into the windrow of snow, which flew up over the engine hood and filled the windshield so Hank could barely see out. Hank could see and smell the steam from the snow hitting the hot engine while he was grappling for the wiper switch. The car bounced back onto the roadway and Hank had to scramble to keep it from crossing the road into the guardrail on the other side. Finally he got it righted and continued on with a sigh of relief that there was no oncoming traffic and a "Thank you God" for the soft snow that cushioned the initial impact. When he met the car coming from Port Hastings, he and Bert quickly examined the right front corner of his car using the headlights of Bert's car, there was no apparent damage. Bert handed Hank the precious cargo, they both turned and went their separate ways and Hank carefully returned to Inverness Hospital with his delivery.

CAR WASH

One hot summer morning Hank was on a Town patrol and stopped by the railway freight shed to pick up a parcel from a mail- order catalogue. It was wrapped in heavy brown paper and hopefully contained some new hand tools Hank had ordered to work on his car. As he returned to the car the police radio was barking a message that a drunken man was 'stemming' (begging) and making a nuisance in front of the liquor store. Hank threw his parcel on the front seat, responded, arrested the man without incident, searched him and put him in the back seat of the two door police car. Since he had come along willingly Hank didn't cuff him and on the short trip to jail, two blocks, he sat up on the edge of the back seat with his folded arms resting on the back of Hank's seat pleading the old familiar

"Aw c'mon gimmie a break. You seem like a nice young fella, I didn't hurt anybody gimmie a f---in break." "You just sit back in the seat and behave and we'll be there in no time," said Hank, so the man stayed where he was and went quiet. Then, without warning, he threw up a stinking, running gush of stale beer over Hank's right shoulder, down the front of his shirt, down behind Hank's back creating a puddle on the driver's seat. Hank was shocked, but didn't stop as he was nearing the jail. For an instant Hank thought if I wanted to cool off on a hot day, this would not be the way I would choose. Hank got out at the jail, around the car, disgusted, reached into the back seat, unceremoniously hauled the man out of the back seat, put an arm lock on him and walked him on his tip toes into the jail.

When Duncan the jailer saw Hank he chuckled to himself, looked at the prisoner and said, "What the f--- am I supposed to do with this mess?" "I don't know, he's your problem, throw a bucket of water on him. I'm going back to the office to get cleaned up" was Hank's reply. At the car, Hank looked in at the wet driver's seat, shrugged and sat in with his already soaked shirt and breeches, and noticed the vomit had also covered his parcel. Back at the office his Cpl. got a good laugh when he saw Hank's shirt, reminded him to hose out the car, leave it to dry in the sun, get changed and ready to go again. For years afterward, Hank swore he could still smell vomit off the plastic handle of his 'new' multi-tipped screwdriver.

Later that year, on a dark, rainy night Hank got a call to an accident on the Strathlorne stretch between a car and a horse and wagon.

Hank drove out the two miles with his siren and red light flashing. When he arrived at the scene some other motorists were already there and Hank asked a man with a flashlight to walk back up the road towards town and flag down other vehicles and warn them of the accident ahead. The only lights at the scene were the lights of other vehicles, the flashing red light on top of the police car and Hank's three- cell flashlight. When Hank approached the driver's side of the black coupe involved in the accident, the lady driver was still behind the wheel, the window was down she had her head on the window sill, and was sobbing

"I couldn't see him I might have killed him, is he O.K.?" Hank asked, "Who's him?" "The man in the wagon" she faintly replied. When Hank went to check the wagon, the man's rubber boots were still sitting on the floor of the wagon, the shafts were broken off and the horse was gone. With the help of a bystander, Hank located the driver of the wagon a man from Mount Young, sitting on the shoulder of the highway in his sock feet. When Hank asked, "Are you hurt?" he chuckled "I'm O.K. but it looks like my horse is gone home without me."

As it turned out there was minimal damage to the front of the car or the black wagon except for the broken shafts. (No triangular slow moving signs for the back of the wagon in those days.) The driver of the car, had her car towed back to town and came to the office the next day to file the accident report. Both she and the man were alone in their vehicles and both received a ride home from a neighbour, the wagon was left in the ditch for the night and retrieved the next day.

Hank later learned the horse that fled the scene relatively unscathed, ran alone in the dark, the almost ten miles home right into the barn and into his stall.

TELEPHONE OPERATORS

Not long after Hank arrived in Inverness he began to realize how valuable the telephone operators were when he was working alone or with another member, they could call 'Central' give the phone number where they'd be for the next little while and the operator would forward any police calls to that number. Also the cheery greeting "operator" when he made the call would give him a 'boost' on an otherwise gloomy day. Remember this was long before 'cell phones' even portables and these ladies were on duty twenty-four hours a day willing to help. When he was in the office typing reports and needed a break and didn't yet know many people in town, Hank could always call the 'operator' and have a friendly chat if she wasn't busy.

Of the four operators at that time plus Regis the boss, Hank liked Christine the best so he 'got up the nerve' one day and asked her for a date. She accepted. Hank picked her up in his car at her father's house; they went to the movies and to the Wonder Bar for a burger afterwards. A tall, pretty brunette Hank's age, with a sense of humour she was obviously happy to be seen with the newest Mountie in town. Her father and her brother-in-law were both coal miners at Evan's Mine in St. Rose who sometimes had to work on their knees in a thirty-inch seam of coal. They didn't have a car so hitched a ride to the mine twenty some miles north of town with a friend or on a shuttle. While Hank dated Christine, he was welcome at her home by both mother and father and on weekends drove them to social events or visiting friends. On a day off in the fall, Hank and Christine would take a drive to a neighbouring town or into the mountains to see the fall colors, without mom and dad.

In stark contrast to the operators in Inverness, eight years later, shortly after Hank arrived in Shelburne, constable Dunsford was off duty and Hank called the operator to tell her that he had to visit the Crown Prosecutor for half an hour to discuss a case and asked her to forward any calls to his number. She responded abruptly "I'm sorry, we don't do that here". Hank recognized her voice as a neighbour he had met just once and appealed to her but she simply said, "We don't make the rules". Although Hank was taken aback, he had to concede that operators were not being paid for this service and accepted the old adage 'When in Rome do as the Romans do' and live with it.

EXPLODING FLASHLIGHT

Whatever trepidation Hank had of being transferred to Inverness, the once booming coal-mining town, was reinforced over time by the stories of the other members previously stationed there. Some were humorous and others not so. Some have already been included in other chapters of this book. One involved a lumberjack who had too much to drink late one night and his family or friends couldn't persuade him to settle down, so they 'called the Mounties'. A young member working alone at the time took the call. Once there, he tried to subdue the offender who didn't fight back, but kept slipping away from the officer's grasp so the officer couldn't get the cuffs on him. In those days 'night sticks' or 'billy clubs' were not issued to help control a culprit. So, at the point of exhaustion and embarrassed in front of bystanders, as a last resort, the young officer swung his three-cell flashlight, striking the culprit on the back of the head. The end of the flashlight with the bulb and glass in it went flying through the air followed by three 'D' cell batteries, much to the delight of the bystanders, even more so when the man didn't drop to his knees. The offender straightened up, put his hand up to his head, peered out under his arm at the Mountie and said "Jees man what'd ya do that for?"

"Oh all right I'll come with ya." He conceded.

The moral of that story is, don't use your three- cell flashlight as a 'billy stick'!

Another story for Hank, the new constable in Inverness, involved the Corporal and an unnamed young constable answering a call to a fight on the street at the North end of town involving several brothers known as the 'the blue boys'. An attempt by the officers to arrest some or all of the combatants was met by resistance so forceful that both officers were assaulted so severely that the constable 'ran for help'. By the time he returned, the Corporal had been beaten so badly that he had to be hospitalized, but recovered. The assailants were later arrested by other members from Inverness and neighbouring detachments, charged, convicted and sentenced to serve a variety of time in jail or penitentiary, depending on their degree of involvement.

BODY ASHORE IN DUNVEGAN

The next morning Hank was nominated by Cpl. Ward to attend the autopsy and collect samples of body parts suitable to send to the RCMP lab in Sackville, N.B. Hank walked the less than a block up the coal dust Railway Street to St. Mary's Hospital. The autopsy was to be performed by Dr. MacLellan who had to drive the hundred miles plus across the island from Sydney that morning. Hank met him in the reception area of the hospital and they went down the stairs to the morgue in the basement, which as the country song goes 'it's dark as a dungeon and damp as the dew'. The attending nurse/nun provided Hank and the doctor with white cotton gowns and rubber gloves. The body was laid out on its back on a marble slab and the doctor chose to first open the chest and examine the lungs. Immediately the air was filled with the smell of rotting flesh. He found water in the lung sacks, which indicated the man probably died from drowning but he continued examining other organs. The examiner took samples, which Hank diligently placed, in bottles containing formaldehyde.

INVERNESS

When the doctor approached the head he asked Hank to stand at the end of the table and hold the head of the body from turning while he attempted removing the cap of the skull with a hacksaw. Although rigor mortise had set in a long time ago, the motion of the saw caused the head to turn and the skin of the head to peel off in Hank's hands, which caused some difficulty for Hank to keep his breakfast down. While Hank peeled off the gloves, the alert nurse/nun seeing the doctor's plight offered to fetch a dremel-like electric tool used to cut casts off patients.

It worked like a charm as the doctor removed the cap from the skull with Hank barely needing to hold the head. Examination of the brain and the rest of the body showed no sign of foul play. As they removed their gowns and gloves, the doctor thanked Hank for his assistance, handed him the samples and they departed.

Hank walked back to the office, found the wooden box with sawdust in it, to pack the bottles in for shipment to the lab, packed it up, put the lock on it, made sure the address was correct, walked across the street to the Post Office and mailed it. Then returned to the office to write the report to send to headquarters.

That evening Hank received a message from Cpl. Anderson at Antigonish that they had identified the body as that of Ronald James Reardon, a fifty-seven year old bachelor from Cape George who had been reported missing eighteen days ago. They had notified his sister, Mabel MacInnis, the only next of kin and she was making arrangements to recover the body.

"That's great news Al," Hank told him and continued with the details of the autopsy. Cpl. Anderson reported that Reardon was a seasonal labourer, fishing and lumbering and lived alone in one of the fish shacks at the harbour. "I'll put my senior man Cst. Batt on this and see if there's anything more to this. How's the weather up there? Did you get your deer yet?" Al inquired.

"No luck yet, just been out once." Hank replied. "Thanks for your help Al, we'll talk later. Tell Mrs. MacInnis to look me up when she gets here, if we can be of any assistance."

Hank knocked on the Cpl's door next to the office and told Cpl. Ward "I just heard from Al Anderson in Antigonish, they concluded that our body is probably a Reardon from Cape George missing since October 2nd.

"We may as well wait and see what they find" Cpl Ward replied. "We'll talk more tomorrow."

The next day Hank did some typing and paper work, took a call from a lady in Broad Cove about someone stealing apples from her mother's abandoned orchard next door, but once there, she could offer Hank little information as to who the culprit(s) might be or what kind of vehicle they were driving. That evening Cst. Batt called to say that he could find no evidence of foul play around Cape George. The deceased was a bachelor who didn't have a lot of friends and he came and went as he pleased. That's why nobody missed him. He liked his drink and may have fallen off the little bridge over the creek with no railing, near his shack, into the harbour and drowned. He also mentioned that Ms. MacInnis had engaged the funeral home in Antigonish to retrieve her brother's body from Inverness and prepare if for burial. They should arrive sometime tomorrow morning if Hank wanted to notify the hospital, which he did.

HAVING A BABY

One stormy winter night Hank was on duty alone at Inverness Detachment when an excited Bobby Williams called from West Lake "My wife is having a baby, we're stormed in and my car won't start. Can you help me?"

"We'll see what we can do, keep calm and we'll call you back." Hank called the switchboard at the telephone office and enlisted the help of Norma the operator on duty to call the snowplough operators Edwin and Earl and ask them to open the West Lake Road, and the lane to the Williams place, if possible. He also asked Norma to call Mr. Williams back and tell him help was on the way. Hank donned his P Jacket and fur cap, overshoes and winter gloves, cleaned off the police car, made sure he had his three-cell flashlight and snow shovel and started out to West Lake some fifteen miles out of town. Visibility was poor but the first three miles out, the road had been ploughed. Now drifts were forming in open places. There were no other vehicles on the road. When Hank turned onto the gravel Lake road, he could see that the snowplough had gone on ahead of him, so he sped up a bit but remained cautious especially on curves and along the shore of the lake, which was frozen over, and heavily snow covered. About five miles in the West Lake road Hank could see between squalls the flashing lights on the back of the snowplough, so he slowed and let them lead the rest of the way. When they came to the Williams place they stopped and opened the side door of the plough. Hank left the car engine running, jumped out, walked up beside the plough, climbed the ladder to the cab and hollered above the wind and the plough engine

"Thanks for coming out on such a bitch of a night" Edwin said

"No problem, get in and close the door." The cab smelled of diesel and cigarette smoke but it was warm and Hank thought to himself what a nice shelter from the storm and what great guys these are to be here, but he wouldn't tell them because they'd only say "we already know that". They decided Hank shouldn't attempt the lane that wasn't ploughed and asked him if the barnyard was big enough to turn the plough around if they went up. Hank said he remembered it was from last fall, as he dismounted from the cab, got back in his car and followed the plough up the lane where it circled and parked as Bobby came out the door of the house. Hank rolled down the window and hollered against the wind "How is she?"

"Hangin in there, but she's gettin close" was the reply, followed by "Do you mind takin her in to the hospital Cst. James, I gotta stay home with the kids?" Hank assured him he'd get her there safely and asked him to call ahead to the hospital to tell them we were coming. By this time the expectant mother was standing in the doorway all dressed in boots and parka and ready to go.

Hank held the car door open and the back of the front seat tipped down so she could get in and lie down if needed. When all was ready the snowplough led the way down the lane and onto the road, pulled over and let Hank go by with emergency light flashing and moving faster with his precious cargo. Twenty minutes later Hank was greeted at the hospital door by two nurses dressed in winter boots and coats to assisted Mrs. Williams into the hospital. "Many Thanks" said the nurses. "Drop in for a coffee later".

As Hank drove away, he thought 'thank God she didn't deliver in the back seat' and 'what wonderful, caring citizens these people are' and he was reminded of the great cooperation the Force had from telephone and snow plough operators, linemen from the Power Commission and Maritime Tel. and Tel., ambulance drivers, medical staff and all those that made his job easier. The baby was a boy, but sadly they didn't name him Hank!

THE TRIALS

Trials were a common part of Hank's duties. Unfortunately, Hank bore the brunt of lawyers like McNeil ridiculing him just once, but swore never again, and later at an inquiry appealed to Crown Prosecutor MacDonald in private to give Hank better support on the witness stand in future.

Another example of McNeil's free-wheeling cross-examinations was when Hank's junior friend Cst. Mike Stinson on patrol alone in a snowstorm arrested an impaired driver who had enough money to hire McNeil. During Mike's direct testimony at the ensuing trial, he had mentioned that the snow was so deep it was as high as the telephone wires. By the time McNeil was finished with him during cross-examination, he had Mike agreeing that the defendant "could have been driving on the telephone wires." Hank witnessed that there was no objection from the Crown Prosecutor and no interruption from Magistrate Chisholm. Besides, rumour had it that Magistrate Chisholm and Prosecutor MacDonald would on occasion 'chip in' on a bottle enroute to the 'trials' and may have even invited McNeil to join them in the hotel room after court was adjourned.

Coincidental or otherwise, the Cpl. in charge of Inverness detachment at the time rarely attended the trials, but left the young constables to their own volition when it came to testifying. Sometimes, if available or involved in a case of his own, the senior constable would attend and be there for moral support to the young inexperienced constables, but not always. This was in stark contrast to Hank's experience in Glace Bay or later in Baddeck where the Crown Prosecutors recognized the plight of some young constables in the courtroom and gave all the support allowed. Hank vowed when he became in charge of a detachment later, he would never allow his subordinates to be exposed to the kind of embarrassment he and Mike had at the hands of McNeil in the court room at Inverness.

MEETING MARY ANN

During the early weeks of Hank's tour in Inverness, John D. and he were having lunch at the counter in the Baltimore Café when through the front door came two tall, stately, well-dressed ladies, one an attractive middle aged lady and the other a tall, younger, drop-dead-gorgeous blonde. They took a table behind John D. and Hank and casual glances in their direction caused Hank to whisper "I gotta find out more about her" prompting John D to joke "Which one, the mother or the blond?"

Two nights later Hank was on town patrol when he met a car with one headlight out, so he pulled it over. The driver, Glen Rossman was surprised to hear that the light was out and explained "I was up-country today on gravel roads and must have picked up a stone, this is a Department of Agriculture car, I'll get if fixed right away". This all became secondary to Hank because, when he shone his three- cell flashlight into the car, there were also two young ladies in the front seat beside the driver, a cute brunette in the middle, and on the far side, there she was, the blonde from the café. Hank wrote a warning ticket to the young man and told him after he gets the light fixed, to bring the car in so he could cancel the ticket and give him a safety sticker. Hank just happened to be in the office typing reports when Glen returned early the next week with the headlight fixed, so Hank asked him about the blonde in the front seat the night he was stopped.

"She's my girlfriend's sister, she's home on vacation from nurse's training in Glace Bay, and she's at her father's farm at Lake Ainslie," he said.

Hank obtained her father's phone number, thanked Glen for coming in with the repaired headlight and gave him a sticker. Hank called Mary Ann that evening, told her who he was, and asked her out on a date Saturday evening. She hesitated for what seemed the longest time, but with his best plea Hank said, "we'll just go for a drive down Margaree Harbour to see an old fishing schooner that was towed in just yesterday. They're going to make a restaurant out of it, I'll bring along a chaperon if you wish."

"Okay, I guess that would be all right, what time?" She asked.

"How's six o'clock, and Oh, how do I find your father's farm?" She gave Hank directions and said "Okay then. See you Saturday evening". Hank couldn't wait for Saturday to come.

Saturday, Hank's car wouldn't start, so he borrowed Jim Riley's '54 Ford, took neighbour Danny MacLeod as chaperon and guide, and met Mary Ann and her family. Danny chatted with Mary Ann's father Alex in Gaelic/English, and Hank answered some questions from her mother Jean. When the visit ended, the young couple dropped Danny off in town, drove to Margaree

Harbour, saw the old schooner, walked and talked along the beach beside the harbour, then took Mary Ann back home. On the way, they picked up two teenage neighbours of Mary Ann's, drove them up the mountain past her home and came back down. When Hank turned Jim's car around in her father's yard, he was so excited he backed into a big maple tree in front of the house. Mary Ann laughed. No damage was incurred to car or tree, just Hank's pride. Hank walked her to the door, they said goodnight, and that's how it all began!

ADVENTURE AT INVERNESS

One night when Hank was off duty, he took Mary Ann and her girlfriend Kay to 'the movies' at Tubetti's theatre. After the movie he took them to the Wonder Bar in Maybelline for burgers, and later drove across town to 'see the sights'. On the way, Hank spotted a local criminal Martin MacDonald walking along the sidewalk. Hank knew there was an outstanding Warrant for his arrest because he had been charged for assaulting his girlfriend. Martin was a strong, young lumberjack who Hank didn't attempt to arrest alone, especially with the girls in his private car, so he cut through the alley beside the Co-op store to go back to the detachment to get a police car and some help from Dave, who was on duty. When the car crossed the ditch onto Church Street and swung to the right, the driver's door on the old car unlatched and flew open. Hank was left halfway out the open door hanging onto the steering wheel with his right hand and frantically reaching for the brake with his right foot, to no avail. Finally he let go of the steering wheel and fell to the ash covered street leaving the girls alone in the front seat as the car crawled slowly up onto Archie Cameron's lawn and headed for the front porch, like something possessed. Meanwhile the two passengers sat awe-struck staring at the approaching porch while Hank gathered himself up off the street, ran to the stopped car and shut the engine off. The commotion woke Archie who came down to the porch and outside in his pyjamas saying, "What the hell is going on here, you knocked me outta bed. I know you son, you'll pay for this!"

Hank tried to explain but Archie wasn't listening. Together under the porch light Archie and Hank examined the front of the car and the side of the porch. There was no damage to either.

Coincidentally, a few weeks before, Archie had had a fender-bender down town and Cpl. Cunning nominated Hank, the junior man, to write a letter to the Nova Scotia Department of Motor Vehicles, recommending that due to his senior age, Archie should have his driving privileges revoked, and they were. The day after Hank's car bumped Archie's house, his son 'Shorty', operator of a small, prospect coal mine on the River Hill on the North end of Town, came to the detachment, talked privately to the Corporal, and they agreed to forget the whole thing. Hank was really relieved because for awhile he thought this whole episode might cost him his career. MacDonald was later arrested at his home by Dave and Hank, and jailed awaiting trial later that week. He was found guilty and sentenced to one month in the County jail at Port Hood.

DANCES AT THE GLEN

Every Wednesday night during the summer, one of the most popular fiddlers on the Island, Scotty Fitzgerald played for square dances at the Glen beside highway nineteen just south of town. The proprietor Donnie D.R. didn't hire bouncers, but relied on the Mounties to visit and keep the peace. Bryan and Hank were the only two on duty, one warm, summer night and dropped in to the dance to check things out. Booze was big at these dances, especially with local young men, home from Ontario and the U.S. on vacation, trying to make an impression. When Bryan and Hank arrived at the front of the dance hall, they noticed a crowd gathered around the back of a new two-toned Dodge Custom Royal, with the trunk open. Young men, including the owner of the car, were drinking beer from bottles, between the highway and the front door of the hall, under the lone light on the wall above the door. They showed little concern at the arrival of the Police, so Bryan and Hank grabbed their three-cell flashlights and walked into the middle of the crowd. Bryan shouted "What the Hell do you think you're doing here? Who owns this car?" At the same time Hank noticed the open trunk was half full of open cases of beer and hard liquor. Meanwhile, Bryan determined who owned the car, put the cuffs on him, and started towards the police car. The young man put up a struggle, so Hank joined in, and together they walked him to, and put him in the back seat of the nearby police car with a warning to "stay put if you know what's good for you." By the time the constables returned to the car with the open trunk, much of the liquor had disappeared, but they seized what was left, found a friend of the owner to take care of the car, and put the seizure into the trunk of the police car.

Now, some of the crowd, bolstered by the liquor and their numbers, gathered around the two Mounties and the police car shouting "Let Billy go, you're not gettin out of here alive". Hank shoved his way through the crowd, jumped in behind the wheel of the police car while Bryan entered the passenger side and checked on the prisoner, who by now had reconciled himself to his fate. Meanwhile, the gathered mob shouted all kinds of threats and obscenities like "You bastards. We'll get you for this". Some grabbed the sides of the police car, rocking it back and forth, trying to turn it over. Knowing the disparity of their situation, Bryan and Hank, both six feet plus tall, grabbed their flashlights and simultaneously swung both car doors open, knocking some of the crowd off their feet, stood up on the doorsills of the car scanned the mob with their flashlights, and Bryan bravely hollered "You people break it up and move away from this car, or we'll come back with help, and arrest the whole damn bunch". A few stragglers remained boldly in the police car headlights blocking the exit to the highway. Hank slipped down behind the wheel. Both constables slammed the car doors. Hank revved the engine of the police car to a pitch, dropped the car into low gear, and floored it. The stragglers scattered like the parting of the Red Sea, and the gravel flew from the rear wheels as it lurched out onto the highway. In town, the constables found Duncan the jailer, deposited the young man into the jail, and headed right back to the dance. They found the crowd had dispersed from the parking lot. They entered the dance hall to a greeting from Katie, the proprietor's wife, "Boys, you sure got away with one that time". She pointed out a sober cousin of the young man in jail, who assured Hank that he would take care of the new Dodge car and get it home to the parents place. He also offered to notify them that their son was in jail in town for the night. Later that night, Bryan and Hank returned again to the dance hall and all was quiet. 'High fives' as they walked back to the police car, breathing a sigh of relief that another close call was behind them.

INVERNESS

DANNY MACLEOD

If ever there was a 'friend of the Force' anywhere, Danny MacLeod, the manager of the Inverness Unemployment Insurance office certainly was one. Before Hank was transferred to Inverness, Danny's office was on the third floor of the old Post Office building on the corner of Railway and Church Streets, while the R.C.M.P. office was on the second floor. By the time Hank got there, the new R.C.M.P. office was diagonally across the street from the Post Office, and the stories of camaraderie, pranks and practical jokes in the old office abounded from the members still stationed there. Stories like the weekly Friday morning 'fatigue day' when all hands would turn out to ensure that the past week's dirt was cleaned up and every room including the single men's quarters was left 'spic and span' for the next week.

One morning when the clean up was about complete, Danny or one of his employees came in off the unpaved, coal dust covered street with winter boots on and tramped all over the freshly cleaned office floor to the howls and threats of the assembled' janitors' before escaping up the stairs to his own office. Another 'fatigue day' Friday morning the third floor neighbours might throw a stray cat or dog into the police office to scurry around and track up the clean floors before being captured and deposited into the office one flight of stairs above. On another 'fatigue day' morning a mischievous constable from Newfoundland who was known to be late at times like this, appeared in the office door from the men's quarters, with his penis hanging out of his pants. When Cpl. Ward asked, "What the Hell do you think you're doing?" he replied, "If you want me to work like a horse, I may as well look like a horse" and scooted back into his quarters to the snickers and laughter of others assembled.

For a new member in town, Danny was always ready with a joke or a story to help him relax and, if deserving, Danny was also a great source of information on almost anyone in central Inverness County, like their correct name and 'nickname', where they lived, where they worked, and sometimes even who their father and grandfather were. However he was careful not to reveal personal Unemployment Insurance information. Danny had a litany of stories of town and country characters including humorous escapades of former members of Inverness Detachment. One young member who was known to perhaps drink too much with his 'buddies' on his weekly day off, forgot to come back to work. After a day or two and many futile trips and enquiries to locate him, frustrated Cpl. Ward 'staked out' the local liquor store. When the young constable and his friends drove up to replenish their supply, Cpl. Ward moved in, placed the 'truant' under open arrest and called headquarters in Sydney. They ordered him removed from active duty and delivered to Sydney for further disciplinary action. As the Force was known to do in similar situations in those days, instead of counselling, rehabilitation or some such help, they transferred the problem, in this case back to his home Province. Like the rabbit in the briar patch, he never looked back. Hank later met him as a senior N.C.O. during an operational audit, and they had a few good laughs about their times in Inverness.

Danny didn't have a car; so on the May 24th weekend when Hank was going home to P.E.I. to visit his family, he invited Danny and his family to come with him for the trip to visit relatives. Danny, a widower, had a teenage daughter; a teenage son Kevin who was the paper boy for the detachment and a younger daughter aged eight. Kevin later joined the Force and served in "O" Division (Ontario) and CSIS his entire career. His youngest sister Marcella married a member of the Force who was stationed in Inverness long after Hank was there.

This was the first ferryboat ride for the children, and they were treated to drinks and snacks during the seventy-five minute crossing to P.E.I. On arrival, Hank dropped them off in the city, and picked them up on the return trip on Monday morning. Some souvenir photos were taken and all had a memorable trip!

Back on the job, Danny was known to exercise his authority in cases where a young man from the area, unable to get work in a once active coal mining town would "get in trouble" with the law. Instead of seeing him charged, Danny would negotiate with the police, supply funds through the Employment Insurance Commission already approved by the Federal Government, buy a train ticket to elsewhere in Canada where the young man could get a job and start a new life. Many such grateful young men either wrote to Danny or came in person on vacation to thank him 'from the bottom of their hearts' for what he had done to 'give them a leg up' and change their life forever. This system worked well for years.

INVERNESS

Danny always made a point to meet new members who transferred in to Inverness. He would shake hands with them and greet them in Gaelic. When they said they didn't understand him, Danny, with a serious look, would ask "How do you expect to work in a community where the first language is Gaelic?" The next day when the Cpl. came in to work, a concerned member, Shorty Jesperson asked for a transfer stating Danny told him he didn't have the native language. Cpl. Ward just smiled and told Cst. Jesperson, "Don't believe anything that man says."

Danny was later a Justice of the Peace. Women whose husbands were charged with being drunk or having open liquor would come to Danny's house and ask Danny to give the husband time in jail instead of a fine, because the fine would take a good portion of the welfare cheque or sentence him to three days in jail to allow the wife time to cash the cheque and buy groceries and other necessities at home. Danny would always give the person charged with a minor offence a choice of either paying $10.00 and costs or $25.00 and costs. Of course they all would choose the former, believing Danny was 'giving them a break' and go away thinking, "What a great guy!"

Another time, in winter, the then Sgt. in charge of Inverness Detachment as a joke gave Danny a brown serge jacket with Staff Sgt. stripes on it that he had before he was demoted. The next day, as a 'return joke', Danny told the Sgt. that a man who liked his drink, was well known to the police, came to Danny's house in short sleeves and he was cold. So Danny gave him the jacket. The man thanked Danny profusely and said

"I'm wearin this to the Legion and then I'm gonna hitch-hike home," all of which was not true. When the Sgt. heard this, he called all available men and cars to find the man and retrieve the jacket before the Sgt. "got in trouble". The members searched the town and surrounding communities but were unable to locate the man or the jacket. Late the next day after he figured the Sgt. had sweated long enough, Danny phoned the Sgt. and told him the man returned the jacket to him because "he didn't look good in brown". The Sgt. was much relieved and offered a few not-so-complimentary words to Danny for his 'caper' with the jacket after which they both had a great laugh.

Three Cell Flashlight

BALER ACCIDENT

One afternoon during Hank's second summer in Inverness, a call came in from the Court House in Port Hood that a farmer had died in Glencoe while working on a hay baler and the constable from Port Hood couldn't be reached because he was out on the harbour water skiing. John D and Hank responded with difficulty, because of the maze of gravel roads in an unfamiliar area. They eventually came upon a farm with a tractor and baler stopped in the field, not far from the farmhouse, with a man standing beside the tractor. Hank drove past the field and up a short lane to the house. Before the police car stopped, a lady came running from the house saying, "Thank God you're here. Alex had a bad accident with the baler, and we think he's dead out there in the field. Sadie is in the house with the children. They're all bawlin, and she doesn't want them to see their father like that."

John D and Hank went to the kitchen door with the neighbour woman to express their sympathy to Mrs. MacInnis. After she suppressed her sobs, John D asked her, "Who found your husband?" "I did" she said and continued, "I was workin in the kitchen and I could watch Alex mowin below the house, and at first didn't think much about it when I saw the tractor stopped, because that happens all the time when you're balin. After a minute or two I looked out again and there was no sign of Alex. I put my boots on and walked down through the field and as I got closer, there he was lyin on the ground under the baler. I ran to him screamin his name and fell down beside him. Neighbour Davie must have heard me and came runnin from the other end of the field.

"He looked Alex over and said "Sadie, I'm afraid he's gone. Looks like the plunger arm got him in the head." He hugged me and said "We can't leave him here like this because of the flies. I'll go home and get a tarp to put over him." He also offered to call you guys and Angus Norman, the undertaker in Port Hastings.'

While John D stayed with Mrs. MacInnis to take some notes and explain the possible need for an inquest, Hank walked down through the field to the man who had come running when he heard Sadie screaming. Hank introduced himself to David McNeil and apologized for taking so long to get there.

Hank knelt down and petted the dog still lying there beside the body. He pulled back the tarp to have a closer look. There was some dried blood on his face and the side of his head and when Hank touched the skull, it was as soft as jelly. He turned to Mr. McNeil and asked, "What do you think happened here?" "I'm not sure, but when I got here the baler engine was still runnin and the plunger arm was still goin up and down. I shut it off. I figure he must have bent down to see what was plugged and got his head jammed between the arm and the frame. I brought the tarp from home to keep the flies off him. Would you like me to start the engine to see how it runs?" "Thanks," said Hank "I don't know much about balers." When the engine started, the plunger that packed the bales started back and forth, the arm that drove it looped down and up between the sides of the frame below the engine every five seconds. There was no guard on it. Hank could easily see how quickly that arm could get you if you got too close.

By the time Mr. McNeil and Hank walked back to the farmhouse, Cst. Simmonds from Port Hood had returned from water skiing and arrived at the MacInnis farm. John D had already filled him in on the details of the accident. Simmonds, being senior to John D and Hank, in his own area and away from the grieving family said, "That's okay fellas. Thanks for your help. I'll take it from here." Hank and John D. got into their police car, said goodbye to Mrs. MacInnis. She and Mr. McNeil, thanked them for their help, and they headed back into their own area in case there was someone else looking for help.

TOWN CHARCTERS

Jimmy Taylor

Another unforgettable character was Jimmy Taylor, a prematurely white-haired operator of the Texaco garage, who sold new and used cars, had a smile that would light up the night, would sweep an unsuspecting lady off her feet, and as they say 'could sell ice to Eskimos'. Both he and his partner John Smith were returned veterans of World War II, and John had a severe limp, a testament to a wound in action. Jimmy had a wife and son who lived in Guysboro, but he rarely ever spoke of them. Like most of his friends, Hank was hooked the first time he met Jimmy. He gave better-priced gas, lube oil and filter for the police cars, than the other two garages in town. He also had a body man,

John MacDonnell, in the basement of the garage, which could touch up little dents and scratches on your car, police car or personal.

In fact, Hank's car Maybelline was black when he bought it, and one day when things were quiet, John said "You and Sonny sand and masque your old car, and I'll paint it for you." What colour?" Hank asked. With a captivating grin came "What colour would you like? I got a bunch of part cans in the shop. I'll just mix them up and see what we get," John said with a hearty laugh. "Okay" said Hank. So Sonny and Hank got the car ready in a couple of nights, and John painted it turquoise the next week. They all laughed together, but the car looked not too bad, Hank thought.

Jimmy had an addiction, alcoholism. He could go for weeks sober, make all kinds of money and then 'fall off the wagon'. But he was careful not to drive drunk, to the extent that near the end of one 'spree' he was seen late at night, crawling on the street headed to Dr. Jim's house to get a "cure". When he was sober and travel was good, he'd canvas three or four drivers to come with him to Sydney for an afternoon, each one to ferry back a new '57 Chevrolet from the main dealer R.J. Logue, to be sold on the western side of the Island. Jimmy already had customers in mind that might like a new car, and could afford it. Hank went with him occasionally on his day off. It was a wonderful trip, laughing and talking with the other drivers on the way to Sydney. Then later, they'd see all the new cars in the showroom and to get to drive one back. A dinner celebration with all the trimmings at Joe's Steak House was how they would end the night.

Jimmy's rule was no booze, because he wanted everyone to return home safely, for them and his new cars, and they did arriving back usually after dark. Little did any of them know what the value of these same cars would be in a few years time, as collectable cars. When Jimmy had a used car on his lot that was collecting dust, he'd ask John to sand it and paint it 'red'. Then one day he'd head down North to the Acadian villages, with the shiny red car, and come back with a trade-in more often than not. It seemed the Acadian men and women had a taste for red cars.

Jimmy also had a twelve foot 'speed boat' with a Mahoney Bay wooden hull, a 25 Hp Evinrude on the back and during sober times, he and Hank would take the boat for a spin out into the Gulf.

INVERNESS

One day on Hank's day off, Jimmy showed up at the wharf with two lunches, a six pack of Cola, and an offer to take Hank to P.E.I. to see his folks, a distance of at least forty miles one way across the Gulf, if they didn't get lost. Jimmy had two life jackets, but no compass, or anything else if they drifted off course. Hank was hesitant, but Jimmy, with his silver tongue and the big smile, persuaded Hank to go. So off they went, Hank sitting up front looking back, first as the shoreline faded away, then the church steeples, until the mountains in the background became a dark blue haze against the sky.

When the wind started to pick up, Jimmy slowed the engine and said, "What d'ya think?" Hank gushed out "I think we better turn back!" and Jimmy reluctantly agreed, and turned the boat and headed back. An hour later, a freighter appeared from the south, which, at first looked like it was almost on the beach at Inverness. Jimmy kept full throttle steaming toward the freighter, and as they neared and Jimmy steered around its stern, the sailors were out on deck screaming at the two adventurous sailors, in their native language, which Hank interpreted as,

"You fools, get to Hell ashore before dark, or you'll drown".

Eventually they did reach the harbour before dark, with smiles and sighs of relief. Each gave thanks and a promise to never again try that! The next day, with Jimmy back on the job at his garage, and Hank back in uniform, they had a private chuckle about their foolish exploit, and an unspoken pledge not to mention it to anyone else.

SONNY

One of Hank's friends while he was in Inverness was named after his father Frederick Marple Taylor Jr., but junior didn't stick as a nickname, in a town of many nicknames. Rather, this youngest brother of Jimmy was known by one and all as "Sonny". Although they became friends, on one occasion, Hank had no choice but to arrest Sonny in the Chinese restaurant one night, for drunk and causing a disturbance, and put him in jail for the night to sleep it off. Hank answered the call and was not surprised when Sonny, although intoxicated, said "Go ahead Bud, do whatcha gotta do." By now, Hank had learned that the only way an officer can give a person a break is, if they are the only two people present, i.e. no witnesses, and neither speaks of it later. There were witnesses in the restaurant. Shortly after that, somebody in town, probably Danny MacLeod, gave Sonny a train ticket to the 'welding school' in St. John, New Brunswick, and Sonny never looked back. He first worked for Babcock, and later got hired on permanently at Scott Paper in Abercrombie, Pictou County, Nova Scotia. Sonny was still there, living in New Glasgow, with wife and two children, when Hank and Mary Ann were transferred to that same town, twelve years later. Their sons played hockey on the same team.

When Sonny, who was renting at the time, decided to build a house in MacKinnon's Brook east of town, Hank helped him set the forms, pour the footings, and erect the forms for the foundation. Hank was also there as part of the barrow crew, when the ready mix trucks brought the concrete. Some of it had to be hauled by wheelbarrows, along a catwalk on top of the wall, and dumped down between the forms.

Although Hank wasn't there, a story he will never forget, happened the previous winter that was characteristic of Sonny, downtown in front of the liquor store. Late one bitterly cold Saturday morning, like all Nova Scotia liquor stores, this one closed at 12:30 PM. Sonny was making a last minute trip for his weekend supply. When he came out of the store, another male customer was struggling, trying to get his car started. In spite of the weather, good-neighbour Sonny said "No problem Bud, I got booster cables in the trunk, I'll pull my car around in front of yours and we'll get her goin."

Singing to himself as he went to his car, he brought his car around, opened the hood, hooked the cables up, started the other car, disconnected the cables and slammed down the hood of his car. At the same time, the other man is standing by his car, thanking Sonny repeatedly for helping him. The front of the hood latched, but the infrequently oiled hinges at the back of the hood left it part- way up the windshield. "You son of a whore", Sonny mumbled as he climbed up onto the hood with his unlaced work boots and open jacket blowing in the wind, walked to one corner of the hood and jumped on it, until the hinge collapsed into position. As he walked across to the other hinge, the man he'd helped is standing with his hands clasped in prayer saying "Please God don't let him do this, I never meant for this to happen, look what he's doing to his car." When the second hinge collapsed in surrender, Sonny mumbled as he climbed down off the hood "I never did like this f---in car anyway," got into his car and drove away. Sonny never did get the hood fixed, but traded the car the next week for a newer one.

Sonny and Hank still kept in touch years later, although Sonny's health was failing, his knees shot from years of kneeling as a welder, not in prayer, still able to laugh and tell stories, curse frequently, and have the odd beer from his living room arm chair, comical as ever.

The author regrets to inform the reader that Sonny has since passed away.

Harry the Greek

The most noteworthy of town characters, owned and operated one of three restaurants in town, named the Baltimore Café. His name, Harry Katapodi, to everyone in town "Harry the Greek". You guessed it he came from Greece. Harry stood five feet- ten inches tall, well built, with a portly front, usually wearing a stained white apron, a new one every day, because he was the chief/ cook and butcher too. He didn't stay in the kitchen, but delighted in coming out behind the counter, butcher knife raised high in his right hand, for emphasis making a point in broken English, to regular customers, in whatever discussion might be the topic of the day.

Hank and the other single guys stationed in Inverness ate their meals occasionally at all three restaurants. But the entertainment seemed better at Harry's. His wife Germaine, also worked in the restaurant when needed, and she could verbally handle any male customer, who might try to make an undesirable remark to her, or any other woman in the place. They had one son, ten year old 'Butch', who had red hair the same as Hank. So early in Hank's tour in Inverness, Harry named Butchie ' Son Numero One' and Hank 'Son Numero Two' and he would announce this in broken English, anytime when Hank was present, no matter how many customers were in the restaurant.

When things went wrong, his favourite expression was "Sul –ofa-bitch-bastard." Harry liked the ponies, race horses that is. He went to the races twice weekly at the track in Inverness in summer, and if possible, or at the last minute, he would recruit a fan or two to go with him, and drive to the night races in Sydney, a hundred and some miles away, on the other side of the island. Some fans never went with him a second time, because it was crystal clear, Harry had never taken a defensive driving course. Rumour had it that he had even owned a 'not so fast' racehorse at one time, and had retired it to his farm in Gillisdale. Hank too liked horses, but never visited the farm or seen Harry's horse. As noted elsewhere in this book, Harry was the cook that volunteered to butcher and cook, the deer that Hank shot during his first hunting season in Inverness. Hank suspected Harry probably served some of the venison, to unsuspecting customers when his larder ran low.

Later on, after Hank was transferred to Baddeck, Harry surprised him by moving into and opening an abandoned restaurant on Main Street, Baddeck, without wife Germaine or son Butch. Hank was happy to see him, but sad as it was not like old times, because Harry had lost some of his gregarious charm and was obviously lonely.

He could still tell stories, make outlandish speeches, and cook as well as he had before, but he seemed sadder than before. In addition, his new venture in Baddeck never took off. Without a word to anyone including Hank, Harry vanished in the middle of the night. Hank sadly never saw him again. Hank heard months later, that Harry was rumoured to have landed in Montreal, but that was never confirmed.

Theft of Bread

During Hank's first winter in Inverness, one evening Hank was alone in the office typing a report, when a call came in from Mr. Yip at the Island Grill that a man had stolen a loaf of bread off the rack by the door, and walked out into the night. Hank responded to the call, talked to Mr. Yip who was upset and asked him,

"Which way did he go?" Mr. Yip came to the door, pointed north into the raw, driving wind, with fresh snow drifting across the sidewalk. Hank, and his three-cell flashlight, could trace fresh footprints as he walked the block and a half to the tavern, where the footprints turned up the steps to the door. Hank followed and when he entered Gerry, the bouncer, greeted him. Hank asked, "Did a man just come in here carrying a loaf of bread?" Gerry nodded to a table about twenty feet away and said quietly "the red hunting jacket." By now the men at tables near the door realized Hank's presence, which was an uncommon sight in their favourite, only pub in town, and started to mumble amongst them. Hank briefly questioned his wisdom about proceeding further, but was not to be deterred, and walked straight down the aisle to the man holding a beer, and a loaf of bread beside him on the table.

When Hank put his hand on the man's shoulder, the whole tavern stood up. Hank swallowed hard and with the bravest voice he could muster and as loud as he could shout, "This man is under arrest for the theft of this loaf of bread. Now, the rest of you go back to your drinks, and there will be no more trouble." Hank half lifted the man out of his chair, grabbed the loaf of bread off the table, turned him and guided him towards the door, waiting at any time to get hit on the back of the head with a beer bottle, or at least get a glass of beer thrown in his face, but it never happened. Hank never even attempted to cuff the man, just get him out of there, and Gerry responded by holding the door open, as Hank and the man went down the steps and out into the blowing snow.

On the way back to the police car with the wind on their backs, the man quietly said as they walked, with the wind at their backs, "I'm sorry officer, I didn't mean to do it, I'll pay for the bread tomorrow. The kids will need it for breakfast. The missus will kill me. She gave me the money for the bread, but I really needed a beer." Hank asked him his name and where he lived. He said Freddie MacLean, down the Red Rows. When they arrived at the police car, Hank told Freddie to get in the passenger side and he'd take him home. "You mean you're not takin me to jail. Oh, thank you officer, thank you, thank you." Hank never went back to the restaurant that night, but stopped around the next day and paid Mr. Yip for the bread. He was happy and so was Hank.

When Hank discussed the case with Cpl. Ward the next morning he commented "You got away with one that time. We don't usually go into the tavern at night. We just let them take care of it themselves. Maybe in future, you should do the same."

HOUSE FIRE IN COLLIN VALE

In March of the last full winter that Hank was in Baddeck, he was temporarily transferred back to Inverness to replace Cst. Hales who was on extended sick leave, while another constable was away on course. Cst. Simmonds, from the neighbouring one-man detachment at Port Hood was also away, so the calls from there were forwarded to Inverness.

At 1:30 A.M. on a foggy winter night, a call came in about a house fire in Collinvale at the southern end of the Port Hood detachment area. Hank got dressed in his winter work uniform, went outside, started the police car and scraped the ice off the windows while the engine warmed up. He double checked his three-cell flashlight and it was good to go. When Hank drove down the street, he noticed a reflection from the surface, touched the brakes and the car started to slide. When he got out onto the deserted highway, it was completely covered in black ice, but he had no choice to continue on, very carefully. In addition to the ice, visibility was so poor because of fog, it took over an hour and a half and several corrective driving maneuvers, to arrive safely at the fire site, beside the highway. At times, he had been the only vehicle on the road.

By the time Hank arrived, all that was left of the modest two storey house was the chimney, remnants of kitchen appliances, hot water tank and a Queen heater wood stove, with wisps of smoke coming from the blackened debris. Hank knew about queen heaters because they had caused many house fires and deaths in the Maritimes. There had been one for part of a winter in his father's house a few years back. The Queen heater was a cheap, lightweight, oval shaped corrugated metal, wood-burning stove with no liner, which when the fire got hot, turned beet red and would ignite anything combustible nearby. That's why his father got rid of his Queen heater back home.

A lone volunteer fireman and neighbour stood in the driveway beside the ruins in obvious sorrow. Hank got out in the dark with his three-cell flashlight, shook the man's hand and introduced himself. Jimmy Chisholm responded in kind.

He said "We got here too late. She was almost gone by then, nothing we could do. The rest of the lads have gone home for a bite and some sleep, before they go to work. A couple of them should be back later." Jimmy and the other firemen believed that the mother and two of the children, a seventeen-year-old son and an eleven-year-old daughter, were most likely still in the smoldering ruins. The father was away working in a mine in northern Ontario. There was no basement under the house, just a cellar. Jimmy excused himself and went to his home nearby for a rest, and some breakfast while they waited for the hot coals to cool down. He offered to bring back a couple of pitch forks and a shovel to search for the bodies. Hank had left the motor running so he crawled back into the police car, left a window open a crack and tried to sleep, but his thoughts of what was beside the car in the ashes, and of his family back home with wood-burning stoves, permitted him only to close his eyes occasionally.

BADDECK

TRANSFER TO BADDECK

In October of his second year in Inverness Hank got about a week's notice that he was being transferred to the neighbouring detachment of Baddeck fifty some miles to the East on the shores of the Bras D'or Lakes. There he would be the single constable on a two- man detachment with Cpl Dave Coleman in charge. Hank had never been to Baddeck because anytime he went outside the Inverness detachment area, he went North to Cheticamp or South to Waycobah or Port Hastings. He had met Cpl. Coleman only once at the annual revolver shoot in Sydney. So, once more Hank packed his bags and drove' Maybelline' to his new home. There he met Cpl. Coleman and Cst. McTavish, the man he was replacing who was on his way to his new post. The Baddeck detachment building was an old two-story house that housed the Corporal, his family, the single man (Hank) and the office. It had a veranda across the front, the one-room office on your right as you entered the front door, a hallway straight ahead to Mrs. Coleman's kitchen, and their living room on the left. The stairs to the second floor was directly ahead, at the top was Hank's bathroom and to the right was his bedroom.

The rest of the second floor were bedrooms for Cpl. Coleman's family, two girls and a boy, the latter being a real mischievous kid who Hank bonded with as much as he ever did with his own sons later. On a morning after Hank had a late night, David Jr., age four, would burst into Hank's bedroom, vault over the steel end of the single-issue bed and land with a 'thud' on Hank. He would snuggle in and stay until Hank begged or threaten him to leave. There was also a black boxer dog named 'Mister' that when he and Dave Jr. joined forces on a stormy winter day, the rest of the family may as well have moved out. On his first day Hank met the whole family including Millicent, Cpl.

Coleman's wife. That night Hank went on patrol alone around the village, visited the Thistle restaurant, had a sandwich where he would later have most of his breakfasts and stopped at the Telegraph hotel where he arranged for lunch and dinner most days while he was stationed there. He also drove the 12 miles to Ross' ferry, the only paved road in the entire detachment area at that time. All other roads were gravel or dirt, but he was told "cheer up", the new Trans Canada highway is scheduled to come by the village one of these years. The only police car was a '58 Pontiac that looked like a goose with two broken wings.

At Baddeck Hank had similar duties as he had in Glace Bay and Inverness except there was an Indian Reserve ten miles south of the village, and the County jail was right in town. The jailer and his wife lived on the ground floor separate from the jail cells. The Court Room and other County offices were mostly on the second floor of the building. A circuit magistrate came to Baddeck every Thursday afternoon to hold Court and hear the cases from the previous week and beyond. On Hank's first full day in Baddeck, Cpl. Coleman came with him to visit the Lands and Forest Rangers, some of the volunteer firemen and their Chief at their workplaces. Also Crown Prosecutor Fisher Hudson, Claude Phillips at the Fina Service Station near end of the detachment driveway where they had the police car serviced, and some other notables about town.

David's bedroom was across the hall from Hank's which had a single white metal Force Issue bed in the corner straight in from the door with the foot of the bed towards the door. It didn't matter if Hank had gone to bed at 11:00 PM or 3:00 AM when David woke up, he 'hit the floor running', across the hall into Hank's bedroom, vaulted over the foot of the bed and landed on top of Hank gleefully waking him up. He might choose to stay or he might be gone in an instant to 'terrorize' someone else. Whether he became a convenient replacement for Hank's younger brother at home or not, Hank became as attached to David as any of his own four sons later in life.

Outside David was never alone either because he had the family dog Buster or across the street were the Morrison twin boys his own age. Many stories could be told of the adventures of this trio but the most memorable of all happened one sunny spring morning with snow still on the ground and no fence between the detachment and the backyard of the manse next door. On such a nice day the preacher's wife decided to clean out her fridge and placed some freezer items on the concrete back doorstep where they would remain cool. Playing in the back yard of the detachment, the three lads couldn't help but notice the items on the neighbour's doorstep and wandered over to take a look. "Wow", among the frozen foods were two part containers or ice cream, so the boys decided to help themselves before it all melted. Both Cpl. Coleman and Hank were away, so they had to rely on the account of the preacher's wife and David's mother whichever one first noticed the 'picnic' on the back doorstep.

The upshot of it all was when the totally embarrassed Millicent asked "David, what were you thinking?" David sheepishly replied, "I thought we'd have some ice cream". Millicent and the preacher's wife had to contain themselves to keep from bursting into uncontrollable laughter.

If work was quiet Hank always welcome in the living room in the evenings to watch the family black and white T.V. especially on Saturdays when Hockey Night In Canada and Esso got together to broadcast the last half of the N.H.L. hockey games. Both Cpl. Dave and Hank were avid Maple Leaf fans and it would have taken nothing short of a murder to pry them away from that T.V. if the Leafs were playing. Luckily, the murder never happened. Before Christmas that year, Mary Ann and Hank pooled their resources and bought a new T.V. from Freddy and Louise at the Baddeck Hardware store for Mary Ann's parents who lived on the side of a mountain in Inverness County. It helped them pass the long winter nights. They delivered it in the trunk of Hank's car and were able to simply hook it up with 'rabbit ears' thanks to the new C.B.C. tower on the top of Cape Mabou.

The next summer the Coleman's were transferred to Port Hawkesbury only fifty some miles away, but that didn't stop Hank from quietly shedding a tear while standing alone as their new Pontiac station wagon rolled down the driveway.

1957 PONTIAC REVIVAL

When Hank first arrived in Bristol the lone police car was a '57 Pontiac two-door six–cylinder, standard shift which looked like a wounded goose. Standing beside it, one could not see the upper half of the front wheels. The

100 lb. plus chrome bumper and grill at times felt like it struck the ground over a railway crossing or deep pothole. The rear end with nothing in the trunk but a spare tire, jack, a set of chains, police radio and a shovel in winter, at times dragged on the ground in rough terrain. At that time there were only 12 miles of pavement in the whole detachment area. Hank was told that one of his predecessors, a young constable when the car was new, had accidently driven it into the front of a large pavement roller on the Trans-Canada highway under construction. Also in that same era when the Force austerity program reigned supreme, the Corporal in charge believed that to get major repairs to a relatively new car with less than forty thousand miles on it, would have taken reams of paper and months of time that he wasn't about to endure.

So with his casual approval, Hank conspired with a young mechanic named George Cheverie, when things were quiet, to first remove the battered front coil springs and replace them with used coil springs from a scraped pickup truck in the yard behind the Fina station where he worked. Hank would over time charge it to a tire repair, a broken headlight which was a frequent occurrence on gravel roads, a muffler repair or an oil change. George and Hank would work at this remodeling on evenings off or on Sundays when the garage was closed. Little by little the front of the car came up off the ground and became easier and safer to drive. Then the two pals focused on the back end of the car by adding an extra leaf from the scrap yard to each of the rear springs and after a wash job and polish by Hank, she looked and ran almost like new. From there the car continued to serve well to the end of the required 60,000 miles and Hank was sorry to see her go when he picked up a new Meteor in Sydney to replace her.

Although George worked full time at the Fina, he moonlighted for Bethune's Garage across the street on the only tow truck in the village, was very proud of the new truck and the extra money and did it well. He was on call for most of the motor vehicle accidents Hank attended. One of the worst accidents that they attended was on a foggy spring near midnight at a new bridge site at Middle River on the Trans-Canada highway under construction. A businessman from northern Inverness County travelling alone from Sydney apparently missed the detour, drove through the barrier into the river and drowned. There were only headlights from vehicles to illuminate the scene and Hank like many other times had to rely heavily on his three-cell flashlight. It took everything George and his little tow truck could muster to get that car out of the river so that Hank and the volunteers from Baddeck fire department could retrieve the body, find identification and ask the police dispatcher in Sydney to notify the next of kin.

Later that year on a Saturday night in mid-summer George came to Hank's rescue while he and John McDowell from the R.C.M.P. Sydney G.I.S. were staked out watching the home of Billy Cameron, a known bootlegger near the foot of Hunter's Mountain

It was a clear quiet night with no traffic to or from the bootlegger and Hank was in full view of the gravel highway leading to the mountain. After awhile Hank noticed George and his tow truck headed up the mountain. A short time later, Cpl. Coleman in the Baddeck police car followed in the same direction and Hank whispered to John "Looks like somebody had an accident up there." Little did he know it was his girlfriend driving his cherished '55 Meteor convertible. Before long down the mountain came George with Hank's car in tow, followed by the police car with passengers in it. With that, John suggested they discontinue surveillance and return to Baddeck. There, Hank found his car sitting in the back lot of the Fina station across the street from the detachment driveway with the left front fender crushed and the left door and side flattened.

Inside the detachment Mary Ann and her girlfriend Lorraine were being comforted by Mrs. Coleman. Mary Ann was remorseful but neither she nor her girl friend was hurt, except Lorraine's right knee was sore from denting the glove compartment door. Not bad, considering no seat belts or other restraints in the car. They had been sideswiped on a left hand curve by a Dodge custom royal travelling at high speed with a carload of Acadian men enroute to northern Inverness County. The driver had apparently lost control and slid sideways into them on loose gravel and pushed Hank's car sideways into a shallow ditch.

George later towed Hank's car to Kaiser's Body Shop on Boularderie Island to get repaired. Hank monitored the progress when he could and retrieved his car a few weeks later almost as good as new. During that interval if Hank was off duty and needed a car, his good friend Gordon MacAulay, the local Ford dealer would lend him a car from the used car lot providing he returned it in the same condition as when he borrowed it.

Three Cell Flashlight

RELIEVING ST. PETER'S

During the second fall that Hank was stationed in Baddeck, he was temporarily transferred to St. Peter's Detachment on the other side of the island to relieve the man in charge, Cst. Ron White while he went on vacation. Hank was lucky that Keith Dunn, aka K.C. the one-man highway patrol would still be there because Hank didn't know the area. Keith had his highway patrol car, a 1958 Pontiac that could really scat and Hank had a well used basic 1958 Ford with well-worn tires but together they agreed to join forces and work together no matter which car they used. An early priority duty was to set the office up the way it should be because much of what was moved into this new detachment building two days before was still in boxes and needed to be filed and stored away properly. They both pitched in and between calls they had the place ship shape in a couple of days. There were two issue beds in the single men's quarters at the back of the office, both men could change from uniform to fatigues and work their own schedule until the job was done, one night they worked until after midnight at this task. K.C. took his meals at the private home of an empty-nest couple, Janie and Findlay Ross. Hank was also welcome there, an ideal arrangement for two hungry young single men, for a reasonable price. During those two weeks, except on their weekly day off which they alternated, they pretty much put their uniform on when they got up in the morning and took it off when they went to bed that night.

One morning an anonymous call came in from Forchu, a small village on the Atlantic coast. The quiet voice told how the night before, two young men had jacked a large buck outside the village and now it was hanging in a small abandoned barn near the center of the village. Hank and K.C. set out in the highway patrol car because the Ford was in for service, and found their way some forty miles of gravel road to Forchu. There it seemed they had no difficulty locating the barn in question and neighbourhood enquiries disclosed the owner of the barn. Ultimately one of the illegal hunters showed up at the barn, admitted he was involved and with little persuasion, named his accomplice. After taking statements from the two night hunters and seizing the rifle, a light and part box of ammunition used in the offence, K.C. and Hank cut down the buck from the rafters of the barn and proceeded to drag it from the barn to the police car. There were no offers from anyone to help.

At the back of the car, it took everything Hank and K.C. had in muscle power to lift the animal up onto the trunk that simply could not hold it inside. The hind legs reached ahead of the doorpost on the driver's side and the front legs did the same thing on the passenger side with the head hanging down over the rear fender. The officers secured both sets of legs to the door posts with short pieces of rope from the barn floor. What a trophy that buck would have made parked outside the local tavern had it been in season. Hank made arrangements with the two 'hunters' to voluntarily appear in court in Arichat the following Tuesday and the two constables headed for the cold storage in the same town to deposit the buck in case it was needed for evidence. The two hunters appeared in court the next week and were each fined seventy dollars and allowed two weeks to pay or spend thirty days in Jail. They paid the fine. The rifle and light were forfeited, the deer was donated to the County to be processed and given to the poor.

ICE TRAVEL

Baddeck is located on a small bay on the western side of the Bras d'or Lakes, which drain out into the Atlantic Ocean and have partially salt content and many species of fish that live in the ocean. Most of the lakes freeze over in winter and while Hank was stationed in Baddeck, in some areas, the ice froze thick enough to drive a car on it. This was convenient for the residents of Iona and Washabuck who needed to come to Baddeck, instead of driving on winter roads around by the Little Narrows ferry and back north on highway five taking at least forty-five minutes, they simply drove out onto the ice, crossed over to the highway a mile south of Baddeck, and were there in ten minutes. In mid-winter, many crossings were made both ways including the Baddeck police car in an emergency, without incident.

Most everyone knew that closer to spring, the weaker the ice, and caution and cooperation reigned supreme. No cars or trucks went through the ice while Hank was stationed there.

As an example of a near miss on the ice, a jock about town named Crossy had an ice boat with sail and one spring morning a call came in to Baddeck detachment that Crossy had crashed it against the cliff at Bien Breagh and might be injured. Hank drove down to the government wharf, took out his binoculars, looked across the channel, could see the iceboat on the shore, but no sign of Crossy. If he was injured and needed help, it would take Hank at least half an hour to drive around the narrow, icy road to Bien Breagh so he decided to cross the ice with the police car. When he got there, the iceboat was crashed on the shore, but no one there. Hank climbed the cliff and learned from the caretaker of the Graham Bell estate, Kenny McDermid that Crossy was O.K. and had hitched a ride back to town. Hank drove back across the ice following his tracks, returned to the office and typed up the occurrence report. He had a talk with Crossy later who just joked about the whole thing.

That night there came a mild spell of weather and within days the channel Hank had crossed with the car was open and Hank realized he had dodged a bullet. During the three winters Hank was stationed in Baddeck he never heard of a vehicle going through the ice on the lakes. Only a private plane, an old Harvard trainer owned and operated by good friend, Cst. Maurice Gaudet. That's another story.

THE SILVER DART 50th Anniversary Flight

In February of 1959 and for months before, the buzz in Baddeck was all about the coming of the fiftieth anniversary of the first flight of the Silver Dart, the invention and creation of Alexander Graham Bell culminated by the historical short flight off the ice on Baddeck Bay by his pilot J.A.D. McCurdy. This directly involved both members of Baddeck detachment in the planning and organization of the event, especially the potential increase in attendance and traffic for that one day. Most winters, it was common for automobiles to travel on the ice of the Bras D'or Lakes when it became thick enough to carry vehicles, and this year was no exception. Also there would be no parking on the shoulder of the narrow highway beside the site. So a construction contractor Howard Cameron who lived across the highway from the site was engaged to clear a parking lot on the ice outside the proposed flight location. He first tested the ice which was over a foot thick and used a small bulldozer to do the job. He also cleared a quarter- mile strip for horse races after the flight took place and prepared an approach onto the ice from the highway for pedestrians and vehicles.

The hotels, motels and restaurants all prepared for the big day and the Post Office even issued special stamps and envelopes to commemorate the occasion. Hank bought some and mailed them home with notes inside to preserve them. Members from nearby detachments like Ingonish and North Sydney were detailed to assist on the day of the event and reported early to help. Hank was ready to go before daybreak the day of the flight which took extra effort because he was not an early riser. He dressed as warmly as he could, long johns, sweatshirt, winter shirt, breeches, jack boots, Pea Jacket and fur cap with ear lugs down. The weather was clear with a light wind, but bitterly cold and Hank was out in it without a break all morning and into the early afternoon. By the time the celebration ended Hank had frostbite on his nose and both cheeks from the sub-zero temperatures.

The flight was delayed past the planned 10:00 AM flight time and when the pilot, a serving officer of the Royal Canadian Air Force, finally got the aircraft rolling into a minor headwind, it lifted a few feet of the ice, bumped back down gently onto the ice, made a few wobbles, the crowd gasped, the pilot accelerated to about fifty feet, flew a quarter mile and set it back down to the applause of the assembled throng.

Following the flight, there were three horse races each with four horses. Hank's favourite was in the second race, a big chestnut horse with a white stripe down his face who had earlier broken his right front knee, was retired from racing and allowed to heal. A farmer out back of Baddeck, Dody Garland had bought him and nursed him back to health, even though the injured knee wouldn't bend the horse still had heart and loved to compete. That's what Hank admired about him, that and Dody's daughter Cassie who always came to see him race, wasn't hard to look at and always had a big smile for Hank. The day of celebration went off without incident after which some of the members from other detachments retired to the one room Baddeck detachment, enjoyed some hot drinks, discussed the events of the day and thawed out after a long cold day on the ice.

BUDDY AND THE LYNX

A few days after Hank arrived in Baddeck, a young forest ranger named Buddy MacLeod got a call from a farmer friend in Big Baddeck that he had discovered a mature lynx in an illegal trap beside a logging road not far from his home. The Lynx was trapped by the front leg and any attempt to approach it was met with a flurry of growling, hissing, jumping and thrashing around that might cause it or the farmer injury. He asked Buddy if he could and take a look at the situation and perhaps offer a solution. Buddy called his boss Sandy who borrowed the department tranquilizer gun and a couple of darts to come and try to set the lynx free from the trap.

On a sunny autumn morning the farmer and Buddy arrived where the lynx was in the trap and Buddy couldn't believe what a big beautiful animal it was. He immediately thought "I'll bet the wildlife park in Schubenacadie might like to have him for display to the visitors." He called Sandy who checked with the superintendent at the park. He replied "We'd love to add a lynx to our collection as we don't have one now, but how are you gonna get it here?" Sandy bravely replied "just leave it to us, we'll call you later." Sandy grabbed a coil of rope and the tranquilizer gun, jumped into his car and headed to Big Baddeck.

There, he sized up the situation, and agreed the animal would look good in the park. The two rangers decided they would tranquilize the animal, tie its two front feet and its two hind feet together, slip a long pole lengthwise between them and carry him out to the road. Sandy had a nearly new Nash Rambler so Buddy, wanting to please the boss and good friend, offered to take the unconscious animal in his not so old Volkswagen bug. So Sandy shot the lynx with a T.Q. dart and while the sedative was working, went into the woods, cut a small maple pole just the right length so it would fit inside Buddy's car. They brought it out, tied the front and back legs of the sleeping cat together, and threaded the pole between the legs parallel to the body. With considerable effort, the two rangers picked the sizeable animal off the ground and carried it out to Buddy's car. With much more effort and assistance from the farmer, they loaded the animal into Buddy's car hanging upside down on the pole, which rested between the ledge at the back window and the dashboard in front.

Sandy offered to follow Buddy the twenty some miles in to their office in Baddeck "in case something went wrong along the way". Sure enough about half way to town, the lynx stared to stir. Buddy wasn't sure if it was too little tranquilizer or the motion of the car on the rough road, but within two minutes, the stir became a growling, hissing and thrashing. Buddy pulled over, stopped, jumped away from the car and slammed the door. Sandy pulled up behind him, walked up and looked into Buddy's car and said with a grin "Well I guess that didn't work," and as they both stood helplessly by, the lynx got its front paws free and was spinning around the pole, claws extended ripping at seat upholstery and tearing the roof liner into shambles, to the delight of the farmer and some neighbours who stopped by to see the show.

CO-OP STORES

A sizeable part of the Baddeck Detachment area while Hank worked there, was a large peninsula near the middle of the Bras D'or Lakes, which was off the beaten path from the new Trans-Canada highway. Although a main line of the CN Railway ran through it and over the only bridge over Grand Narrows at Iona. Also available to the public was the cable ferry at Little Narrows for twenty-five cents, vehicle and driver. There are several stories to tell about one ferry terminal at Little Narrows but that is covered in another chapter. The driver's other choice was to drive around the Bay via Orangedale which was fifteen miles further. There were no paved roads in that part, just gravel on a mostly gypsum base which, when the frost came out of the ground in the spring made them almost impassable. The first spring Hank was in Baddeck, he and Cpl. Coleman had an urgent call to Iona, some forty miles by ferry. When they crossed on the ferry they had to stop and put chains on the rear wheels of the '57 Pontiac and plough through mud with the front bumper in low lying places. The travel wasn't much better on the return trip. After they arrived at Ottawa Brook they learned the call was a false alarm so they continued on to Iona, a quaint little village, with population of less than five hundred, beside the Grand Narrows where a larger car ferry ran towards the industrial side of Cape Breton.

Iona was the largest community in that part and a center for the Roman Catholic Church where the priest reigned supreme as he did in other small communities on the island. It was the custom for R.C.M.P. members on patrol in such communities to visit the priest if they had time to have a cup of tea and discuss the welfare of the people and the news of the day. Most of the residents were hard-working, peace-loving citizens, so police calls to the area were rare.

During Hank's first fall in Baddeck, Steeltown G.I.S. alerted Cpl. Coleman that they had confidential information that two criminals from the industrial area were planning a break, enter and theft at the Iona Co-op, a large general store with everything from groceries to sewing needles to nuts and bolts. Cst. John McDowell would be coming to Baddeck to assist in a stakeout on the alleged night of the attack. Hank was assigned to accompany him in old clothes and an unmarked car that Cpl. Coleman had arranged to have parked in a private garage not far from the Co-op.

John and Hank arrived in Iona shortly after dark, parked the car in the assigned garage, spoke to the owner and walked to the store trying to look nonchalant in the small village. They entered by an unlocked door, briefly checked the interior with a hand over the lens of a three-cell flashlight, found a place behind a counter in view of front windows and both front and back entrances. Their senses on high alert, lying on heavy blankets and men's work clothes from the shelves on the floor, their plan to take turns on watch while the other slept never materialized. Due to the old store creaking in the wind and the odd vehicle sweeping its headlights through the front windows as it made its turn at the 'T' intersection, there was no rest all night, and NO visitors.

THE LADY MOONSHINER

In most areas where Hank was posted during his ten years in Cape Breton, there were throw backs to the prohibition days who still practiced the art of making moonshine. In some cases it was probably out of necessity and the artists were mostly men. Hank was involved in apprehending several of them but in other cases such as this one, he was part of the stake out team, but not the arrest. One of the most memorable was a robust country woman from Estmere known locally as Annie Rob N. She had chosen a piece of isolated woodland a number of miles from home, several hundred yards off the road and not visible from any occupied home. When she was planning to run off a batch, she would have her boyfriend drop her off with equipment and supplies and alone would carry them to the still site. She would carry water from a nearby stream and mix the mash in wooden barrels, cover them, and let it set for up to a week, before it was ready to run. Later that day at an appointed time the boyfriend Lennie Northern would pick her up and drive her home.

Her ex-boyfriend in an act of jealously, told Cpl. Coleman about the operation, so early one morning, took him into the woods and showed him the 'still' site. There were three wooden thirty-gallon barrels full of mash that they estimated would be ready to run in the next two or three days. Cpl. Coleman requested a member of the Sydney G.I.S. for he and Hank to set up surveillance on the still the following day. Before daybreak the next day John and Hank were dropped off by an unmarked car to remain at the site for two days and two nights, to be replaced if necessary by two other members. With little effort, they found the still site as described and located a secluded spot to set up camp at the base of a large pine tree within sound of the still, on the side opposite the trail from the road. They were dressed for the clear autumn weather with an extra jacket to use as a pillow as they did not have sleeping bags. Later for a bed they cut small evergreen branches from new growth several hundred yards away from the still. It didn't rain the next two days, only a few drops one night that the upper branches of the tall pine easily deflected. John and Hank had each packed a lunch which they hoped would last the two days and were pleased to find that the water from the small brook near the still was fit to drink.

They surmised that was why Annie chose that location in the first place, a ready supply of water for her mash. For their nature calls, they simply went alone to a secluded spot in the woods and did what they had to do using moss, dried grass or leaves to wipe their behind.

To prevent boredom during the day, they each had a small pocket novel that they read sparingly. They also took turns checking the still for activity and exploring the shore of a nearby lake. Hank found a small cranberry bog and had to take care not to get his feet wet while he picked a few for he and John to eat. They were fresh and tasty but sour.

We were relieved by our fellow Mounties who were able to apprehend Lady Moonshine.

Three Cell Flashlight

COURT DAYS

When Hank first arrived in Baddeck, the Cst in neighbouring Ingonish detachment was a Scout named Bob Steven. He and Hank occasionally worked together on crimes or incidents close to the detachment boundary at North river. But within months Bob was transferred to Inverness detachment from where Hank had just departed. He was replaced by a young rosy cheeked native of P.E.I. like himself named Willard MacDonald, nickname 'Spud'. The nickname Hank had worn all through training and into Cape Breton. That nickname deserted Hank over time, but stuck to Willard all his adult life. Hank and Spud soon became close friends and a weekly convenient meeting place turned out to be in the driveway of the County Court House in Baddeck Thursday afternoons after Court was adjourned. In those days private cars were a status symbol. For his private car, Spud had a 1958 Ford sedan, black with gold panels on the rear quarter panels. Off duty Hank drove a 1955 Meteor Convertible yellow bottom, black top. So, late in the summer, they decided to trade cars for a week just to give the ladies in each community a different look. The plan almost backfired because Hank's girl Mary Ann fell in love with Spud's car and Hank had to persuade her to give it back by reminding her of the many attributes of his car. It must have worked. Hank later married her.

Besides being the County seat, Baddeck was also the home of the shared County Crown Prosecutor Fisher Hudson who Spud on occasion came to town to discuss charges or to prepare for trial. That also afforded Spud and Hank a chance for a coffee together and catch up on the adventures in each other's area. When the circuit magistrate R.J. MacDonald came to town Thursday afternoons, he required everyone to be there and ready to proceed at 2:00 PM sharp. Unlike Inverness, spectators in the Court room were rare, perhaps a family member or friend for moral support for the accused, but most days there were accused, defence lawyers, police and prosecutor.

Some days, depending on his mood, it was obvious the 'The Judge' was pro- R.C.M.P. and a supporter of what they were trying to do, keeping a lid on the entire county. One example was when a bold young man from the Ingonish area appeared before him without a lawyer and pleads "Not Guilty" to a charge of dangerous driving which had been laid by Spud. After a brief pause and a bone-chilling stare at the defendant, Judge R.J. said in a loud voice "What do you mean Not Guilty. Do you think these young officers have nothing better to do than risk life and limb travelling at high speeds at night on the Cabot Trail, of all places, to apprehend the likes of you and bring you before me?" "No Sir" meekly came the reply.

The Judge continued "Cst. take this man outside the Court Room and speak to him." Spud obliged, they departed, and returned shortly with the defendant who asked if he could change his plea to guilty. He was sentenced to one month in the county jail "to think about it" and one year's prohibition from driving a motor vehicle. Spud never did tell Hank what he said to the cocky young defendant out in the hall of the Court House.

Baddeck was also the head office for the Forest Rangers of the County who frequently worked hand in hand with Spud and Hank chasing poachers, fighting forest fires, searching for lost people, saving people from drowning and recovering bodies. These men were not only good friends but valuable contacts because they knew most everyone in the County.

During the summer of 1959, Baddeck and Ingonish, both two-man detachments had an exchange of men in charge. Baddeck got Cpl. Simmonds who Hank already knew, and Ingonish got Cpl. Vance. Both had a reputation of 'hail fellow well-met' and both in spite of being married with children, had a playboy attitude of independence and only worked when they absolutely had to. This only served to have Spud and Hank spending more time in police cars, especially at night. Because of the hierarchy in the Force at that time there was little recourse for the constables to take. Thank God for the three-cell flashlights with fresh batteries. Off duty, Vance drove a pink Cadillac hard top and according to Spud behaved like a fox in the henhouse in his resort mecca of summertime tourists, some of whom were young bikini-clad females. Simmonds drove a normal family car but relied on his duty uniform, police car, sneaky grin and a roving eye to win over unsuspecting females.

Now after Court on Thursday afternoons, when Hank and Spud sat in one of the police cars most of the conversation hinged around which one was blessed with the most harmonized Cpl. and joked about placing bets with each other who was most likely to climb a rock pile to get at a snake.

In spite of their bosses, Spud and Hank managed to get their one day off a week, sometimes the same day to drive to Steeltown for a taste of city life,

Three Cell Flashlight

some shopping, see a movie, visit friends or the Sgts Mess at Victoria Park. Unfortunately like most young Mounties on their day off they were inclined to behave like young calves let loose in springtime and bend the laws they were sworn to uphold. An example was a beautiful spring morning Spud picked up Hank at Baddeck in his '58 Ford all shined up for the occasion and headed for Steeltown fifty some miles away. Once across the car ferry at Big Harbour on a winding paved road in the North Sydney detachment area, the exuberance of the moment transferred to Spud's right foot and they came around a sharp curve, drifted over the center line and almost met Cst. Jack Burbridge of the highway patrol head-on. Not impressed, Burbridge U-turned, overtook the two freedom-seeking young constables, stopped them, proceeded to chew Spud out royally and for a time debated charging Spud with careless driving, but didn't, nor did he report Spud and Hank to Sub-Division headquarters. Both thanked Jack profusely and went not-so-merrily on their way.

On a similar trip in the spring on a Sunday afternoon, Hank was driving his '55 Meteor convertible with Spud in the passenger seat, rosy cheeks and black hair blowing in the wind. In Steeltown, they picked up Dick and Harry, two fellow constables on their day off with not much else to do and proceeded to cruise around town. It was not long before Harry suggested "We should get a bottle. "Spud replied, "but it's Sunday, you dumb fork, the liquor store is closed." "We're not going to a bootlegger!" Hank chimed in.

"You're not drinkin anyway, you're drivin," chirped Dick from the back seat to everybody's laughter. "Drive me to Victoria Park and I'll see if Buddy is workin today," said Harry. So, Hank delivered him to the back door where Harry disappeared and later returned with a concealed bottle of rum and got into the car. "I told him I'd replace it as soon as the liquor store opened tomorrow" Harry explained. "We'll all chip in" said Dick "I'll collect" and he did.

Instead of seeking a quiet, secluded place to have a drink, they all voted on such a beautiful day to do laps down the city's one-way main street with all the stores closed but hoping to spot one or more beautiful ladies in another car or walking along the sidewalk. Then continue back along the harbour on the same street as the R.C.M.P. headquarters with the three passengers sneaking sips from the brown bag concealed under the seat. On one of the laps down main street, they did overtake a carload of young women, but they chose discretion over valour and resisted the open invitation from the handsome collection of the male species in the convertible. All had a few good laughs but in general careful not to attract attention of the City Police Force who as good luck would have it, must have been otherwise occupied in another part of the city.

As Hank and Spud dropped the other two off at the single men's quarters and headed home with promises to do it again sometime but never did. They reflected happily on their day together. But admitted they had not been very smart and counted their blessings that they had not been stopped by the city police or had some citizen call in a complaint while they cruised the city having fun with open liquor in the car.

THEFT OF DRESS

On a hot summer afternoon of Hank's first summer in Bristol, Cpl. Coleman was away when a call came in from McIver's Store in Nyanza from a clothing peddler who excitedly stated, "She stole my dress."

"Who are you and where are you calling from?" asked Hank. "Jack Asaph from Sydney Mines" came the reply in a foreign accent, and he continued that he had his truck parked on a road on the Reserve and a young 'squaw' (Indian woman) had stolen one of his best dresses and ran.

Hank drove the twelve miles of gravel road out to the reserve and located the young man standing by his one ton truck with a covered plywood box and steps at the back leading up into it that served as a mobile store. He was angry and upset and wanted action. He related how earlier that morning three teenage girls visited his truck; one had bought a dress and one a pair of jeans. While he was distracted, the third girl grabbed a dress off the rack and ran. What did she look like?" asked Hank. "Young, Very pretty" he said as he demonstrated her figure with his hands, "and bare feet" he added. "Can you describe the dress?"

The man led Hank to the back of the truck, opened the door and pointed to a rack of dresses on hangers on the left side and pointed to a cotton dress with low neckline, large yellow flowers on a green and white background. "Like that one" he said. "Will you lay charges if I recover the dress?"

The Cst enquired. Hesitantly he replied "well, yes, do I have to?" "Yes, you do" came the reply. "Which way did she go?" the Cst. asked. The man pointed

Three Cell Flashlight

to a dusty road leading up into the reserve and added, "I think the other girls called her Briget".

Hank took off his hat, wiped his brow, tucked his notebook and pen into his left shirt pocket, put his hat back on, locked the police car and headed up the road on foot with the dust collecting on the toes of his shiny brown jack boots. His presence on the reserve always caused a stir and today was no exception. A hundred yards or so up the road, three young boys stopped playing when Hank approached.

"Hi there" said Hank "Would any of you happen to know where Briget lived?" The smallest one pointed to a small unpainted house on the right side near the crest of the hill. "Thank you very much" said Hank as he continued. At the house on the hill Hank found sixteen year old Briget at home with her mother and four small children. She was still on bare feet and wearing the stolen dress which complimented her ample figure partially visible through the thin material of the dress. Mr. Asaph was correct. She was tall and slim, tanned with jet-black hair and even on bare feet, a shape that Hank thought would have garnered her a position on a fashion runway in any city in the world.

For a moment Hank was speechless, then collected himself under the strict gaze of the mother's eyes. "What's the trouble?" she asked. "The peddler in the truck down the road says she stole that dress from him" Hank replied. "I paid for it" Briget interjected in a loud voice. "What with?" the mother asked.

From there the discussion led to the ashamed mother scolding Briget and telling her to get changed into other clothes and go with the Cst. to return the dress to the man in the truck. At the same time pleading with the Cst not to take her to jail and assuring him that this would never happen again. At the truck Mr. Asaph was noticeably pleased to see the young woman carrying his dress apologizing and begging for mercy.

When her tears started to fall, the hearts of both Hank and the peddler melted and forgiveness was in the air. Up until now, Hank had never encountered a situation exactly like this, and was reluctant to arrest her and questioned the wisdom of taking a sixteen-year-old girl to jail with him alone in the police car. Besides, the radio in the police car might not reach any one else from this location, not even the dispatcher in Steeltown who might not know what to do in these circumstances anymore than Hank did. The whole thing would have been frowned on by the citizens, especially Martha Campbell the jailer's wife. Mr. Asaph, now brave, warning Briget not to steal, said he didn't want to press charges, the tears stopped, she smiled and headed home with thanks all around. Hank headed back to the detachment to write his report, wipe the dust off his boots and wait for the next call.

GONE FISHING

Since he was a boy, Hank loved to sport fish and the only spring that he was stationed in Inverness he went fishing a few times at West Lake with Sonny or Lawley or Dr. Risk. Some days, the only fish biting were small perch and Hank or friends would unceremoniously toss them back into the woods behind them while muttering some not-so-complimentary words about bait-snatchers while re-baiting the hook. Some days the trout would be biting and the excitement of fighting and landing one big enough to keep would make the trip all worthwhile. But the real purpose of each trip was getting away from the job and having a few laughs in the privacy and tranquility of the great outdoors. Hank and friends all used spinning gear and worms as bait, but there Hank was introduced to metal lures with not one but three hooks on the back that didn't need bait and he thought to himself "I must get me some of those."

He ordered some from the Canadian Tire catalogue and especially liked the 'Al's Goldfish' lure because the first time he used it, he caught a pound plus speckled trout and Dr. Risk took his picture holding it and his rod beside his car. Unlike other lures that came stapled to a piece of cardboard, the goldfish came in a clear plastic case with a hinged cover and a plastic cap to cover the hooks when not fishing. It was a bit more expensive than the others but Hank thought it as 'real class'.

Before his transfer to Inverness Hank had acquired a used fly rod and reel and ordered a card of cheap flies made in Japan. Hank asked a friend John Dougal who lived near the Middle River

"How about any spots along the river where I'd have room to practice casting and maybe catch a trout or two?"

"Well, there's an old gravel pit along the river about two miles up from the Trans Canada on the Dublin Line, you can drive your car right down into it and nobody can see you from the road." "That sounds good John, I'll give it a try next day off, thanks a lot."

John and his wife Lena were a middle-aged couple with no children who were friends of Mary Ann's parents and always made Hank welcome whether on duty or off and who respected Hank's need for privacy in a small community. That day Hank drove directly to the gravel pit and found it to be exactly as John had described it and on his next day off drove his car there and parked. He found a shallow spot between pools where the river flowed over some small gravel stones and no trees to obstruct Hank's beginner casts. He chose a fly with a yellow tail, pulled some line off the reel like he had seen fishermen do on T.V. and cast out over the river. In no time he had a strike, reacted too fast, the fish spit the hook, but the fly was still intact. Hank cleared more line from the reel and this time when the trout jumped for the fly, he was more patient, let him run with it, and set the hook. He landed a nice pan-size trout and three or four more that he took to John's wife who cleaned and cooked them for lunch while he and John went to the barn to see John's new foal.

With homemade bread, tea and cookies and John and Lena's hospitality, that was a memorable lunch and a welcome change from village restaurants where in uniform or not, Hank felt he was always under someone's watchful eye. This scene, thanks to John and Lena was repeated many times during the next two years, even with Mary Ann after she came to work in Baddeck. She was their friend long before Hank came along.

When things were quiet, and Hank was alone on duty, which was often the case, and the fly rod mysteriously appeared in the trunk of the police car, he would visit the gravel pit, leave the radio on and make a few quick casts. If he caught anything, Lena was less than five miles away, he'd drop the fish off as a treat for them. That summer Hank was asked to do a favour for Lena when she unofficially mentioned that recently a middle age bachelor neighbour of theirs had hidden in the bushes and watched her while she was alone picking blueberries. She had not confronted him but asked Hank if he could pay the man a visit to let him know that Hank knew what he was doing rather than investigate, perhaps charge him, and create fodder for the local gossip mill. So the next time Hank was on duty in the area, he obliged, the man got the message and nothing more was said.

BADDECK

That same summer when Hank and forest ranger Sandy were on patrol checking beaver dams, Sandy said, "I hear the salmon are runnin up North River. The season isn't open yet, but have you ever seen a lot of salmon in a pool just layin there keepin cool?"

"No, I haven't, can we go someday and have a look?" Sandy replied, "They're catchin some trout up there, we should go. When's your next day off?" "Next Tuesday, let's do that" Hank replied. Sandy invited Buddy along and on Tuesday the three drove to North River, parked Sandy's car off a woods road and walked up the river wearing only old sneakers on their feet. The two had done that before because the river was shallow and this was a lot easier than slugging through the woods and rocks on the high ground on both sides of the river. Besides, fishermen know that if you fish going upstream, you are less likely to disturb them before the bait gets there. It was a hot summer day with few flies, the scenery was beautiful, there was no one else on the river, the men were dressed for it and the water on their feet helped to keep them cool.

When the trio came around a curve in the river, sitting high above in a dead tree on the North side was an eagle which wanted no part of the intruders, spread it's huge wings, lifted off and flew further up the river. It was a Great American Bald Eagle a protected species about which Hank had to submit a monthly report on sightings to the Canadian Audubon Society. About two miles up the river, they came to a small pool with a few mid-size salmon just lying there facing up steam moving the odd fin to maintain their position in the cool water from the high country. Further on up, there was a larger pool with an evergreen deadfall at least ten inches in diameter lying across it three feet above the water. Sandy was the first to climb up onto the trunk and walk out over the pool.

"Look at the size of those babies just layin there" he yelled as he got down on his belly to get a better look. When he came back, Buddy and Hank took turns walking out over the pool. None of them had a camera, but the depth of the water and the reflection of the sun on it would have distorted any picture. Just for the hell of it, when Hank had his turn, he lowered a hook with a worm on it onto the nose of a three-foot long salmon and the fish never budged. It probably would have pulled Hank overboard into the water. Try to explain that to the Fisheries Officer. By mid-afternoon, they made it back down the river, with no trout, tired and hungry, but with stories to tell.

Three Cell Flashlight

LOST AT BELL LAKES

On a quiet Sunday morning in Baddeck, a call came in from Sydney, a Mrs. Foreman crying that her brother had taken her two young sons age twelve and ten fishing at Bell Lakes twenty some miles out back of Baddeck early Saturday morning and she had not heard from them since. They were supposed to be home Saturday night. Hank called his Forest Ranger friends Sandy and Buddy to see if they could help and also Kenny the chief of the village fire department. All agreed the weather looked good overnight and those that could, offered to meet Hank at the Fire Hall at six A.M. the next day. Sandy said "I can take two in my car" and Hank had already arranged to take two more with him. Sandy reminded "Wear a good pair of boots, waterproof because there'll be some swamp in there, and don't forget your fly dope." Hank thanked him and continued making plans for the next day.

The next morning, both cars went as far as they could to the end of the Big Glen road, parked the cars and set out on foot the last six miles overland to the Lakes, which are about 1,500 feet above sea level. At times they could find the remnants of a wagon trail built originally for Alexander Graham Bell when he needed a secluded spot to go and think, fifty years ago. Hank had chosen a new pair of Logan's he had received in a shipment of new kit the week before because they were rubber bottoms and leather tops. Two miles in Hank realized his mistake, when one of his heels started to ache, that this was not the time or place to break in a new pair boot. When he took off his boot and sock at the next stop, the broken water blister and the angry skin beneath emphasized the folly of his decision.

Some salve and a gauze bandage from Buddy's first aid kit helped but didn't fully relieve the pain. But they were all spurred on by the thoughts of what may have happened to the man and his two nephews to prevent them returning safely from their trip.

The six men went single file most of the way and at times one man had to boost the man ahead of him over a particularly steep incline. When they finally reached the open barren near the lakes, Sandy offered to set his compass in the direction of where at least one of the lakes might be and go ahead until he couldn't see the man behind him. Then that man would move up to his spot followed by another in an effort to prevent wandering off course until

Sandy was in the lead again. This was repeated several times until they came to the first lake where all sat down, had some lunch and, as there was no response when the men took turns calling out enroute, they moved on.

From there, they split into three groups of two, to search for the other lakes and the lost fishermen. Hank had his revolver and Buddy had a single- barrel twenty gauge shot gun, so they agreed that if they came upon the missing trio, they'd fire a single shot to notify the others. In less than an hour, Buddy and Jimmy came upon the uncle charging through the woods, eyes bulging, bare-foot with knees and elbows sticking out of his pants and shirt. As soon as they got him stopped, sat him down, gave him a chocolate bar and some water, they asked where the boys were. "They're just back here, on the shore of the lake" he said confidentially. " Which lake, what direction?" Buddy asked. The uncle broke down and started to cry. "It's O.K." Buddy assured him. We'll find them." Buddy forewarned the uncle before he picked up the gun and fired a single shot into the air and listened. Within seconds he heard another from the other searchers behind him and in no time he heard Hank's loud voice farther off to his left. Buddy and Jimmy waited until the others joined them and the uncle during which time Hank and Buddy shouted back and forth to make sure they were on the right track. After a brief rest they again split into the three groups, the uncle with Buddy and Jimmy, to try to locate the two boys, hopefully on the shore of one of the two remaining lakes.

By now, it was getting close to Noon, and before one o'clock Hank and Gerry came out on the shore of another smaller lake, scanned the shores and there on the far side were the two boys just like their uncle had told them. Hank hollered across "Are you O.K.?"

"I think so." one replied. "Stay there till we come around to get you" Hank shouted back. Then he and Gerry started the trek through water, rocks and weeds in their direction buoyed by the thought that the boys were still alive. On the way Hank took his revolver from its holster and fired a single shot into the air to let the others know the boys had been found. Buddy fired a shot in response and he and Jimmy started in the direction of the sound as did the two volunteer firemen, shouting back and forth to each other as they went. When they finally reached the boys, they all sat on the ground in a circle, Hank and Gerry opened their lunch packs, gave each boy half a sandwich and some cookies followed by small drinks of water all of which were wolfed down like they really hadn't eaten for a day and a half plus one night. "What's your name? Hank asked. "Billy" said the eldest, "Junior", replied the other. "Did ya catch any fish?" Gerry asked. "No, not a one" said Billy, and the conversation continued until the others arrived.

What a joyous reunion when the uncle first greeted his nephews, hugging them, blurting out apologies and thanks at the same time. What great satisfaction for each member of the search party as they made plans for their return to the top of the glen, hopefully before the weather changed or darkness set in. But with Sandy in the lead and everyone moving as fast as they could between stops, they all managed to reach the top of the Glen shortly after dark to be met by Duncan and his sons and two other farmers who cheered as the entire party came into view, tired and haggard but happy to be there.

Hank thanked his fellow searchers profusely, shook hands all around before they got into their vehicles and drove back to the village. The first thing Hank did was call Sydney dispatch and request they call Mrs. Foreman and tell her that her brother and two sons were found safe and were headed home the next day.

LESSON LEARNED

For an instant, Hank's whole world flashed in front of him as he envisioned getting shot in the groin by his own gun, then with lightning reflexes he grabbed her right wrist with his right hand, ripped it and the gun out of his breeches and in the same motion flicked the gun from her grasp. It went slithering across the floor stopping with a dull thud against the wall. Luckily it did not discharge. In the same circling motion of the two combatants, the jug of goobie struck the edge of the steel stove top and exploded sending 'mash' all over the kitchen floor leaving Hank with the neck of the bottle on his right index finger. With a sigh of relief he gave the woman one last thrust away from him so he could retrieve his revolver before she did. She slipped and fell in the gory liquid on the floor. She sat up rubbing her wrist of the hand that once held the gun. Hank picked up the revolver, opened the chamber and dumped the five rounds out into his hand and dropped them and the gun into the right hand pocket of his breeches. He reached down and helped the woman to her feet at the same time telling her "You are under arrest for assaulting a peace officer, you're coming with me." The slurring retorts, "F.U. police officer, I'm not going anywhere."

Hank, now with his temper aroused, grabbed her and threw her out over the high doorstep where she stumbled and landed on the ground face down. Hank jumped out beside her while taking the handcuffs from the belt behind his back, bent down grabbed one wrist and slapped the handcuff on it. He rolled her over and tried to cuff her behind her back, she resisted so he grabbed the free wrist and cuffed her in front. Hank grabbed the link between the cuffs, picked her up off the ground and tried to steer her up the hill to the police car. She twisted, collapsed and threw herself onto the ground. Hank paused to catch his breath then said, "C'mon lady, get up, you're coming with me one way or the other." She mumbled a slurred reply which indicated she was still resisting. Again Hank crouched down and grabbed the link between the cuffs and walking backwards dragged her squirming up the hill and into the back seat of the two- door police car. Before Hank got in behind the wheel, he looked into the back seat and told her "Settle down back there and behave or I'll make you walk to town."

Surprisingly, other than some name-calling and at times questioning Hank's parenthood, she succumbed and went quiet until they reached the county jail ten minutes later. There the jailer's wife Mrs. Campbell took over, Hank followed into the jail, removed the cuffs and watched as with one glance from well-known Mrs. Campbell, the wildcat became a pussycat. The next morning Hank took the woman from jail before Justice of the Peace J.P. Hall charged with Assaulting a Police Officer and manufacturing illicit spirits. She was unable to arrange bail, so was remanded back to jail until the circuit magistrate came to town three days later. There she was convicted and as she had a previous record, was sentenced to thirty days in the County Jail.

During this exercise, Hank learned two valuable lessons, one: 'always keep your revolver in the holster' and two 'a woman can fight just as dirty as any man' and is just as dangerous if not more so.

Three Cell Flashlight

GAELIC MOD
ST. ANN'S

Every year in early summer, the week-long Gaelic Mod was held at St. Ann's approximately 15 miles north of Baddeck overlooking the shore or St. Ann's Bay. Each year Chieftain Dr. A.W.R. Mac Kenzie requested R.C.M.P. presence in boots, breeches, long sleeve shirt and Stetson every day of the week if one of the members of Baddeck detachment was not otherwise occupied. Hank was always volunteered and one year the Corporal was away on vacation, which meant he could get a call anytime to the other end of the County, and there was no backup.

The tasks at St. Ann's were menial such as directing vehicle traffic and pedestrian safety, which was critical as the Gaelic College, was situated on one side of a sharp curve of a twenty-foot wide two-way highway while the cabins and dormitories for the students were on the other side. There were no traffic or warning lights and no crossing guards, only Hank when he was there, but as good luck would have it, there were no mishaps the three summers Hank served there. That time of year, the highway was very busy due to people attending events of the Mod and summer tourists seeking the eastern access to the Cabot trail, a popular attraction. Besides the motoring public on this stretch of highway there were pulp trucks, logging trucks, and fish trucks hauling product to market, Tour Busses and Recreational Vehicles, other trucks delivering supplies and equipment to communities on that part of northern Cape Breton.

The only accident during this assignment was in South Haven one fine summer morning while Hank was driving to St. Ann's, and he was in it. Travelling over an elevated part of the new gravel highway soon to be the new Trans Canada Highway, without warning a small deer jumped into the air having climbed the embankment on the right. Hank braked hard but the car slid on the gravel, the deer collided with the top of the right front fender of the 1961 Meteor police car, which had sharp chrome molding along the top and over the front parking light. The impact flipped the deer back in the direction it came and disappeared down over the thirty-foot bank. Hank got out of the car, checked the broken parking light, looked down over the bank where the deer lay motionless possibly with a broken back. Hank reported the accident to dispatch in Steel town by police radio who recommended he obtain the usual three competitive estimates and forward them later.

Hank continued to St. Ann's where he notified the department of Lands and Forests who later determined the meat would be unfit to donate to a County charity due to the damage to the carcass. This accident happened to be Hank's third collision with a deer in two and a half years, the first two having occurred in Inverness detachment area. This generated an official memorandum in someone's wisdom from Sub-Division headquarters suggesting "more care be taken while driving where deer were known to be prevalent." Both Hank and his corporal got a chuckle out of the memo because in those years, most of Cape Breton Island had an abundance of deer because it was the end of a seven-year cycle. Easy to write from the comfort of a swivel chair behind a desk. For instance the previous spring, Hank had counted just before dusk one evening in Bucklaw near the County line in two open fields that separated the highway from the woods, nearly one hundred deer grazing just like cattle.

ANNUAL REGATTA WEEK

To Hank it seemed the Gaelic Mod just ended in St. Ann's one-week and Regatta Week started in Baddeck the next week. For this event, even if the corporal was away, he had some help from the men on the police boat 'The Interceptor' with the captain and three-man crew out of North Sydney who came and tied up at the government in Baddeck the day before the week started. They came there to assist with safety on the water and crowd control on land if Hank deemed it necessary. Like all regattas, there were races for all sizes of boats from prams for children to snipes with two-man crews. It was also an opportunity for friends, families and tourists to come, by land or sea to cheer on the competitors. By land in R.V.s, campers, cars and trucks, by sea in large sailing ships and yachts some built right there in Baddeck's Pineau's Boat Yard.

One year, early days and nights of Regatta Week passed uneventfully but as the week wore on and more visitors stayed later at the Yacht Club, one of two watering holes in town, the need for police presence increased. That made for longer days for Hank and the boys from the boat, especially those days when Hank put his uniform on when he arose in the morning and took

Three Cell Flashlight

it off when he went to bed that night. The Yacht Club was right beside the approach to the government wharf and no vehicles were permitted on the wharf after dark, pedestrians only. Late one night the crew from the police boat had packed it in and Hank was about to do the same when he received a report of a drunken man causing a disturbance on the wharf. Hank parked his police car as close to the wharf as he could and walked out onto the poorly lit wharf using his three-cell flashlight. Hank found the intoxicated young man leaning against the freight shed, approached him, shone the flashlight in his face and recognized him as Harvey Campbell, a young man his own size and age whom he had arrested before. When Hank spoke to him the retort was "Go f--k yourself!"

Hank said, "That's not nice, you're under arrest for creating a disturbance" and reached for him. Harvey spun away, lost his balance and slid down the side of the shed. Hank had his cuffs ready, grabbed the closest arm and snapped one cuff on it.

Harvey tried to rip the cuffed arm away, but Hank held tight and said "Get up!"

"F—k you cop, make me" came the reply. With that Hank reached down grabbed the other wrist, slapped the loose cuff onto it and tightened both as he pulled the arms together. Hank then rolled Harvey onto his back pulled his arms above his head, placed the flashlight crossways between the two wrists and started dragging him off the wharf towards the police car some thirty yards away. Meanwhile Harvey is cursing Hank, calling him every nasty name he could lay his tongue on and screaming police abuse. Hank stopped at intervals to catch his breath, change hands on the flashlight and appealed to the prisoner to get up onto his feet, but to no avail. Also, there was no help offered from bystanders. The struggle continued until Harvey was rolled end over end into the back seat of the two-door police car. When Hank arrived at the jail, a short distance away, he dragged Harvey out of the car and was greeted by Helen the jailer's wife who happened to be Harvey's aunt. She was a large well-built woman who gave Harvey a severe scolding and slapped him hard on the side of his head before Hank could get him onto his feet and steer him towards the jail and a cell for the night. After that Aunt Helen took over.

BADDECK

BODY AT BELL LAKES

Late Sunday afternoon one spring a call came in from Duncan Buchanan, a farmer in Big Baddeck who gave the phone to Ben Murphy from Sydney. He said, "Me and me buddy Lornie Smith were on a fishing trip up in at Bell Lakes and I think he took a heart attack and died."

Hank asked, "Where is he now?"

"I left him on the shore of the lake, it took me almost two hours to walk out, but I can show you where he is." Hank thought for a moment "I'm sorry for your trouble Ben, but it will take us the rest of today to round up some men to carry the body out. Can you find a place to rest because we'll need you strong in the morning? Can you call Lornie's family and tell them what happened?" "O.K., I'll do that." Ben handed the phone back to Duncan who told Hank not to worry; he'd find a place for Ben for the night.

Hank called ranger Buddy MacLeod to come and help the next morning he added, "I'll call the boss. Maybe he'll come too. It's gonna be quite a lug, we'll need a few strong backs. Have you thought about a seaplane?" "No, I hadn't, that's a great idea. Do you have anybody in mind?"

"There's a fella in Sydney with a float plane who I hear flies into the lakes. I think his name is Rogers. What time are you thinkin of leavin?"

"In the morning around eight o'clock perhaps, is that O.K. with you?" "Sounds good, I'll call you back."

The Corporal and Hank spent most of the evening with their dispatcher in Sydney trying to locate Rogers who was away for the weekend. When they reached him, he said "I've got a short early morning run tomorrow but I can be at the lakes by Noon. See you there."

That night Hank dug out some gear including an old pair of issue sneakers that were well broken in and he didn't care if he got them wet, dirty or not. He also packed a lunch and lots of insect repellant. The next morning Hank, Buddy and his boss Sandy headed for the top of the Glen. On the way they stopped at Buchanans and picked up Mr. Murphy and the four set out on the two-hour hike. It was a cool, clear morning and the sun was battling some low-hanging clouds. The old trail was visible in some places but overgrown in others that required a welcome pause to discuss the next move because the elevation increased twelve to fifteen hundred feet from the Glen to the lakes over some rough terrain of rocks and swamp.

On one steep incline of ten feet, all four men had to get down on hands and knees to make it to the top. The men stopped for several breaks along the way to drink water and replenish the fly dope. Those black flies were relentless.

Shortly after they arrived at the lake and Mr. Murphy got his bearings, they found the body and confirmed rigor mortis had set in. Silently the men gave thanks that wild animals had not paid a visit overnight. The men moved away, sat on the ground, had a bite to eat and rested. Before long the stillness of the woods was broken by the far-off sound of an airplane approaching and within minutes the float plane appeared, did a fly-past, turned into the wind and made a smooth landing in the middle of the small lake.

Rogers turned the plane and taxied back to the group on the shore, shut down, stepped out onto the left float, jumped ashore and greeted each man with a firm handshake and a smile. He turned, bent down and touched the body and said "I'm afraid I can't get him inside the fuselage, he's stiff as a board. How long has he been here?"

Hank had heard during the hike into the Lakes that Rogers was a bit of a dare-devil and was impressed when he greeted him, not suspecting he would prove it to Hank later. After all present deliberated this predicament Rogers said "Maybe we can lash him to a pontoon." And together they picked the body up, carried him out to the left pontoon, the one nearest the shore where some men got their feet wet but didn't mind. Most of the party including Hank thought quietly. "I sure hope this works because that will save us from carrying him all the way out to the Glen."

Sandy and Hank helped Gordie tie the body securely to the strut above the pontoon before Gordie got in, fired up the engine, turned and taxied out into the lake with a wave to those on the shore. By now, the wind over the lake had picked up from the West, so Gordie taxied to the far East end and turned. He sat there for a moment or two, revved the engine, came down the lake at full throttle, tried to lift off but the left pontoon wouldn't break clear from the water.

Before reaching the end of the lake Gordie wisely cut the power, slowed, turned and taxied back to the far end of the lake. "I need more wind; I'll wait awhile and try again" he hollered from the cockpit as he went by. Fortunately, the wind continued to increase over the next half hour, almost to white caps in places. "That should help to free the pontoon from the water this time" Buddy said as all on shore agreed and crossed their fingers as Gordie fired up the engine again and the plane started to move. As he came down the lake this time he was almost standing in the cockpit rocking the plane back and forth trying to free the heavy pontoon from the water. Very near the end of the lake, the pontoon broke free, the lopsided plane lifted off. But from where the men stood on shore, it looked like the plane might not clear the treetops and for a few seconds it disappeared. Everyone held their breath until the plane rose triumphantly above the treetops, banked to the left and headed for Sydney. On shore all raised their arms and cheered wildly as they gathered in a circle of mutual relief.

They gathered up their stuff and one by one started back to the Glen each expressing their own fear of what he might have done as they went, had the plane crashed. As they departed from the lake they could see where Gordie must have steered the plane down a small river at the end of the lake until it was able to clear the trees. Back in the car at the Glen, Hank called R.C.M.P. dispatch in Sydney to report the rescue party had returned from the lake before dark and got a return message that Gordie and his 'cargo' had arrived safely at the airport. Hank never saw Gordie again, but a few years later he asked a friend about him and learned that the previous spring, Gordie had dropped off a charter of salmon fishermen for a couple of days fishing on an isolated river in Newfoundland and had gone on to another secluded spot to fish by himself. He had such good luck that he strung his catch on a wire along one side of the fuselage to show the fishermen when he returned to the fiord off the coast to pick them up. As he did the flyby to display his catch, he caught an air pocket, lost control, crashed into the fiord wall and died. Hank was saddened to hear that, but reflected on the persistent, daredevil display by Rogers he had seen on their rescue from Bell Lakes years before. "Only the good die young" was the only comforting thought that Hank could muster.

JAIL BREAK

Early one morning in February Hank got a call from Fred Campbell, the jailer, that two prisoners had escaped from the same cell overnight, and were gone when his wife took their breakfast in to them. One was a Micmac, Isadore Bernard, from the local reserve in Nyanza, awaiting trial for assault causing bodily harm, and the other, a young white man from North Sydney named Arthur Thomas, serving time for a second offence of Break and Enter and Theft. Cpl. Simmonds and Hank went to the jail and found a hole in the wooden floor of the cell, just big enough for two slim young men to slip down between the joists into the basement, and escape through the unlocked coal chute. They left behind a short flat steel bar that looked like part of a small leaf from a rear spring of an old car that undoubtedly was the tool they used to tear up the floor. Two sets of footprints in the snow led from the coal chute out the driveway, ended at Main Street and became totally obscured, by vehicle traffic and the snow plough. Cpl. Simmonds decided not to call the Police Dog, as in his opinion, they probably headed out to the reserve, ten miles outside the village. Hank was of the opinion that if they hitched the right ride; they could be on the mainland by now or even further.

When they returned to the police car, Hank drove while the Corporal called dispatch in Sydney, and requested an all points bulletin be sent to mainland Nova Scotia and southern New Brunswick. He gave the description he had been given by the Jailer of the two escapees, and that they were not believed to be armed or dangerous. At Bernard's home on the Reserve, they interviewed his mother, and she and his sister swore they had not seen the two escapees. The mother expressed humour in the fact that her son had escaped, but was not surprised. The Corporal and Hank also visited the self-appointed Spl. Cst. Francis Gould, who had not yet heard of the break but felt sure he would have heard, had they stopped on the Reserve. He suggested an abandoned logging camp that Bernard knew of, some five miles out behind Hume's Station, just North of the Reserve. Back in the police car, Cpl. Simmonds told Hank that he knew a farmer South of the Reserve, with a team of horses and a sleigh, that he owed a favour to, so they dropped in to hire him. After the officers explained their suspicions to him, he agreed to take them to the camp as soon as he got the horses hitched and ready to go. Hank didn't agree with this maneuver, and in private mentioned it to his Corporal, but he was the boss, and Hank conceded.

By the time the horses were ready, the wind had picked up and it was snowing harder, which only accentuated the bitter cold. When they reached the road to the logging camp, the snow drifting across it had already obliterated any tracks the escapees might have made. Although the farmer and the officers were dressed for the weather, there was no place to sit on the sleigh. Standing on the slippery, wooden platform, that was the floor of the wood sleigh, and turning their backs to the biting wind, provided little relief. The snow was almost up to the horse's knees in places, so the progress was very slow, so at times, Hank stepped off the back of the sleigh, and ran behind in the deep snow, for two minute intervals, just to keep warm. When they finally arrived, they checked the interior of the unlocked camp, and there was no sign of anyone having been there. Back on the reserve, the officers checked with Francis, and there was still no word of the escapees. They also called dispatch in Sydney, and there was no response from the bulletin that they had sent out earlier.

Later that night, an alert Cst. Upshall on the Trans-Canada highway near Jemseg, New Brunswick, overtook the two escapees hitchhiking and shivering cold. When he stopped and got out of the car with his three-cell flashlight, they didn't run. When he checked them out, he concluded they were the subjects of the bulletin; he arrested them and took them to jail in Fredericton. They were tired, cold and hungry, happy to get into the warm police car. Upshall notified the dispatcher in Sydney that he had apprehended the two escapees, who in turn called Baddeck detachment, and assisted in setting up a relay, to return the escapees to Baddeck the next day. Late afternoon of that day, Hank met Cst. Downey from Port Hastings, with the two escapees, took custody and returned them to another cell in the Victoria County jail, where they came from. The following morning, on the direction of Crown Prosecutor Hudson, Hank charged both with 'escaping lawful custody', and they were remanded in custody until the circuit judge came to town Thursday of the next week. They both plead guilty, and were each sentenced to two years in the penitentiary at Dorchester, New Brunswick. Sheriff George MacAulay delivered them two days later.

STRESS LEAVE

The week after the jailbreak, Hank started losing his appetite, had difficulty sleeping, was irritable, and on edge most of the time, so he paid Dr.

MacMillan a visit, the only doctor in south Victoria County, and a friend. Prior to the visit, the doctor had noticed the same symptoms on Hank, and reached a diagnosis of, 'the verge of a nervous breakdown'. "You need some time off, can you go home?" asked the doctor. "Not this time of year, I'd have to drive all the way around through New Brunswick to get to P.E.I." said Hank. "Well then, is there anywhere else you can go, to get away from here?" "I could try Mary Ann's parents at the Lake."

"Good then, I'll sign a pass for one week sick leave, and tell the Corporal I said you needed the break." Offered Dr. Mac Millan.

Hank returned to the office, told Cpl. Simmonds, who was obviously not pleased, because that meant he'd be alone, and that might cramp his 'extra-curricular' activities. Hank phoned Mary Ann's mom, and explained his situation. "By all means", she said "you can come here, rest and relax and do whatever you please".

"Thanks, I really appreciate that." That afternoon, Hank packed his winter work clothes into his '55 Ford convertible and drove the fifty-some miles of snow covered gravel roads, to the Lake, arriving just before supper. "Convenient eh" said younger brother Winston in jest. After a delicious, hearty meal, a friendly evening chat, Hank excused himself, went to bed upstairs and slept like a log in the warmth and comfort of the old farmhouse, under woolen blankets made from the wool of the sheep on the farm.

The following morning, Hank was already starting to feel better, and with the constant care of Mary Ann's mom, Hank did little more than eat and read all day, a stark contrast from the job, with only a couple of phone calls. That evening after dark, Mary Ann's brother, and his good friend Donnie Cody came home from cutting pulp all day, and teased Hank about "living off the fat of the land", while they worked so hard in the woods. Hank couldn't refuse their invitation/challenge, to come with them the next day. "C'mon to the woods and help us pile brush, it'll be better medicine than hangin around the house all day, we won't work you too hard" they both said with a boisterous laugh.

Hank's competitiveness came to the fore, "Damn right, I'll go with you, and I'll bury you both under the brush." They were both young teenagers, smaller than Hank, but at that stage a lot tougher, mentally and physically outranking him. Hank found that out the next morning, on the nearly one mile trek to the woods, some places in knee-deep snow, but he wouldn't give in. Hank stayed and worked until Noon, but was one tired puppy, walking home beside the farm dog 'Rip'. After another robust dinner, Hank had a nap, and then went to visit neighbours in a sleigh ride with Mary Ann's father, behind an old racehorse he had recently acquired in a trade.

That evening Hank also helped feed the animals, and milk the cows by hand, before supper. That night, Hank had another great sleep, and went back to the woods with the boys every day for the rest of the week, except one, the day after a big storm, when the snow was too deep to work in the woods. That happened to be Mary Ann's day off at the hospital back in Baddeck, and she called and said "I'm off today, how about you guys, if you're not workin,' comin over to get me?'

Jokingly Hank replied, "It's still stormin here", a lie, "and the roads aren't ploughed yet", the truth.

The boys were eager to go, and together they dug Hank's car out of a snow bank at the bottom of the lane. Hank got it going and warmed up, threw the shovel in the trunk, got it pointed towards the main road, and took off down the lower road, beside of the South -West Margaree River. The road still wasn't ploughed, but Hank and the boys were in high spirits, and they were the only vehicle out there. Hank pushed the car to its limits with its new suburbanite snow tires, as they sped along, with light snow flying over the engine hood, as they broke through small drifts. They were doing fine, until they hit a big drift, too deep and too long to make it all the way through. The car stopped, buried in snow right up to the door handles. Hank tried to back up but the rear wheels just spun out. He shut the engine off then rolled down the front windows, and, one at a time, crawled out. They got the shovel out of the trunk, and took turns on it, for what seemed like an hour, all the while hoping a truck, or a snow plough would come along and rescue them. No chance.

By and by, Hank was able to get the driver's door open, get in and start the engine, and with Winston and Donnie pushing on the front, backed the car up to a bare patch of road. Then they shoveled out the rest of the drift ahead of the car, Hank had left the engine running so she'd stay warm. They got in, shovel and all. Hank dropped the car into low gear, revved it up and took off through the remnants of the drift, continued on to South West Margaree, where they found the paved road was ploughed, and the sun already melting the snow on it. They drove to Baddeck, never went near the detachment, picked up Mary Ann at the hospital, and brought her home, over the now completely- ploughed river road. They had many stories and laughter about the trip for Mary Ann that Hank and his two sidekicks just had, coming to get her. At home, the stories were repeated for the benefit of Mary Ann's parents and younger sister Mora. The following week, Hank returned to work in Baddeck, a brand new man, with many fond memories of his winter week on the farm at Lake Ainslie.

RELIEVING ST. PETERS

During the second fall that Hank was stationed in Baddeck, he was temporarily transferred to St. Peter's Detachment, on the other side of the Bras d'or Lakes, to relieve the man in charge, Cst. Ron White, while he went on vacation. Hank was lucky that Keith Dunn, aka K.C., the one-man highway patrol was still there, because Hank didn't know the area. Keith had his highway patrol car, a 1958 Pontiac, that could really scat, and Hank had a well-used basic 1958 Ford, with well-worn tires. They agreed to join forces and work together, no matter which car they used. An early priority duty was to set the office up the way it should be, because much of what was moved into this new detachment building two days before, was still in boxes, and needed to be filed and stored away properly. They both pitched in, and between calls, they had the place ship shape in a couple of days. There were two issue beds in the single men's quarters at the back of the office, both men could change from uniform to 'fatigues' and work their own schedule, until the job was done. One night, they worked until after midnight at this task. K.C. always took his meals at the private home of an empty-nest couple, 'Janie' and Findlay Ross. Hank was also made welcome there, an ideal arrangement for two hungry young single men, for a reasonable price. During those two weeks, except on their weekly day off, which they alternated, they pretty much put their uniform on when they got up in the morning, and took it off when they went to bed that night.

One morning an anonymous call came in from Forchu, a small village on the Atlantic coast about forty-five miles southeast of town. The quiet voice told how the night before, two young men had 'jacked' a large buck outside the village, and now it was hanging in a small abandoned barn, near the center of the village. Hank and K.C. set out in the highway patrol car, because the Ford was in for service and new tires. They found their way over the gravel road to Forchu. There, they had no difficulty locating the barn in question, and neighbourhood enquiries disclosed the owner of the barn. Ultimately, one of the illegal hunters showed up at the barn, admitted he was involved ' jacking' the deer, and with little persuasion, named his accomplice. After taking statements from the two 'night hunters' and seizing the rifle, a light, and part box of ammunition used in the offence, K.C. and Hank cut the buck down from the rafters of the barn, and proceeded to drag it from the barn to the police car. There were no offers from anyone to help. At the back of the car, it took everything Hank and K.C. had, to lift the animal up onto the trunk lid. The carcass was so big; it would not fit inside the car. The hind legs reached ahead of the doorpost on the driver's side, and the front legs did the same on the passenger side, with the head hanging down over the right rear fender. The officers secured both pairs of legs to the doorposts with short pieces of rope from the barn floor. What a trophy that buck would have made, parked outside a local tavern, had it been in season. Hank made arrangements with the two 'hunters' to voluntarily appear in court in Arichat the following Tuesday, and the two constables headed for the cold storage in the same town, to deposit the buck, in case it was needed for evidence. The two hunters appeared In Court the next week, and were each fined seventy-five dollars, and allowed two weeks to pay, or spend thirty days in Jail. They paid the fine. The rifle and light were forfeited, the deer was donated to the County, to be processed and given to the poor.

Early in Hank's stay in St. Peters, K.C. introduced him to the only general store merchant in L'Ardoise, (anglicized 'Lordways' by the locals) Quentin Sampson who seemed to be a jovial, friendly sort, genuinely pleased to meet Hank. He pointed to a bench across the road from his store with a couple of older men sitting there whittling small pieces of wood with their jack knives and said, "around here we call them 'the chippers'" and added a hearty laugh. A few days later in the early afternoon K.C. and Hank arrived back at the office and as they got out of the police car, Quentin slowed, wound down his truck window and shouted out "I just saw the most beautiful buck you've ever seen come up from the canal and go right up there into the woods behind the detachment." The young constables thanked him at the same time and hurried in to the office, glancing at each other' smiling, one saying "What do ya think, shall we?" answered by "You betcha!" while changing from uniforms to old clothes and boots, grabbing a rifle, some ammunition, and Hank's hunting knife & sheath which met his belt as they went together out the back door. They started to run against the fairly steep hill and realized they were making too much noise so slowed to a fast walk careful not to snap any twigs. At the top of the hill they broke out into a small not so recent clear-cut, stopped at the edge and scanned all 360 degrees while they both gasped for air. K.C. quietly whispered, "Looks like we missed him."

The words weren't out of his mouth, when Hank pointed to the far corner of the clearing, and this magnificent buck got up from where he was laying, and shook himself. Hank slowly offered the already loaded rifle to K.C. who shook his head, so Hank quietly cocked it, braced himself against a stump, and because of the long distance, aimed just above the base of the neck and pulled. The legs of the buck folded under him like an accordion, and he went down onto the same spot on the ground where he had been, only moments earlier. Instant jubilation, as Hank racked the old shell from the rifle, and injected another as the two off duty hunters, ran and stumbled towards the buck, expecting at any time for him to get up and try to run away, but he never moved. Once beside him, they realized the fatal blow had cut the jugular, and the blood was already pooling under his neck. Hank set the rifle down, took the knife out of its sheath and finished the job the bullet had started. The rack was a good twenty inches across with twelve points in all. Now the work began! K.C. had never shot a deer before, so knew very little about gutting the animal. Hank had only shot two before, but had helped both times from experienced hunters. Now, he was the head surgeon, so he proceeded to split the buck down the center of the belly and open him up, so he could retrieve the heart and liver, being careful not to contaminate good meat, with anything from the reproductive organs. When the time came to empty him, both men rolled the buck on its side and dragged the guts out onto the ground. During the process, Hank straightened up and asked K.C. "What are we gonna do with him?" Came the reply "I'll bet Janie (at the boarding house) would love to have him." K.C. agreed to stay with the deer while Hank went to retrieve the police car and the deer tag he had forgotten in his bedroom, in his haste to the hunt.

Hank hurried back down to the detachment, checked for calls, all was quiet, grabbed the keys to the Ford car, and drove up the road beside the canal, within fifty yards of K.C. and the prize buck. Reminiscent of the similar situation at Forchu with the seized deer, the two really struggled to drag this one over the brush and between stumps to the car. Once there they repeated the same lift to get the deer similarly loaded onto the trunk of the car, and fastened so it wouldn't fall off, going down the narrow, rough, canal road and over town, to Findlay and Janie's yard. When K.C. called them out to see the deer, they beamed like two kids in a candy store, and Findlay went directly to his barn and cleared out an area, where they could hang the deer from the rafters, to allow the meat to 'cure' for two or three days. Hank slit the two hind legs above the hock, so Findlay could insert two meat hooks from his old butcher days, and between the three men and a block and tackle, they managed to get the deer high enough so that its nose was off the barn floor. Later that week, with the help of a long time friend and neighbour, Findlay butchered the animal, gave some away, packed and wrapped the rest into his freezer. At dinner soon after, K.C. and Hank were the first guests to try their venison, and agreed it was the best they had ever tasted. Memories are made of this!

Four years later in the summer, Hank was chosen happily to relieve once again at St. Peters detachment for two weeks. In spite of the fact that he was now married with two boys and was obliged to get back into uniform after two years in plain clothes. His wife Mary Ann was not unhappy about this transfer either, because it gave her the chance to visit her parents in Inverness County, with the only grand children they had, at that time. This time, Hank relieved Cpl. Avery Stairs while he and his family went on vacation, to his native New Brunswick. This time Hank was ably assisted by the now highway patrolman Dave Maloney. He and his wife Marilyn made Hank welcome, even though Hank was again able to take his meals at Janie's. There were also memorable events, on this tour to St. Peters, but none so remarkable as those already mentioned, all with due respect to the Maloney family. Perhaps it was partly because Hank was now married with children and maybe the events of these two weeks didn't stand out quite as much in his memory.

SYDNEY

WEDDING BELLS

In June of that year, Hank married Mary Ann at her home church in Strathlorne. Spud was his best man, and K.C. was one of the attendants. The reception was at Mary Ann's home on the side of Shaw Mountain, on a rainy day. Many high heel shoes and shiny boots got a taste of mountain mud, before the day was out. To accommodate Hank's parents, the party was supposed to be dry, but if Mary Ann's father extended an invitation to the stable to see his horses, perhaps a 'wee dram' could be found on a concealed shelf. The newlyweds drove to Boston in the golden rocket for their honeymoon, visiting friends and relatives along the way, almost missing the ferry from Yarmouth to Bar Harbour, Maine. Back home in Sydney they had rented a tiny one- bedroom bungalow, with a fireplace and a coal fired furnace in the basement, in a quiet residential part of the city. They lived there one year, during which Hank came down with the mumps, which garnered him, two weeks sick leave, and the loss of sixteen pounds, but recovered without any lasting effects. A year later, Mary Ann became pregnant.

Another memorable event one frosty, winter night, Hank came home late from work on slushy roads, parked the unmarked police car in front of the house and locked it. A '58 Ford, the engine hood closed and locked in front of the windshield, and the release was inside the car. In the wee hours of the morning, Hank and Mary Ann were rudely awakened by the howl of a siren, outside their bedroom window. Hank finally realized the sound was from his car, rushed out to shut it off, only to remember that the siren was under the hood, the car was locked, and the release for the engine hood was inside it. He ran back into the house for the keys, grabbed them and his three-cell flashlight, returned, unlocked the car, released the hood latch, opened it to allow the siren to scream louder, and surely wake all the neighbours. In desperation, Hank reached in and pulled the wires off the siren with his bare hands, to stop the noise. The next morning after the ice thawed, Hank and John McNeil the technician who installed the siren, discovered that the terminals on the dimmer switch that activated the siren, were outside under the floorboards, and had been covered in slush the night before. They concluded that when the slush froze, it connected the terminals and activated the siren.

Hank bore the brunt of many good natured remarks, from his fellow workers. Two of his neighbours offered an understanding chuckle, when Hank met them later but there were no complaints. And yes, John installed a new and different switch on the siren, so that late-night disturbance would never happen again.

IT'S TWINS
LOCAL MOVES

The next summer, Hank and Mary Ann moved from the tiny bungalow in the city to a new basement apartment in the outskirts, motivated partly by the fact that Spud and K.C. were already in similar apartments, in other bungalows, on the same street. On Christmas Eve, Mary Ann went into labour, and Hank delivered her to the Sydney City hospital where she had worked part time. Two days later after a long struggle she gave birth to twin boys in a snowstorm. The parents named them Craig and Curtis, the first grandchildren to Mary Ann's parents. When Hank tried to reach the grandparents by phone to tell them the good news, the lines were down due to a snow storm, so Hank called the Post Office in Inverness and asked their mailman, Peter John Lauchie, a large gregarious man, to pass the news on to them on his way home. Due to the storm, he couldn't get his truck up the driveway, so he walked in deep snow up to Mary Ann's old home, right into the kitchen, stuck his hand out to Mary Ann's dad and said "Congratulations Grandpa". Let the celebration begin!

Other than Hank, the first visitors to the maternity wing were good friends and fellow members, Bryan and Gordie from Glace Bay detachment. They came to the hospital on duty, in uniform, in the Christmas spirit, just to see Mary Ann and her twin boys. Mary Ann's long-time friend Donna MacGregor, a long-time resident of Sydney, also came to see the new boys, and was a big help many times later at home, when she was not working. Mary Ann's sister Joyce flew in from Boston for a week, to assist with the new family, while Hank continued working. Over those next few days at home, many friends of the new parents dropped in to see the twin boys, which seemed to be a novelty to some of them. The stay for the new parents in the suburbs was short, as that apartment had only one bedroom, now with the crib in the corner of the parent's bedroom. In the spring, a larger three-bedroom second floor apartment became available in the city, when friends and fellow member, Jones and his wife Grace, got transferred to Newfoundland. With the new apartment also came two boarders, young nurses, Debbie from Inverness and Jennie from South Bar.

In those days when members of the force moved within the city, usually on a Saturday, they simply borrowed a truck, a favorite being a cube van, either from Buddy, the bread man, or Allister, the egg man, both friends of Hank from his days in Glace Bay. Days before, the member moving would invite fellow members with strong backs, to come along and help. A nucleus of those who had been helped before, or banked favours for future, would gather on Saturday morning, assemble at the departure point, and by Noon, the move would be completed.

Two reasons were, small items could be moved by car, and larger items were at the basic minimum. The reward was usually a taste of 'bubbly' when the job was done. Most moves were uneventful, but Hank will never forget a move, where friend George refused to empty his freezer before the move. It was relatively easy to move from the basement up the wide stairs and out the back door to the van. However, the destination was a second floor apartment in the city, part of an old three storey house, with coal fired furnace and cast-iron hot water radiators. Three able-bodied men and Hank, with considerable effort, managed to get the freezer from the van, in the front door and up the stairs. When they reached the second floor, one of the lads on the front hollered "I can't hold on, she's gonna go", not wanting to risk a back injury, all four dropped the freezer at the same time. Unfortunately, it was right beside the end of a tall cast iron radiator. The freezer, on its way to the floor, snapped the two feeder pipes at the bottom end of the radiator, like dry twigs in summer. Instantly, the black water in the lines under pressure, no doubt for many years, shot up to the ceiling and the walls, leaving the four 'movers' scattering for cover.

SEARCHING SHIPS

During Hank's five years on G.I.S. there were many searches that yielded little or no contraband at all. One such search was aboard an empty Liberian freighter at anchor in Sydney harbour. The day was clear but there was a chop on the water. The search party was taken from the government wharf out alongside the freighter, by the police boat 'Interceptor'. Usually when a ship is at anchor, a stairway is lowered for visitors. This time, showing utmost distain for the visitors, the crew lowered a 'Jacob's ladder' from the highest point of the bow of the empty ship, thirty some feet above the water. With the ship rolling back and forth and the police boat bobbing up and down, it was a real challenge for the faint of heart to start up the ladder, but all five made it to the top. Hank didn't mind because he had done that before.

No contraband was found during the search, the first three men made it safely down the ladder to the deck of the police boat, but Cst. Ring was seized by a severe attack of acrophobia. The crew didn't offer to help rather some got a chuckle out of his dilemma. Hank took several minutes talking Ring into crawling over the side, and starting down and promised him Hank would go first and place Ring's feet on the rungs of the ladder, if necessary. With the men below cheering him on, Ring struggled to climb over the top edge of the bow, swing his legs over, and with Hank's guidance, place a foot securely on the top rung of the ladder. Then one rung at a time, they slowly made it down to the deck of the police boat and all breathed a sigh of relief. Although it was part of his job, Cst. Ring vowed he'd never volunteer to do that again, and all had a good laugh.

As junior man on the Sydney G.I.S. and as a get-acquainted exercise to the job, days he was in town, Hank drove through the steel plant to check the steel and coal piers for recent arrivals of freighters from foreign countries, as well as any new foreign ships waiting at anchor in the harbour. Some days, it was also a chance to visit with Hank's first boss in Glace Bay, Bill House, now retired, and in charge of steel plant security. G.I.S. also had several plant workers on different shifts, who might keep them informed, of any new arrivals selling contraband liquor. To verify this, of course, they would first be required to purchase their own sample. Whereas most ships stayed in port only one or two days, when smuggling was confirmed, a search party had to be assembled quickly, calling on four to six constables available at the time in mufti-plain clothes. In Hank's early days, he was one of the constables 'learning the ropes' and he did manage to find his share of illegal liquor on board some ships.

Then one day in his third year on G.I.S, Hank was delegated to organize and lead the search, with four other men, of a Norwegian freighter, loading steel rails. Information was that the smuggler went to the bow area, out on the deck, to retrieve the bottle he sold. Once on board, Hank checked the bow, and noticed a number of forty-five gallon steel drums outside on the front deck. Close examination by he and a young constable, revealed that the top of one drum had been modified, so it could be opened with a slight twist. When they removed the lid, the drum was almost full of quart bottles of Bacardi Rum, packed like cordwood. Among the rest of the barrels on the deck was one other barrel, with a similar top, and thirty some more bottles of the same rum in it. Hank went to the wheelhouse and notified the First Mate of the find. He, in turn, located the crew member responsible for the stash. He also offered three heavy burlap bags, in which to carry the seized rum ashore, twenty some bottles per bag, seventy-six bottles total, so many that the officers had to take turns carrying them, the full length of the 'steel pier', because of the weight. Before he left the ship, Hank arranged with the Mate for that same young crewmember to be available the following day, for a hearing before the ship's Chandler in the city.

The next morning Hank and George met the handsome young blond-haired man on board the ship. He, by the way, couldn't speak English, and an interpreter was not made available. He seemed quite at ease being led ashore by the two officers, no cuffs, so as to remain unnoticed, and into the back seat of the unmarked police car. Much to the surprise of the officers, as soon as the car started moving, he put his hands behind his head, sat back in the seat, and began singing a current popular song "Send me the pillow that you dream on" in perfect English, and on key. He appeared before the Chandler, was assessed a fine of one hundred and fifty dollars, which the ship paid, and would be later deducted from his pay. He was returned directly to the ship, as happy as when he departed.

This seizure was part of the liquor that George and Hank took to Halifax, in Hank's car, during the Navy Court Marshall. Also the same rum that earned them an audience with the Commanding Officer of the R.C.M.P. Nova Scotia after the encounter with a fire truck, the night before.

PORTUGUESE WHITE FLEET

An Annual event that brought smuggling to the shore of Cape Breton in June was the arrival of the Portuguese white fishing fleet, on their 'spring break' from the Grand Banks off Newfoundland. The fishermen were poorly paid, and each year some stocked up on pints of cheap brandy before leaving home, to sell when they came to Canada. Hank was told that the fleet usually set sail from home in March then spent three months fishing from one-man dories by hand and came into North Sydney for a few days rest and to replenish supplies. There were between ten and fifteen two-massed schooners, and one hospital supply ship in the fleet. In port, they would tie up beside any available wharf space, sometimes four abreast. The schooners were old style, and labour intensive, with rows of one-man dories stacked on the deck like paper cups, enough for thirty or forty fishermen. Each dory was large enough to carry one man, a large wooden tub of baited trawl line, a large wooden box in the center to hold the fish, a bailing can and oars to row the dory. On the fishing grounds at daybreak, each man and dory would be lowered over the side, with distinct orders not to return without the trawl line intact, and a full box of fish. This was in all kinds of weather, rain, sleet, snow or fog, except a severe storm or hurricane.

If a surprise storm erupted while the men were out, the mother ship would sound intermittent blasts on the ship's horn, but if the wind was too high or the fog too thick, some fishermen wouldn't hear the horn. Rumour had it that only the medical officer of the fleet or the captain would know for sure how many men didn't make it back to the ship.

Another night, perhaps the next year, Hank received a call at home that North Sydney detachment had information about fishermen from more than one ship in the White Fleet were selling contraband liquor on the main street.

SYDNEY

If Hank could lead the search, they had one detachment member and two men from the Interceptor to assist him. Hank met the other three at North Sydney detachment and all four drove in Hank's unmarked car to the waterfront. On the way they agreed to search two ships at one time, the two men from North Sydney as one team and constable King from the Interceptor with Hank as the other. Each ship in the fleet carried between thirty and forty officers and fishermen, although not all men were smugglers or might be on board at any one time, especially in the evening.

The two teams agreed to meet after each search before they went on to the next two ships and after the first four ships, they had found no contraband. But Cst. King had found out that some irate fisherman had confided in him that the contraband was coming from one of four ships moored side by side at the Government wharf. The four policemen walked the short distance over to the Government wharf and found the four ships mentioned to Cst. King. As they had already been there almost two hours, it was getting late, and the four suspect ships were side by side, they agreed to each man searching a ship alone. Hank offered to take the ship further away from the wharf and the other three constables chose a ship as they walked across the decks. Normally as the police boarded a ship, they found the Officer on Watch and identified themselves and the officer would accompany him during the search and act as interpreter if there was a problem.

When Hank found the Watch Officer on the ship he boarded, he was busy with another problem on board, seemed indifferent, told Hank to go ahead and he'd catch up later. In most ships in the white fleet the fishermen's sleeping quarters were below deck in the bow accessible only by one hatch, down a perpendicular ladder into a room full of bunks, some two bunks high and some three, one above the other. When Hank appeared below deck, he identified himself; most fishermen present seemed to understand and cooperated as he searched their bunk. As he progressed farther into the sleeping quarters away from the exit ladder, the spirit of cooperation seemed to dissipate, led by a small vocal fisherman who had a following of equally vocal, more irritated friends. Hank shone the beam of his three-cell flashlight directly into the eyes of the small vocal one and raised his voice to try to impress that he was in charge here. As the dozen or more men closed in around him, Hank waved the flashlight in the air, shouted some non-descript obscenities and shoved his way through the knot of men in front of him. He ran towards the upright ladder and took the eight steps in three leaps with the 'hounds' nipping at his heels. Once on deck he located the watch officer who, when he learned what happened below deck, had difficulty stifling the smirk on his face. He surmised that Hank was probably getting too close to the smuggler and since he was alone the 'mob' decided to chase him. That was the only time in his twenty-five years of service that Hank ever ran from a dangerous situation.

The other members of the search party also had no luck finding contraband liquor, but had a good laugh as they walked back to the police car after Hank told them about his narrow escape.

Later while stationed in Shelburne, Hank's friend Ed Turner, a Forest Ranger told Hank how when he was a teen, he fished on a schooner just like the ones in the Portuguese fleet, out of Lockport, Nova Scotia. He had similar stories to tell as the other fishermen, about being alone in a dory out in the Atlantic in fog so thick he couldn't see any other dories and for sure he couldn't see the mother ship. A memorable day while he was out there alone, a sudden storm came up, the mother ship blasted the horn to tell him and other fishermen to return. When he tried to haul the trawl into the dory, it was snagged on the bottom, and try as he might he couldn't free it. He knew not to go back to the ship without the trawl and he also knew he did not want to spend the night out there in the storm. So as his dory tossed in the sea, he waited until it dropped into a trough between waves, tied two quick half hitches around the bow sprit and when the dory rose on the next wave, the trawl line snapped. He was at least able to retrieve some hooks and line to take back to the ship and as he rowed hard through the rough seas and saw the ship come into view he thanked God he made it back. He still had to wait his turn alongside the mother ship to offload his minimal catch and then get hoisted aboard.

One year while the white fleet was in North Sydney, after dark, George and Hank were on foot in old clothes just mingling with the residents and the visiting fishermen. One young fisherman stood out in the crowd, short in stature and wearing a new beige trench coat that almost touched the ground. Hank first noticed him in the distance talking to another man and appeared to be exchanging something. So Hank stepped into an alley and waited for the fisherman to come closer. And sure enough this time Hank could see him open the coat, take a flask from an inside pocket, hand it to another man who quickly gave him something and departed.

Hank moved swiftly towards the man in the trench coat who spotted Hank, turned and ran between two buildings toward the waterfront. Hank could run fast then, and soon overtook the fisherman who seemed burdened down with a load. Hank closed in, tackled him from behind and they both fell sliding along the ground. When Hank dragged him to his feet, identified himself and opened the coat, there were eight pockets hand- sewn into the inside of the coat. Two of the pockets were empty but six each contained a pint of Portuguese Five Star brandy, and the miracle was none had broken during the fall. Hank arrested him, had him point out his ship, returned him to it, found the officer in charge who assured Hank the young fisherman would be available the next day to go before the Court and pay the fine for smuggling.

BOOTLEG COAL AND MOONSHINE STILL

In November of '61, Hank had his first experience inside one such mine, when an 'informant' took Hank's boss to an underground 'still' site, in the old No. 11 workings. There he saw seven 30 gallon wooden barrels of 'mash', set to mature at different times, and the mash in two or three of the barrels looked like it was ready to run. Hank and two other members, Jim MacDowell and Don Bentley, were hastily assembled, and under the cover of darkness, dropped off at a new entrance to the mine. It was a 'cave -in' at the end of a coal seam, just below the surface of an isolated field, on the side of Steele's Hill. Both outside and inside the mine, the 'three- cell flashlights' were vital to make a safe decent over the 'cave-in' rubble, into the mine. Then to follow each other some ten city blocks, which they were of similar size, to the 'still' site deep underground. Enroute, there were puddles of water on the floor of the mine, which also left wet tracks from the feet of previous passersby. These were valuable when the trio came to an intersection, to see which way the footprints went. The wet footprints became even more valuable when they came upon, what at first glance, looked like a solid wall. Closer examination disclosed a cave-in of the roof above, over which the wet tracks led, so, with trepidation, the trio followed up through the hole vacated by the cave-in and down the other side. The officers had no hard hats or miner's boots, just three-cell flashlights, ball caps and work boots, and enough food and water to last two days.

After a couple of wrong turns, they found the stable, and were amazed at the size of the operation. Besides the barrels of mash, there were two forty-five gallon metal oil drums welded together and lying on their side, on two steel frames from old kitchen couches, which made up the boiler.

On the ground nearby were, four or five hand-held flame throwers, used to burn brush on the side of the road or railway. They could be easily lit and propped up beside the boiler, when the still was operating. There was a third forty-five gallon barrel sitting upright full of cold water, likely to hold the 'worm' which was not present. After they scouted the immediate area, the trio found a secluded spot where they could rest on the ground, in full view of the entrance to the still, and hopefully not be detected. They then settled in for a restless night, anticipating that perhaps tonight was the night the 'moonshiners' chose to come down and run some 'shine'. They never showed. The only activity came from a couple of rats, chasing each other either in fun or attempting to mate. One scurried right over Jim's foot, and was gone.

The Old coal mine sites in and around Glace Bay showed various heaps of slag on the surface, and underground was a source of bootleg coal to men who had small trucks and the means to extract it. They also needed a following of regular customers and an absence of Coal Company police or the R.C.M.P. who were both obliged to enforce the Mines Act. Hoping the police would either be at dinner or off duty, the 'bootleg' miners would usually deliver their loads at noon or after dark. By the time Hank got posted to Glace Bay most of the wooden pit props in the mines had rotted and fallen away. Also, some illegal miners had carelessly chipped away at the large columns of coal that had been left to support the roof of the mine for safety when the mine was in operation. Both these conditions made the abandoned mines very dangerous to enter. But not all-illegal activity in the old mines was mining coal because one year, three enterprising young men decided to set up a 'still' in an abandoned pony stable where there was a ready source of water.

In November of '61, Hank had his first experience inside one such mine when an informant took Hank's boss to an underground still site in the old No. 11 workings. There he saw seven 30 gallon wooden barrels of mash set to mature at different times, and the mash in two or three barrels looked like it was ready to run. Hank and two other members, John MacDowell and Ron Bentley were hastily assembled, and under the cover of darkness dropped off at the entrance to the mine which was a cave in at the end of a coal seam just below the surface of an isolated field on the side of Steele's Hill. Both outside and inside the mine the three-cell flashlights were vital to make a safe decent over the rubble into the mine and to follow each other some ten city blocks, which they were, to the still site deep underground. Enroute, there were puddles of water on the floor which also left wet tracks from the feet of previous passersby. These were valuable when the trio came to an intersection and could see which way the footprints went.

The wet footprints became very valuable when they came upon, what at first glance looked like a solid wall, but on closer examination was a cave-in of the roof, over which the wet tracks led. With trepidation, the trio followed up through the hole vacated by the cave in. The officers had no hard hats or miner's boots, just three-cell flashlights, caps and work boots and enough food and water to last two days.

Once at the stable, after a couple of wrong turns, they were amazed at the size of the operation. Besides the barrels of mash, there were two forty-five-gallon metal oil barrels welded together and lying on their side on two steel frames from old kitchen couches, which made up the boiler. On the ground nearby were four or five hand-held flame throwers used to burn brush on the side of the road or railway. They could be easily propped up beside the boiler when the still was operating. There was a third forty-five-gallon barrel sitting upright full of water likely to hold the worm which was not present. After they scouted the immediate area, the trio found a secluded spot where they could rest on the ground in full view of the 'still' and hopefully not be detected. They then settled in for a restless night anticipating that tonight was the night the moonshiners chose to come down and run some shine, but they never showed. The only activity came from a couple of rats chasing each other either in fun or attempting to mate. One scurried right over John's foot and then was gone.

Three Cell Flashlight

WINGER GEORGE – DRUG SQUAD

When Hank first arrived at Glace Bay detachment, he replaced George as Junior Man. Still, at times they both worked together, on mundane tasks like filing Gazette index cards, cleaning office floors and washing police cars. It wasn't long before they became good buddies going on patrol together, answering calls in the middle of the night, to fights outside the Wagon Wheel dance hall, in Reserve Mines, and double dating on evenings off. Little did they know five years later, they would be stationed in Sydney together, on the three-man General Investigation Section? As the two constables on a plain clothes section, with a corporal in charge, they worked together for the next five years on investigations all over Cape Breton Island. As a team, it wasn't long before they knew at a glance, what the other was thinking. The Corporal in charge, Doug Wright soon became an idol of Hank's, because when he was present, he was flawlessly decisive, and would never ask Hank to do anything he wouldn't do himself.

A large, gentle man most of the time, when combined with George and Hank, if the situation required, they were a force to be reckoned with.

At the time, the financial services in Headquarters wouldn't pay for motel accommodation out of town, after a long day at work, but expected all members working out of Sydney, to drive back home the two or three hours, in the middle of the night. Usually, George would drive a few miles at the start of the trip, then hand the reins over to Hank, slump over in the passenger seat, and sleep the next hundred miles or more, while Hank struggled to stay awake behind the wheel. On some of these trips, it was nothing short of a miracle, that they survived without accident, in all kinds of bad weather and road conditions. Realizing their concern, Doug went to bat for them at headquarters, but he was unable to get the policy changed.

George was second generation Czechoslovakian from a southern Alberta prairie farm, who knew hard work from an early age, and the value of every penny earned. With similar background, Hank was not unlike him in his beliefs. Pre-Christmas, both would be watching for deals on children's clothing and small toys, to ship home to their younger siblings. Then would come the early wrapping of presents, packing them into used cardboard boxes

SYDNEY

destination marked clearly on both sides, tied securely with issue brown paper and twine, and shipped to arrive in plenty of time for Christmas.

In tasks like searching an ocean-going freighter for smuggled goods, or hiking through the woods looking for moonshine stills, George was like a blood hound, with the stamina of a good racehorse. Hank learned early to let George lead, and he would try to keep up. When it came to stakeouts in bitterly cold temperatures, which were not uncommon, George would be determined to stay until the last gun was fired while Hank, with teeth chattering and stomping his feet to stay warm, would be hinting that "don't you think we should call it a day/night". In interrogation of suspects, George was usually the bad cop, while Hank assumed the role of good cop. In long, tough cases, occasionally they'd reverse roles. Whatever, the common goal was getting all the facts and wrapping it up in the shortest period of time, as taught by Cpl. Wright.

In the police car, George always liked to be at the helm and was probably more cautious than Hank. When Hank, who had more country road time under his belt, would demonstrate his driving skills, George would frequently deploy his imaginary brake pedal on the passenger side, citing his favourite warning "for cryin out load Hank, take it easy will ya!"

Both practiced, to a degree, the beliefs of their first boss on G.I.S., Cpl. Wright "The shortest distance between two points is a straight line, guilty until proven innocent, and sometimes we have to bend the rules a little." Even though George and Hank didn't always adapt these methods to the letter, they really missed him, when he got transferred to Halifax. They both remained loyal to their new boss, in fact George, two years later, took over the section, when that boss was transferred out. With hard work and dedication, eventually George was commissioned, and returned to Sydney as the Officer In Charge of the Sub-Division. In the end, George and Hank had worked together for almost seven years.

During the five years that Hank was on Sydney General Investigation Section in the early sixties, he could count on one hand, the number of drug cases he was involved in. Drug traffic simply hadn't reached Cape Breton Island, or the police hadn't yet heard about it. Either that or the traffickers of the day were being very careful.

Three Cell Flashlight

In one case, a report came in from Dr. Dan Shepherd in Whitney Pier that someone was stealing morphine from his 'black bag' in the back seat of his unlocked car, while he was making a house call on Howard Street at night. Winger George and Hank went to visit Dr. Shepherd the next day, recorded the pertinent details, and arranged to stake out his car, during his next evening house call. The first attempt, two weeks later yielded no activity, around his car, parked on the same street under a streetlight. Ten nights later, George and Hank were back at the same location on a calm, bitterly cold night, when the exhaust from passing cars hung in the air like miniature clouds, and the tires crunched softly on the snow covered street. The visibility was really clear around Dr. Shepherd's car, parked under a streetlight, and there was very little traffic. Shortly before seven-thirty P.M., a tall, stooped-over man wearing a fedora, scarf and long winter overcoat, appeared on the sidewalk walking in the direction of Dr. Shepherd's car. As he approached it from behind, he slowed right down, opened the back door, leaned in and in a few seconds, straightened up, walking briskly now, back in the direction from which he came.

By the time George and Hank exited the unmarked car, and crossed the street, in plain clothes, they needed the light from their three-cell flashlights, to intercept the man, and identify themselves in the darkness, between two streetlights. He was a well-dressed, polite man who was outwardly embarrassed to be caught in this situation. At first, he denied having taken anything from the doctor's car but a quick search of his overcoat pockets, revealed a small, slender vile of five, even smaller, tablets. There was no clear label on the vile, but the two detectives concurred the pills were morphine. The man, who identified himself as James Graham, retired Mayor of Sydney city, was unable to supply a valid source of the pills, and finally admitted to taking them from the bag in the doctor's car. Because of the extreme cold temperature, George invited Mr. Graham to come and sit in the warm police car, until they obtained his personal information.

"You're not going to arrest me, are you?" deeply concerned, he asked. "Not unless you give us reason to." George replied.

The three men crossed the street, entered the police car, George and Mr. Graham in the back seat and Hank behind the wheel, to start the engine and keep the car warmed up. Now, somewhat relaxed, Mr. Graham related how two years ago, he and his wife Margaret had been involved in a bad car accident that took her life, and left him with injuries so severe, that between the pain, financial loss and loneliness, he could not continue without a lot of strong medication. As such, he resorted to stealing from the doctor's car. The two detectives were so sympathetic with the plight of the man, that they decided to drive him home just three city blocks away, and to 'confirm his street address' at the same time. The next day, George and Hank discussed the case with their boss, and later the Crown Prosecutor, who instructed that Mr. Graham be charged with theft from a motor vehicle, to appear alone before Provincial Magistrate Doug MacDonald who knew him, and understood his situation. When told of this decision, Mr. Graham was pleased and said with a smile "I'll throw myself on the mercy of the Court." Magistrate MacDonald dutifully sentenced him to one-week house arrest, and to report back to him at the end of the week. Dr. Shepherd was advised of the action taken, was satisfied, and later received from the police, the morphine taken from his car.

MURDER AT BARRA HEAD

One weekday morning in early spring, a call came in to Sydney G.I.S. from Cpl. Stairs at St. Peters detachment. He advised that a sixty-nine year old woman named Isabel Bernard had been murdered the night before, in her home where she lived alone, on the Indian Reserve at Barra Head. As he was already involved in two other cases, he requested the assistance of Sydney G.I.S. Cpl. Marshall detailed George and Hank to go out to the Reserve on Highway Four, approximately forty miles south of Sydney, on the east side of the Bras D'or Lakes. George called Avery, and arranged to meet him at the Reserve. Hank was familiar with this Reserve, having relieved at St. Peters, twice in the past four years. At the time, it had a population between one hundred and one fifty well-behaved citizens, quite unlike Nyanza on the other side of the Lakes, where Hank had served for over two years.

George and Hank met Cpl. Stairs at Barra Head about 10:00 AM He explained that he had done a preliminary investigation, and visited the scene with the victim's sister Evelyn, who had already called a funeral home in Sydney, to remove the body. Cpl. Stairs had also notified the Coroner, and Cst. Dornan from Sydney Identification to attend. The Coroner, unable to attend the scene, asked that the body be delivered to the morgue at St. Rita's hospital in Sydney. Cpl. Stairs gave the detectives clear directions to the scene, and to the sister's home.

The inhabited Reserve covered approximately one square mile on both sides of Highway Four, not including Chapel Island, one hundred yards from shore, accessible only by boat, or on the ice in winter. Hank drove the police car up into the Reserve to the end of the gravel road, and the two constables, with the victim's sister, walked the rest of the way to the scene. The body had already been removed. A small two-room cabin, nestled in the woods, not visible from other homes, showed signs of a struggle in the kitchen, with the furniture in disarray, including a couch with soiled blankets, and pieces of clothing. Besides cupboards, the kitchen had a counter, sink, a small wooden table, four chairs, stove with a hot-water tank, in the middle of the room, and a hooked rug on the floor in front of the stove. On the counter beside the sink, were two water glasses with stains. While the victim's sister was still there, George asked "Do you have any idea who might have done this?" She hesitated, then replied with an unconvincing "No, I don't," and departed.

George and Hank agreed it was better that way, so she would have time to think, and went about searching the cabin. Hank chose the bedroom, and noticed behind the bed, against the wall, on the floor, was a ten pound brown paper bag, almost full of dried Irish moss. He showed it to George and both wondered what it was for. George had already lifted the floor mat in the kitchen, and discovered a small triangular piece of, what appeared to be human flesh. Later, sister Evelyn explained the flesh was probably from the side of the victim's head, where she fell or was pushed against the sharp edge of the hot water tank, on the end of the stove. She also told them that her sister, in spite of her age, was still having menstrual periods, and used the moss as an absorbent pad. Later, George and Hank searched around the outside of the cabin, and found an empty gallon jug, that looked and smelled like fresh native home brew called 'Goobie'. They retained it to have Cst. Dornan check it for fingerprints.

When Cst. Dornan arrived from Sydney, George and Hank accompanied him to the scene. He took some photographs, dusted for fingerprints, and seized, for further examination, the water glasses and bottle that showed signs of home-brewed 'Goobie'. Back down the hill, George and Hank went door to door, one on each side of the road, conducting neighborhood enquiries. Hank had no success, but George received a hint of a boyfriend of the victim, but nothing else. After awhile the sister, who had been watching from her home, called the detectives to come over, and with confidence, named Isabel's boyfriend as a suspect, Tom 'Spook' Isadore. "He's about nineteen years old, lives with his mother down near the highway, doesn't work all day, and prowls around at night." She described his mother's home, so the two men could easily find it.

George and Hank walked back to the police car and drove down to the Isadore house. He was outside, behind the house splitting firewood, looking up as the car approached. When he saw the two plain-clothes officers, he secretly knew the jig was up, thought about running, but changed his mind. As the officers approached him, Isadore was still holding the axe. Hank ordered him to put it down. George went directly to him, told him to put his hands behind his back, cuffed him, and told him that he was wanted for questioning in the murder of Isabel Bernard. In front of the house, Tom's mother came to the door and asked, "What's going on here?" Hank replied "We're taking him to St. Peters detachment for questioning about the death of Isabel Bernard."

At the detachment, Cpl. Stairs suggested they use his office for interrogation, and offered to be available if needed. George and Hank had agreed to first question him together where he said "I never killed Isabelle. I was home at Mom's all night." The officers then implemented the good cop/bad cop routine which exposed some discrepancies in Isadore's story. In less than an hour, he confessed "Okay, it was me. I went to see her last night. We were a secret you know. It was her idea. We drank a bottle of goobie. She liked to tease me. She sat down on the couch and opened her shirt, said C'mon big boy, come and get some. I wanted to do it, but I couldn't get it up. She really laughed at me then and I got mad. I grabbed her and picked her up off the couch. She was still laughing and she fought me. I pushed her away. She fell and hit her head on the stove, landed on the floor. She was knocked out. I got scared."

After a pause, with tears in his eyes he continued. "I got down beside her and shook her, but she didn't wake up. I felt for a pulse, she wasn't breathing." Now sobbing, he said "Honest, I didn't mean to kill her!"

Meanwhile, Cpl. Stairs checked his index cards that showed an 'assault causing bodily harm' charge against Tom Isadore two years before that had been dismissed, but his fingerprints were still on file. Later, Cst. Dornan confirmed that he had lifted Isadore's legible fingerprint from one of the water glasses at the scene. From there, Cpl. Stairs took over the case, taking the suspect to jail in Arichat, and charging him with second degree murder. He later pleaded guilty to the charge, and was sentenced to twenty years in Dorchester penitentiary.

CAREFREE MAURICE

During Hank's last year in Baddeck, a new member arrived in the radio room in Sydney named Maurice Gaudet, a native son of Miscouche, P.E.I a suburb of summer side. A young constable, Hank never heard where he transferred in from, or why he was assigned to the radio room full-time. If his reputation preceded him, Hank could only conclude that he got in 'ca-ca' somewhere previously. Hank was still driving out to MacAulay's Hill three miles north of Baddeck, twice a day to send or receive messages on the radio in the police car. He introduced himself to Maurice, a fellow 'Islander' over the radio, and all he got was a snide remark about Hank's hillbilly village on the eastern end of the island, followed by a hearty laugh.

Another day shortly after, Hank had the police car window down on an exceptionally windy day, and with his loud voice, was trying to make himself heard while giving a lengthy message. Finally an exasperated Maurice's loud retort was "Stick your head out the winda," followed by another hearty laugh, to which Hank couldn't resist joining in. When Maurice was on the night shift, and Hank was out on patrol alone, Maurice always had a joke, or a story to tell, where another member had gotten into difficulty on patrol, but managed to 'right the ship' before he got in too deep. All in all, Maurice was a refreshing voice in the wilderness on an otherwise boring night patrol.

When Hank got transferred in to Sydney G.I.S. a year later, he finally met the effervescent Maurice, and see firsthand the gleam in his eye, the charming grin, and hear his general disregard for the "establishment", who had thought they were punishing him, by transferring him to the radio room. On the contrary, he bragged about the luxury of his confined workplace, the warmth of being inside, just a few short steps from his bedroom on the second floor, instead of out on the road in all kinds of weather.

Maurice was allowed only a fifteen-minute break, in an eight hour shift, away from the building when another constable, usually Ned Hallet, would relieve him. He could then drive downtown in his 1950 some Packard, pick up a sandwich and drink to bring back to the radio room to eat. In summer, he wore an issue shirt with no badges, a clip-on tie which he removed when he went on his break, issue brown serge pants, and issue black boots, which no one but a fellow member would recognize as police uniform. In winter he wore a storm coat, with no badges and maybe his issue fur hat. Some breaks, on his return, he'd brag that he even had time for a service call with some young lady he had recently met over the phone.

On his days off, he spent most of his time taking flying lessons or just hanging-out at the Sydney airport, between Glace Bay and Sydney. In fine weather he rode his used ex-Army '45 Harley motorcycle, which needed frequent self-repair to keep it operating. He didn't own a toolbox, just the top drawer of his dresser, so he was always borrowing tools, some that never found their way back to the rightful owner. As expected, he was frequently in need of a loan "just till payday", and he was so likeable that some lenders rarely collected, Hank included. In fact, at one time Hank even owned, not on paper but, half of Maurice's Harley Davidson motorcycle. Mary Ann never knew about that either.

In the early sixties, long before Hank arrived in Sydney, the Sub-Division headquarters was domiciled in a large wooden three-story building, acquired from the Royal Canadian Navy after World War II. It was over a hundred feet long and at least forty feet wide, with a firing range in the basement, in addition to storage, furnace and other necessary equipment. It was located below the Esplanade parallel to the East side of the Sydney Harbour, with the Government Wharf in front and to the West. The parking lot in front of the building was gravel, large enough for the men from the Portuguese White Fleet to play soccer in the evenings and on weekends, the first time Hank saw the game played. Ten or twelve concrete steps led up to the front door of the Headquarters, which opened onto the ground floor with Sydney detachment office straight ahead. To the left was a washroom and John MacNeil's radio repair room, to the right on the ground floor was office space and exhibit

Three Cell Flashlight

lockers, occupied mostly by the Highway Patrol and G.I.S. The stairway to the second floor was in the center of the building and contained administration offices, some single men's rooms, a washroom, a large recreation room and the Radio Room with a telex machine. Maurice lived in one of the bedrooms on the north end of the second floor. The stairway continued to the third floor where there was a large seldom-used meeting room, with single men's quarters at both ends of the building. In early 1961 Hank from Baddeck, Spud from Ingonish and K.C. from St. Peters transferred in to Sydney around the same time. They shared a three-man bedroom in the South end of the third floor, until Hank got married. They, already good friends, were "as snug as bugs in a rug", and pleased to be together, after years of being alone on two-man detachments. In spite of, now working different shifts and going in different directions on their time off, they were as close as any trio of brothers.

Although most of the single men in quarters had their own car, there were times between monthly pay cheques, that some of the single men, on both floors, would be happy to stay in on weekends to relax, visit, play cards or watch T.V., if there was one. Sometimes there would be liquid refreshments available, but most times not. Hank will never forget a quiet Sunday afternoon when some 'pal' filled a condom with water on the second floor, tied a knot in it and threw it at another 'pal'. It didn't matter if the object connected, or just splattered against the wall, the game was on! More balloons and condoms filled with water mysteriously appeared, and within twenty minutes the industrial covering on the second-floor hallway, had a half-inch of water on it.

Any member with leather soled shoes or boots, had difficulty running or stopping. The floor was as slippery as ice. Hearing the noise on the second floor, Spud, K.C. and Hank became definitely involved, as was Maurice, who probably was the instigator. At one point Maurice was fleeing from Spud, when he reached his end of the hall, tried to stop, his leather soled boots lost traction, went up in the air, Maurice landed on his back, his head hitting the floor. He gathered himself up, went into his nearby room mumbling to himself, opened his top dresser drawer, took out a live round of .38 caliber ammunition, picked up a pair of pliers and pulled the lead out of the shell.

Meanwhile, Spud had been standing in the hall near the washroom, laughing heartily when Maurice fell. This stopped abruptly and Spud ducked into the washroom, when he spotted Maurice coming out of his room with his police revolver. Hank, who had witnessed most of this action, followed Maurice who forced his way into the washroom, and without a word, pointed the revolver at Spud from a distance of about six feet, and fired. Some bits of the powder spattered on Spud's bare chest and stung a little, he grabbed his chest with his right arm. With a look on Spud's face Hank will never forget, and his wide eyes open in pure shock, Spud said "You bastard, you shot me". Simultaneously, Maurice and Hank said "Don't worry, it was a blank". Relieved, all three had a nervous laugh, and the water fight ended, as other combatants gathered round, upon hearing the shot. That was the first and last time that 'game' was played by those men, especially when Identification boss, Bill Haines opened the door of his office near the washroom, Monday morning and was greeted by a minor flood. From the radio room across the hall, Maurice appeared, explaining, begging forgiveness, as he helped clean-up, and they both had a good laugh. No official report of the flood or the 'water fight' was ever made, much to the relief of the participants.

Meanwhile, Maurice, in spite of his financial situation, managed to acquire his private pilot's license at the Sydney Airport. He also was in contact with the people who stored old war planes, in a small desert compound in Alberta. Over time he bought a single-engine Harvard trainer there and arranged to take delivery of it himself.

Weeks later he flew to Alberta, checked out his nearly new aircraft, and flew it back to Cape Breton alone, by making frequent stops along the way to refuel, and ensure it was still airworthy. Near the end of his journey, enroute to Sydney, he took the time to fly under the new Seal Island Bridge at Big Bras D'or, which had been built high enough to allow ocean-going ships to pass beneath at high tide. He tipped his wings to the few workmen on the bridge, who were not amused by this maneuver. They had two or three heavy chains hanging below the center span, that could have terminated the flight, and left behind a lot of unanswered questions.

Early the next spring, Maurice flew to Baddeck on his day off to visit his good friend Neil Hallet, who was now stationed there. He landed safely on the Bay ice, taxied and parked beside the Government wharf, hitched a ride to the detachment, and managed to persuade Ned to come with him for a ride in his 'new' two-seater plane. Ned, a somewhat nervous individual, reluctantly accepted, accompanied Maurice to the wharf, climbed into the back seat behind him, and buckled up. Ned was not pleased, when Maurice slid the overhead canopy forward and latched it. Ned was ready to abort the flight, but Maurice consoled him, fired up the engine, and taxied out onto the bay ice, parallel to the highway running north out of Baddeck. A few hundred yards out from the wharf, as Maurice was increasing speed for takeoff, the plane shuddered, slowed abruptly, the two front wheels punched through the soft spring ice, and the plane settled on its belly, stopped! Maurice didn't know how Neil did it, but claimed, later with a grin, that by the time the plane came to rest, he looked and "there was Ned, standing on the shore."

Now the work began. Ned and Maurice walked back to the village, told some of the locals about the mishap, invited as many of them that were able to come and take a look. Once there, the assembled men had different opinions how to get the aircraft out of the ice, and some, reacting to the Gaudet charm, offered to help the next day. Ned and his boss arranged a relay with North Sydney detachment, and another member from Sydney Highway Patrol, to get Maurice the sixty some miles back to Sydney. Hank doesn't know the exact details, but in the next few days, Ned and the volunteers from Baddeck with raw muscle, pulp wood, jacks and pry's, managed to get the plane's landing-gear lifted up out of the hole, and back onto solid ice. Maurice came to help when he wasn't working, removed, had repaired a bent propeller blade, and ultimately certified the plane fit to fly. On a bright spring day, a heavy frost the night before, and a strong wind to lift the craft off the ice, Maurice, after a long run over the Bay ice got airborne, and back to a warm hanger at the Sydney airport. To no one's surprise, after a night in the hanger, the wings on the plane started to weep a substantial amount of partly salt water, from the Baddeck Bay onto the floor. This caused some of Maurice's cronies at the airport to stand in awe of his flying skills, to ever have gotten the plane off the ice, with all that extra weight on board.

Much later, on return from a weekend visit to Hank's family on P.E.I., the first year they were married, Mary Ann and Hank stopped at the New Brunswick ferry terminal, late one Sunday night to gas up and have a coffee. When they returned to their car, in a busy parking lot, Hank noticed Maurice's car a short distance away, and went to investigate. Maurice, also returning from a weekend family visit on the 'Island', was sound asleep on the front seat. Hank opened the driver's door and hollered "Wake up you sleepy-head, it's time to hit the road." Maurice half-sitting up on one elbow, squinting into the dim light, groaned "What the Hell are you doin here?" At the same time Hank detected a burning smell and asked "What's that smell?" Half asleep, Maurice explained to Hank that his car's electric fuel - pump had 'shorted' and caught fire, when he tried to start the car.

He continued "I was able to beat it out with an old blanket that I had in the trunk. I'll have to leave the car here. I just don't know how I'm gonna make my shift in Sydney by 6:00 AM."

Hank offered, "We'd take you, but we're only goin as far as Mary Ann's place. Besides, I doubt if we could make it by 6:00 AM anyway" "Aw never mind. Don't you worry, I'll figure something out." says Maurice, as he patted Hank on the shoulder. Now near Midnight, Hank wished Maurice good luck, as he reluctantly walked back to his car and Mary Ann, to face his own six-hour plus journey to her parent's farm.

A day or two later back in Sydney, Maurice related to Hank how, shortly after they left the ferry terminal, he hitched a ride to the Moncton airport, located a pilot friend of his, who dug out his own plane, and flew Maurice to Sydney, in plenty of time to be there for the start of his shift. Hank can't remember how or when, Maurice retrieved his car from the ferry terminal in Cape Tormentine, but he did, with a grin!

Maurice was selective when he drove his motorcycle, because it was not completely up to standard as far as the Motor Vehicle Act was concerned. He chose mostly evenings and weekends when there were no brass around. The lot in front of the Sydney Sub-Division headquarters was gravel surface, and if there was an audience when Maurice departed, he would extend his left leg to the ground, lay the bike halfway over, accelerate into a circle, cut a couple of donuts, straighten back up, and wave with one arm, before departing full throttle, up the hill to the Esplanade and gone.

Hank is sure there are many more stories to tell of Maurice's adventures, but after Hank was transferred out of Sydney, he learned that Maurice was discharged from the Force as unsuitable.

Much later Hank heard that Maurice had found his way to British Columbia. Then word came back that, while working underground as a shot fire in a mine, Maurice and a buddy, to relieve the boredom, played chicken, to see who would stay longer at the face while the other pushed the plunger to detonate the charge before it exploded. One time, Maurice stayed too long, and sadly that was the last we heard about him!

NAVY FRIGATE IN DRYDOCK

On Sydney G.I.S., much of the Customs Act enforcement occurred in Sydney Harbour and adjacent waters. In this case, it was not a commercial vessel, but a Canadian Navy frigate, on its return from winter exercises in the Caribbean Sea. These trips were an annual tradition, a tempting opportunity for the crew of the ship to stock up on duty-free liquor, before returning home to dry-dock. Especially with the holiday season approaching. This time, on arrival in Canada, they failed to declare the bulk of their liquor purchases, when the frigate arrived for refit, at the Point Edward naval base across the harbour from Sydney.

Days later in Dartmouth, while retrieving something from her locker in the basement of her apartment building, a senior lady tenant noticed a trickle of liquid running across the floor, from an adjacent locker. She called the superintendent who determined that the liquid was liquor, many boxes of it that almost completely filled one locker. He called the Mounties, who contacted the lessee of the locker, a young navy seaman who, when questioned, gave the names of sixteen other officers and men, shipmates from the frigate involved. Further interrogation of the young seaman revealed the liquor had been hauled to Dartmouth in a Navy van. Halifax G.I.S. seized the liquor in the locker, called Sydney G.I.S. with the names of offenders, and Cpl. Marshall detailed George and Hank to visit the frigate in Point Edward and investigate. Some of the seventeen navy personnel involved in smuggling the liquor were still on board, and made available to the two policemen by the Chief Petty Officer assigned to the case. Now the work really began, interviewing each and everyone involved, and taking written statements from them, which took several days. Back at the office, the work continued sometimes into the night, typing the statements and the accompanying reports, which eventually were mailed to headquarters in Halifax.

Weeks later, George and Hank learned that the Provincial Attorney General had agreed to a request from Naval Command not to charge the personnel involved, in civilian court. Rather, to deal with the offenders by a Navy Court Marshall in Halifax. The result was that months later, for six consecutive weeks, George and Hank boarded the train to Halifax on Sunday afternoon, stayed over at Thornvale Barracks, and attended as witnesses at the Court Marshall during the week. On Friday evening, they caught the train home to Sydney, and on two occasions worked Saturday nights while home. Between the fifth and sixth weeks, the Officer Commanding Sydney Sub-Division gave permission to Hank to drive his private car to Halifax, instead of riding the train. The official explanation was that Hank would take several cases of Bacardi rum, that Hank and others had seized weeks earlier, to the Nova Scotia Liquor Commission in Halifax for resale, rather than pay the cost of shipping it. Hank and George were pleased with this arrangement until Sunday evening, while stopped at a red light, at an intersection in Halifax, a fire truck passed them on the right and clipped the front bumper of Hank's car. The damage was minor, but Hank reported it to the Fire Station, several blocks back from the scene. Word of the accident reached Commanding Officer Tony MacKinnon of the R.C.M.P. Nova Scotia by Monday morning. Now, instead of going directly to the Court Marshall, George and Hank were summoned to headquarters and paraded in front of him.

When they asked the C.O.'s assistant who met them at the door, what this was all about, he replied in a whimper, "I don't know, but you'll be lucky if you're not in big trouble." With knees trembling, both young men climbed the stairs, were paraded before the 'Commandant' who asked "Who authorized you two to drive your car in here instead of the train?" Hank explained that Insp. Glendenning, Officer Commanding Sydney Sub-Division had, and they were returning cases of seized liquor to the Liquor Commission in Halifax. This seemed to mellow the angry little man, who had made his reputation during the 'Rum Running' days years before. With that George and Hank were summarily excused, and allowed to return to the Court Marshall.

According to Hank's friend Duncan Campbell, a senior retired member of the Force in Baddeck, who had worked with MacKinnon in the 'Prohibition Days', Tony was not always present at the beginning of a 'raid', but was quick to report it to his superiors, and receive the recognition, if the raid was successful. As abruptly as they entered, George and Hank were dismissed, with his approval for following in the same role that made him famous, and "holding high the probation torch." The two 'rebel' constables continued as planned, first to deliver the seized rum to the head office of the Nova Scotia Liquor Commission, and then to their final week of testimony at the Court Marshall. Not every hour of the six weeks, or sometimes not every day, were they required to testify but they had to be present, in case they were called. To cope with the boredom, George, Hank and other witnesses played darts, and in the process, managed to wear the center out of the only dart board in the room where they waited. As for exact disposition of the accused involved, Hank is unable to recall the detail, except that all seventeen were found guilty of smuggling, and received different sentences. None were fired.

NEILAND JOHN H.

Hank's time in Sydney was NOT all work and no play. He still attended the Annual R.C.M.P Sub-Division Ball where all members got dressed in Red Serge, Banana pants, and Wellington ankle boots with spurs. The ladies wore formal dresses, special hairdo's, high heel shoes with nylons and a corsage of flowers. It was held on a Saturday night, at the Isle Royale Hotel, and tickets were sold to civilian couples, dignitaries and friends of the Force. There were also less formal parties, and dances during the year, morale boosters, which gave a chance for the old guard to meet new members, and their wives/girl friends, who were recently transferred in. Sports jacket, shirt and tie and shiny shoes, were still required for the members, while ladies displayed their latest, best dress. These events were usually held at the Sgts. Mess in Victoria Park, or at the Air Force Base in Lingan on the outskirts of the city. Single members and others could also get their noon meal for a nominal fee, at the Sgt.'s Mess in Lingan, and use unmarked police cars to travel to and from the base. In summer, Hank and other interested members were welcome to field a team in the Air Force fastball league, which was much appreciated. In Sydney the Force didn't have a ball field, or anything else in sports equipment or facilities. Members bought their own bats, balls, gloves and spikes.

In that era, Esso credit cards were used for the first time, for gasoline and servicing of police cars. The nearest Esso station was on the Esplanade, a quarter mile from the Sub-Division headquarters, and recommended as a 'preferred supplier'. The proprietor of the station was a jolly, memorable character,

SYDNEY

Neil MacLeod, who befriended Hank and some other members of the Force. Neil and his wife Catherine, a telephone operator, were basic country folks from Framboise, on the Atlantic coast, could speak a bit of Gaelic, a little older than Hank and some of the members, with no children. Together they were great hosts for a party. They also had a great sense of humour, liked a good laugh, and were not above pulling a 'prank' on an unsuspecting guest. They both liked a little 'gillach' of rum or rye, Neil preferred Black Velvet, but neither drank to excess.

They also practiced the Las Vegas slogan "What happens here, stays here" which was so relaxing to off-duty policemen and their ladies. Neil and Catherine were also invited back to some members' homes, in return.

Neil had many friends as customers, and one, a tank truck driver, Charlie Wells who delivered gasoline regularly to Neil's service station, where Hank met him. Days later, Charlie was delivering fuel to a foreign ship in dry-dock, and acquired a large porcelain penis from one of the sailors. He gave it to Neil who showed it to Hank, and they agreed it would be good for a laugh, at the next party. When the penis was standing at the end of a table, one side showed the Virgin Mary in a long flowing gown, with hands clasped in prayer. The other side was the real thing complete with testicles as the base. It was hollow inside, with a hole in the end so it could be filled with water, which poured out into a toilet. At the next party at his place, Neil introduced the Virgin Mary to his guests, and everyone admired the colors and the craftsmanship. Later he disappeared upstairs and called out to Hank and Spud, like he was distressed. When they arrived at the top of the stairs, there he was in the bathroom, with the giant penis in one hand and the other hand braced against the wall, as he bent over the toilet. The penis was sticking out the front of his pants, with water pouring out of it into the toilet, and him calling "Help, I can't control this thing". When Spud and Hank stopped laughing, they invited other guests up to see the performance, and all had a great laugh. Oh the memories!

Another time in late winter, after dark on the spur of the moment, Neil invited Hank in his car, Spud and Huey in Spud's car, to go ice fishing on a small pond near his summer home in Crooked Lake. Hank drove Neil's car, and Huey went with Spud. When they arrived at the pond, Hank drove right out onto the ice, parked with the motor running, and the head lights on. Neil got an axe out of the back of his station wagon, and with some flair, chopped a hole in the thick ice in front of his car. It was a beautiful, clear night with stars in the sky, which was so much better than the sky in the city with the steel plant going three shifts a day, but it was cold. Meanwhile, Hank retrieved two short fishing poles with hook and line attached, from Neil's car together they baited them, and lowered the lines into the hole. Huey, not to be outdone, flopped down on his belly and stuck his face into the water to check if Neil and Hank had done everything right. When he came up for air, the fur on his parka hood was instant ice and everyone had a great laugh. They put chunks of ice on the poles to keep them from falling into the hole, and all four got into Neil's car with the heater on, where a bottle of Black Velvet mysteriously appeared.

Everyone was cold from being outside, so they all agreed a small sip from the bottle would help warm them up. So pass the bottle, each one had a sip, and then another, and another, except Hank who wasn't much of a drinker, one was enough to warm him up. Hank started singing along with the radio and everyone joined in, so time passed, they each took a turn, getting out and checking the lines, but it seemed the fish took the night off.

On the way back to the city, Hank drove Neil's car and Spud followed on the very crooked highway, for a while. Traffic was light, so Spud passed Hank on a straight stretch, and cut in front of him. Hank was not to be outdone, so he passed Spud, at the first opportunity. Spud did likewise, and before long, speeds increased. Both sides of the two lane highway were stacked high with the winter snow, and when Spud cut in front of Hank this time, his right front wheel caught in the snow, started to climb the embankment, but dropped back down onto the bare highway, where Spud was able to get his car under control. That little scare was the end of the fun and games on the highway, and both vehicles made it back to the city safely. Thank God for no oncoming traffic!

Later that year, in September, two of the four fishermen were invited to Gordie Birt's wedding in Grand Falls, Newfoundland. Neiland offered his Ford station wagon and invited Hank, and three other attendants to join him. They left Sydney after work Friday, caught the car ferry out of North Sydney for the six-hour overnight trip, across the Cabot Strait. Arriving in Port Aux Basque early Saturday morning, they took turns driving the five hours to Grand Falls, over a well-travelled paved road as far as Deer Lake.

Then it was gravel roads the rest of the way, arriving in time to get cleaned up, and dressed for the wedding rehearsal. They all attended the wedding and the reception afterwards, during which time Hank switched the new bride's suitcase, as a prank. She was not pleased. However, Hank later confessed, returned the suitcase, said he was sorry, and the bride and groom left on their honeymoon. Much later, the weary travelers slept well, in the hotel, and got on the road early Sunday morning. They retraced their steps, caught the last ferry to North Sydney, and made it to work Monday morning.

Hank had many more such adventures with Neil, during his five years in Sydney. Like the Christmas tree hunt in the country, after dark, with Hank and his three-cell flashlight, in knee-deep snow, groping through the woods looking for the perfect tree. Meanwhile, Neil drove beside him on the isolated country road, giving him directions, and 'laughing his head off'. The rest are too numerous to mention.

DESTRUCTION OF EXHIBIT

In the years that Hank was stationed on Sydney General Investigation Section (G.I.S.) there was still the odd safe-cracker and his band of forty thieves, trying to separate big business from their hard-earned cash, while they slept at night.

Such a group came from the mainland to Sydney in the winter of '65, while Hank was away on an Advance Training course, and brought along a six-ounce glass bottle of nitroglycerine, to pour around the door of a target safe. To avoid blowing up their vehicle in a mishap, or being stopped and searched by Police, they chose after dark, to hide the bottle under the front doorstep of the United Church on Bentick Street in a residential part of the City. An alert female resident across the street from the Church witnessed this activity and called the City Police, who in turn notified Hank's cohorts on G.I.S., who staked out the front of the church. Sure enough, two nights later, the safe cracker and a friend, returned to retrieve their prize nitro, and were arrested before they got their hands on the explosive, which became an exhibit at their trial. From that time forward, the nitro sat quietly in a wooden exhibit box wrapped in excelsior in the R.C.M.P. exhibit locker next to the G.I.S. office. The locker was across the hall from the Highway Patrol office, where upwards of twenty members worked shifts, sixteen hours a day. Directly above the exhibit locker, on the second floor, five days a week were the offices of the brain trust of the Sub-Division, including the Officer Commanding.

Later, Staff Sgt. Ferney, during his quarterly 'destruction of exhibits' visit, in the presence of Hank and others, declared the bottle of nitro no longer required as an exhibit, and ordered it destroyed. This was followed by a huddle with the dominant questions when, where and how? The conclusion was: Call the Coal Company Police in Glace Bay, and have them destroy it. Hank, being the junior man on G.I.S., although recently married with two sons, drew 'the short straw', because he had been stationed in Glace Bay, and knew the Chief of the Dominion Coal Company Police. He was volunteered to contact the Chief, and arrange for an experienced shot fire member, to accompany Hank to an isolated part of company property, to destroy the nitro. Hank, through all this, maintained a stiff upper lip and set about to carry out the instructions, despite being assigned the oldest unmarked car in the Sub-Division, which smacked loudly of in case something goes wrong!

On the potentially fateful early winter day, Hank retrieved the wooden box with the wrapped glass bottle from the exhibit locker, carried it out to the 'disposable' car, set the box on the floor of the front passenger side, with no restraints, and drove the twelve miles on dry roads to Glace Bay without incident. He parked across the street from the Coal Company office, entered and was greeted by the Chief who assigned an acquaintance, Fred Chutney to accompany Hank to an isolated piece of company property, at the east end of South Street, overlooking the Atlantic.

Fred, familiar with explosives and a great sense of humour, came with Hank, brought along two sticks of dynamite, some caps, a plunger and a hundred feet of wire, all of which he placed in the back seat. He then climbed into the front seat, placed the wooden box between his two feet, and with a grin said, "Let's get this over with!"

Hank drove to the foot of South Street, parked the car, and with Fred, carried the box and other necessities across the barren land, leaning into the wind to the lee side of a lone ventilation shaft. Leaving the plunger there, Fred and Hank strung the wire along the ground to where Fred took the bottle of nitro out of the box, gingerly taped two sticks of dynamite to it, placed a cap in the end of one stick, and hooked the end of the wire to it. They walked back to the lee of the ventilation shaft neither one wearing hearing or any other protection. Fred hooked the wire to the plunger and when he was ready, pushed the handle down. The ensuing explosion was deafening. When the two men peeked out from behind the shaft, the sky above the site was filled with debris and beach rocks. When the noise subsided, and the ground around the site settled, Fred and Hank walked back down, and saw a crater thirty feet in diameter and eight feet deep at the centre, an instant basement for a two-storey house. They walked back to the ventilation shaft, and gathered up their gear. Hank drove Fred back to his office, thanked him profusely, then returned to the City, quietly counting his blessings that he had lived to see another day with Mary Ann and boys. Hank never even told her about the assignment beforehand in the event she'd only worry.

CAREER- MINDED MEMBERS

From Hank's early days in the field, he began to see and study some of the different personalities and characteristics of his fellow members. As he got to know them better, he naturally gravitated to the ones he liked. Not all, but some were from a rural background like Hank, with similar inherent habits, values and beliefs. Even in training, Hank may not have shunned all his city slicker troop mates, but he was more at home with country boys like himself. Early in his career, Hank tended to favour small town postings, not that he had any real say in his transfers, but he seemed happier there. At times when still single, with the mandatory five years before marriage in effect, he suspected he might be more easily exploited by headquarters personnel, who arranged short-notice transfers, both at division and sub-division levels. All headquarters had to do was send a radio message, or pick up the phone and Hank, with his own car, could be at the chosen new destination, either temporarily or permanently the next day. Hank did that, several times during his first six or seven years of service in the field, and he witnessed other members do the same.

All too often other members in the field, with the personality and charm, who did not care for the small towns and being on call 24/7, even at a young age, longed for the cushy office job and bankers' hours in Headquarters. After five years of service, and perhaps with fashion-conscious girlfriends or wives, who may not have been country girls at heart, the headquarters hero pressed even harder for that office job. With enough time devoted to his career plan, and grasping at opportunities that presented themselves, this astute member could eventually find himself driving a desk in the city. Instead of being alone in a stinky police car, in the middle of nowhere, in all kinds of weather, often with a prisoner, and still receiving the same monthly pay cheque. At headquarters, the simple joy of having a secretary available to type his memos and reports, regular coffee and lunch breaks, with card games, if he wished, and carpooling with fellow members to and from work. Evenings, weekends, especially long ones, off duty with friends and family, while the men in the field were urged to, get out there and prevent motor vehicle accidents and other tragedies. Also, the field man had many other duties to protect the general public from others and even themselves. Here, Hank must confess that while posted in a small town, his second detachment, he watched his first ever World Series game, on black and white T.V, in 'The Mayor's' living room with appetizers and drinks, in the afternoon while on duty. Now, that's living the good life, for a short time anyway.

If the career-minded member in Headquarters wished, he could partake of golf and baseball/fastball or tennis in summer, and swimming, volleyball, racquet ball or hockey in winter and on occasion even rub elbows with 'the brass' socially. Being closer to the horse's mouth and the inside track, when job descriptions were first introduced, afforded a much better chance for a transfer of his choice, or earlier promotion than the man in the field.

Much later in service, Hank did get a transfer to headquarters to drive a desk for a couple of years, and even a promotion to boot. That's how he finally was able to partake of some of the above noted perks first hand.

EARLY SIXTIES

In the Fifties and Sixties in the ranks of the R.C.M.P. in Cape Breton, with a few exceptions, male chauvinism was still alive and well. The wife stayed home, if not working, toiled with domestic chores, taking care of the children, or talking on the phone, or in person with lady friends and neighbours. Exceptions were store clerks, postal employees, telephone operators, bank tellers, or nurses, some of whom worked shifts. Meanwhile the man went to work in the fields, the forests, the mines, the steel plant, driving trucks, mechanics, out to sea, doctors, lawyers, bankers, warehouse men and policemen.

Most men avoided domestic chores, at all costs. This was the world into which Hank brought his new bride, Mary Ann, including the possibility that, he could get a call to duty or come home from duty, anytime in the day or night. To Hank and his friends, everybody else in the Force was doing it. So, why should he expect to be any different? Life seemed simpler and more structured then, but maybe sometimes, because of their youthful exuberance and ignorance, they thought they were happier than perhaps they really were.

The story is told in those days of the steelworker who lived in a second-floor apartment, coming home early off-shift one afternoon. When he opened the front door, his wife was on her hands and knees with her back to him, scrubbing the bottom steps of the stairs. Closer scrutiny of her position revealed she had no panties on, under her housedress. Suddenly the weary husband became alert, set his lunch pail down, opened his zipper, lifted her dress and proceeded to do his manly duty. There was no noticeable reaction from her, so when he stood up, zipped up his fly, he gave her a gentle kick on the ass with his boot. She immediately turned her head and snapped "What was that for?"

He replied, "That was for not lookin to see who it was". They both sat beside each other on the stairs and had a good laugh.

Although some social events with neighbours and fellow members were well planned, some invitations were on short notice, and often turned out to be the best party ever. This was especially true in the late fall and early winter, when the days are shorter and the evenings longer. The surprise invitation became more welcome, even if you had to bundle up, leave the car in the driveway and walk, through knee-deep snow to the destination. Then walking home, feeling much better after the visit, and a few warm drinks, not caring how deep the snow was. Memories were made of this!

RECREATION AND TRANSFER OUT

As mentioned in another chapter, the job was not all work and no play. In his first full summer on G.I.S., Hank was welcomed to the R.C.M.P. fastball team as an outfielder in the league at the Air Force Base. Most players still wore baseball shoes with steel cleats. Luckily no one got spiked. Hank played all three outfield positions, but mostly center field on a quasi-regulation ball field for adults. There were no banks of lights for night games, in fact, no lights at all, and the outfield fence was a snow fence, with infrequent posts and wooden slats.

Hank could run like a deer, and one evening during a close game in the playoffs with two runners on base and two out, the batter hit a sure home run to center. Hank ran to the fence, continued partway up the fence, caught the ball in the tip of his outstretched glove, held onto it and jumped down off the fence, for the out.

In winter, Hank was one of the organizers and taxi driver for fellow members to play shinny hockey, at the Sydney Forum at 10:30 P.M. on Wednesdays, when he wasn't working. Everyone chipped in five dollars to pay for the ice time and occasionally a member would invite a civilian friend, for example 'Dugga' MacNeil, brother of Al MacNeil, then a star defenseman for Calgary in the National Hockey League. Dugga was no slouch himself, having played in the Cape Breton Senior league, which was not for sissies. Another regular guest was a character from Westmount named Johnny Power, who didn't have a pound of fat on him and could skate like the wind. He, like most others, did not wear full gear, just skates, shin pads, elbow pads, hockey gloves maybe, and a stick. Johnny's stick had no tape on it, just the remnants of a blade that came to a point, could shoot the puck through the eye of a needle and at your Adam's apple, if you wanted to play him dirty.

Johnny also ran a successful business, first out of his basement, and later out of a large garage in the backyard. He claimed he started out by, he and his wife fastening ballpoint pens, which were new on the market, and which he ordered in bulk, to cardboard cards in sets of ten. They were for display and sale in convenience stores throughout Cape Breton. At first, he drove an old station wagon loaded to the gunwales with trinkets such as key chains, signature coffee mugs, school supplies, work gloves, kitchen ware and such. When Hank met him, he had three relatively new station wagons, one for him, and one for each of his travelling salesmen, one being Buddy MacDonald who Hank knew from his days in Inverness. The other salesman was Joe Basker from Port Hood. They would leave Westmount Sunday night or early

SYDNEY

Monday morning, every week of the year except vacation, or a bad storm in winter. Usually they'd return Friday night or Saturday morning, weather permitting, with a mostly empty wagon. Now, Johnny was selling everything from vacuum cleaners to baseball gloves, and would "give a deal" to members of the Force, if he liked you.

Hank was on Sydney G.I.S. for five years when he got a memo, without consultation or staffing interview, to he and eight or ten fellow members in the Province, specifically advising Hank that he had been transferred in charge of Shelburne Detachment, on the south shore of Nova Scotia, effective July tenth. Herein fail not!

There was no time for a farewell party for he and Mary Ann, just well wishes from fellow members, neighbours and friends the night before they left. Hank cried when he drove over the causeway from Cape Breton, but was consoled by the fact that he had with him, a beautiful young wife and three healthy sons. The promise of a promotion to Corporal was on the promotion list, if he succeeded in 'turning things around' in Shelburne.

SHELBURN

HEADING TO SHELBURN

In July, for the first time in his career, Hank had a moving company, paid for by the Force, come into his home, pack his personal effects and load them onto a truck. Hank felt like a king, sort of. Their last night in Sydney Hank, Mary Ann and three boys stayed in a motel, with a pool, outside the city where the boys could splash around in the shallow end before bedtime. Good friends Neil and Catherine dropped in with a taste of Black Velvet to reminisce, say goodbye and have a safe trip. The next morning they headed out for Shelburne, some eight hours away, in their first ever brand new Ford sedan. In an hour they crossed the Canso Causeway to the mainland and stopped in a parking lot near the toll booth where everyone got out, and the older boys could let off some steam. Hank and Mary Ann stood side by side, held hands and looked back across the causeway and shed a tear to be leaving Mary Ann's parents and their many friends behind. In fact, only a few months later did it really sink in how many good friends they did have on Cape Breton both in the Force and out. Such was the life of a member of the Force subject to transfer.

The rest of the morning was spent motoring along through mainland Nova Scotia on a hot sunny day past Truro and Halifax stopping once for a break and something to eat, the older boys chanting "are we there yet?" The first real stop was in Chester to visit good friends Spud, Beth and daughter Tracey, roughly the same age as their son Mark. By now Spud had been there on Highway Patrol for over a year and he introduced Hank and Mary Ann to his new sidekick Derek White, a Newfoundlander and fierce Canadians fan, and his wife Bonna, an unforgettable couple. They later became real good friends when they were transferred to Liverpool, the detachment next to Shelburne, some fifty miles to the East. There Derek was obliged to cover the east section of Shelburne County on Highway patrol as Shelburne detachment had only one police car at that time. Another constable, soon to become a good friend, Harry Wheaton of Yarmouth Highway Patrol covered the west half of the county for the same purpose. Neither one rarely came into the County without stopping in at Shelburne detachment for a visit, coffee, a chance to 'pull Hank's chain', and bring some news from the 'big 'towns down the road.

After an hour or two in Chester, they shared goodbyes and promises to visit again soon, Hank and Mary Ann continued on down old highway three through scenic Mahone Bay to Bridgewater where Hank had to ask directions to get out of town. Next came Liverpool and Lockport along a highway, which seemed to curve around every cove and large boulder on that part of the Atlantic coast. Finally before dark, they arrived in Shelburne, found the detachment and Cst. Dunsford waiting for them. A jovial young man who seemed happy to have a new family move into the married quarters next door to the office and his single man's quarters. He was especially pleased when he heard that Hank also came from his home province, P.E.I. As their personal effects hadn't yet arrived, he had already made reservations for Hank and family at the Oxbow Motel on the outskirts of town. There, they met the proprietors Jane and Peter Strange who were later to become good friends for the next four years. Hank and family enjoyed a home cooked dinner in their restaurant and a good night's sleep after a long day on the road. Mary Ann and the boys liked the place so well, they stayed two more days until their personal effects arrived and were set up in their new home next door to the detachment.

The next day Hank joined Cst. Duford at the office, to get acquainted and to prepare for a visit from Patrol Sgt. Stevens from Halifax. He arrived mid-morning and after his brief introduction gave an explanation why Hank's predecessor, whom Hank had never met, had been transferred out under a cloud. He proceeded to hand over the control of Shelburne detachment to Hank. Hank had done this several times on a temporary basis, but this was the first time permanently. Everything went relatively smoothly until they opened the door to the exhibit locker, with liquor bottles in disarray on shelves and some with a noticeable faded colour to the contents, indicating dilution. Sgt. Stevens was not surprised, and offered to destroy those whose expiry date had arrived, during this visit. Standing in one corner was an old dry tree branch three feet in length, and when Hank checked the record in the ledger, it was an exhibit from a murder trial nine years ago. Sgt. Stevens agreed to allow Hank time to confirm the necessity to keep it, and he would condemn the branch during his next visit, if no longer required. Other exhibits such as firearms and ammunition matched the records in the ledger.

Shortly before Sgt. Stevens' arrival, Hank had sat down on the chair of the only desk in the main office, and opened the drawers to check the disorganized contents. On top of everything in the middle drawer was an 8"x 10" black and white photo of the front of their only police car, with a hole in the windshield from a high-powered rifle bullet, directly in front of the driver's seat. When the initial shock passed, Hank surmised this was likely his predecessor's sadistic way of saying "Welcome to Shelburne!"

Later after Sgt. Stevens departed, Cst. Duford explained he was off duty the evening the windshield was shot out several months ago. According to his previous boss, he had allegedly answered a domestic call alone, had driven up to the front door of the suspect house, when the culprit opened the door and fired one shot at the windshield. The boss allegedly dove onto the passenger side of the front seat and escaped injury. The culprit was arrested, charged, convicted and was currently serving two years in Dorchester penitentiary. The windshield had been replaced and there was no evidence of a bullet hole in the upholstery.

Later that day, Cst. Dunford took Hank around town to meet Chief Vince Helpard and his lone Cst. George Aulenback, Mayor Ken Morten, Justice Hobie Blades, and other available notables. Gradually Hank settled into his new surroundings and became acquainted with how 'we do things around here'. Basically like any other two-man detachment of the day if one member was off duty, the other was on, and if you were inside the detachment building, in uniform or not, you were on duty. Before Hank went to bed and Cst. Duford was out, Hank or Mary Ann unplugged the telephone from the jack in the kitchen, carried it upstairs and plugged it into the jack in the master bedroom. After a long, hard day this was not an easy task, and if you were inclined to stare at the phone waiting for it to ring, you would drive yourself berserk. Hank avoided that practice like the plague. And if both men were out in the police car at night, as was the custom of the time, in most detachments, Mary Ann was expected to perform this duty herself, answer the call, go downstairs through the door into the office, and call the police car on the radio. Cpl. O'Connell, in charge of Liverpool detachment fifty miles to the East, refused to allow his wife to do this. Thirty some years later, the Force recognized this service by honoring the wives who had performed this duty with a "Second Man" award. Mary Ann was never notified about this and went unrewarded.

NEW NEIGHBOURS

After almost ten years on Cape Breton, Hank's transfer to the south shore of Nova Scotia was somewhat of a culture shock at first. Members of the general public, whom he encountered through the job, showed a variety of responses, most of which Hank had already seen or heard. Overall there seemed to be an undercurrent of distrust, and an attitude of 'Oh well if we have to have a boss Mountie here in Shelburne, I guess you'll do.' Hank's position of authority was compounded by Mary Ann's part-time job at the Roseway hospital, as evening supervisor.

Hank wondered if some of this attitude of the public may have been fostered by his predecessor, but didn't want to place direct blame. Meanwhile Cst. Duford with his happy-go-lucky attitude, seemed to require more supervision than a member with three year's service, and Hank speculated that he may have adopted some of his previous boss's bad habits. About three weeks after Hank's arrival, he was off duty one evening, and Duford was on patrol alone in the police car, in a rural area outside of town on a gravel road, the police car mysteriously ended up in the ditch, and had to be towed out. A motorist, who stopped to help, told Hank the next day he could smell liquor on Duford's breath. When Hank asked Duford about this, he flatly denied it and laughed it off, reminding Hank there was no visible damage to the car. Hank reported the incident to Sub-Division headquarters in Halifax, and within days Duford was transferred to Halifax. He was replaced by a young recruit, fresh out of training named John Simonds. He was mature in appearance, outwardly happy to be there, and willing to learn. Coincidentally, he arrived the same day that Hank received his promotion to Corporal.

Hank and Mary Ann made a few hasty preparations, and sent radio and telephone invitations to a promotion party the next night, at their home. Members came in from neighbouring detachments, including Cst. Williams from a one-man detachment seventy some miles away, whom Hank had never met. Neighbours from the street, and some of the 'who's who' from town that could make it on short notice, also attended with their wives or partners. As a 'door crasher' Cst. Aulenback from the town police brought his guitar and harmonica and led the party goers in a sing song. Cst. Simmonds tended bar, in uniform in case a call came in, but abstained from consuming. Some ladies brought food, and pitched in to help Mary Ann serve it. All in all the party seemed a success, except late in the evening Cst. Simmonds went in to his quarters to use the bathroom, and discovered Cst. Williams in his single bed with another man's wife. He came back to the party, quietly called Hank to one side, and told him what he found. When Hank went to investigate, he met the two instant love birds in the office, coming back to join the party, with sheepish looks on their faces. Cst. Simmonds for a time wondered what he had gotten himself into. His discovery was the source of several private chuckles among other policemen days later but was soon forgotten.

Before the party, Hank and Mary Ann had already met some of the immediate neighbours. On one side, Mac and Glenna Oxner and daughter Sandy who was a year older than their two eldest sons. On the office side of the detachment, was Mac's brother Don, his wife Carolyn, daughter Susan and son Robert. In the back yard was Charlie Wall's blacksmith shop, where the ring of the anvil would wake Hank and Mary Ann early some mornings and take Hank right back fondly to his home village, where there was a forge next door. Next to the shop, was Charlie's barn where his grandson Bill Dolliver based his one-man contractor operation, and repaired his equipment?

Charlie and his wife Carrie lived on the ground floor of a two-story house and grandson Bill and wife Marieta, a telephone operator, lived on the second floor. At the time they had no children but before Hank and Mary Ann transferred out, they had a baby boy. Charlie, a senior at the time, had two gardens, one beside his house and one behind the barn. As he had done with Al Palmer years before, he gave Hank a piece of the garden behind the barn if Hank would help him with the cultivating and weeding. Hank agreed and also drove a tractor that Charlie had built out of an old truck he cannibalized to a smaller size, capable of making short turns and pulling disc harrows or a cultivator. Charlie had access to cow manure from a farmer friend and liberally spread it on both gardens each spring.

One summer Hank had enough yellow and green beans to feed the neighbours and a bumper crop of strawberries that he was able to give away and freeze the rest. When Craig and Curtis were four years old they went to the barn to help Bill work on his backhoe and dump truck. Before long they learned the difference between a 'spanner' and a 'box end' or half inch and nine sixteenth wrench and could hand them to Bill while he was under the vehicle or the engine hood. If Bill had to go somewhere in the truck he'd take them with him, stop in front of the detachment, toot the horn so Hank or Mary Ann could look out and see the two blond heads beside Bill in the front seat. Small in stature, Bill worked alone and was known to load the truck by hand with a round pointed shovel from a gravel pit.

Across the street lived John Hardy, M.L.A., his wife Pearl and three young sons. They were society who hosted frequent house parties to which Hank and Mary Ann were sometimes invited and attended occasionally. They were good neighbours with well-mannered children who were older than Hanks boys but tolerated them if outside together. Further up Harriet Street was the Roman Catholic Church and glebe house occupied by Father D'Entremont who became a good friend to Hank in spite of a difference in religion. They both found solace in a morning or evening fishing / hunting trip out of town from under the watchful eye of some town's people. The second spring that Hank was in Shelburne, one of the guys on the fire department told him about the spring run of sea trout in Clyde River and offered to call him when he heard the run was on. Hank told Father D' and they planned to go together.

When Hank got the word, one cool spring morning Father D' and Hank drove the thirty some miles to Clyde River and in less than an hour they had their limit of beautiful half to one-pound speckled trout, firm, with pink insides just like salmon. They tasted delicious too. Father D' had a beagle hound named Scooter and together on a mild winter day with snow on the ground they would bag two or three rabbits in open woods near Indian Fields. Skinned and cleaned, Father D's housekeeper Emma would cook them in a stew and invite Hank and his family over for a 'feed'.

The first year Hank was in Shelburne Father D., Jane Strange and Hank resurrected a baseball 'little league' that had been dormant for seven or eight years. They built the diamond and backstop by hand on donated land, acquired bases, balls and bats enough for a four-team league that grew to eight teams the year before Father D. got transferred to the Valley. Father D. later left the priesthood, got a job with the Province in rehabilitation, married an ex-nun from Cape Breton and raised a family. Jane continued to run the Oxbow Motel with her husband Peter and was steadfast in keeping the Little League going with Hank and some dedicated parents.

Further up the street across from the church were Graham Pentz, his wife Dorcas and two teen-age daughters Ginnie and Judy who babysat for Mary Ann when she was working or for both she and Hank if they went out for an evening. When the furnace in the detachment was converted from coal to oil, Graham was the man who did the job and his neighbour Frank Acker helped with the heavy work like cutting a trench for the oil line in the concrete basement floor with a sledge hammer. Big Frank played fastball in the same six-team league as Hank on a makeshift ball field on the exhibition grounds. One evening Frank's team was playing Hank's team and Hank was in center field when Frank hit a fly ball over Hank's head. Everyone on both teams thought "Home Run" but in spite of no outfield fence and rough terrain Hank tracked the ball down and caught it. One spectator was heard to remark "I wouldn't want to be comin down outta Indian Fields with a gallon of shine on my back with that fella chasin me."

NEIGHBOURS POOL CHAMPS

On that same part of Harriet St. lived Graham Harrison, his wife and family. Graham had a cute little girl, the same age as Hank's twins. One day after school when the twins were in kindergarten, Mary Ann was in the kitchen, when Craig came in with the cute little blond girl his age, and proudly said with a gesture towards her, "Mom, this is Deidra". For a moment mom was speechless, then smiled and said "Nice to meet you Deidra." Her father Graham owned and operated the Volkswagen dealership, on the north end of town. There are people in town who eventually became friends with Hank, too many to specifically mention, especially the great guys on the volunteer fire department, to which Hank, as a Mountie, automatically became a member. Hank will never forget the afternoon every available member including Hank, were invited to the Fire Department recreation room, on the second floor of the Town Hall, to celebrate Chief Morton's father's eightieth birthday, and have some coffee and cake. Several members carefully placed all eighty candles on a round ten inch cake on the end of the regulation pool table, and without much thought of danger, all cheerfully sang Happy Birthday to 'Mr. Morton', as two or three members lit the candles from the inside out. By the time the last candle was lit, the intense heat gathered all available oxygen and in one flash torched towards the ceiling, quickly sputtered out, leaving smoke and melted candle wax in a pool on top of the icing on the cake. Everyone jumped back, and most thought "quick where's the nearest extinguisher?"

Many thought "please, don't let it damage the felt on the pool table". All later reflected on the embarrassment of an actual fire in the 'fire department' hall, of all places. Many a chuckle and comment were made by the citizens, when the story got out around town, but most present did have some cake when the melted wax hardened, and was removed with wax-icing attached, all thankful that no real damage was done.

For Hank and his constable, that hall and the pool table was a special place to meet for a game of eight ball with the Town Police, late in the evening after the town and County were put to bed, and before they went home for the night. Sometimes a call would come in that interrupted the game, and that would be all for the pool table that night, but most nights things remained quiet. More than one night, when he was off duty and the competition was fierce, Hank would be walking home alone, the three short blocks through the quiet residential area, in the wee small hours of the morning. Hank had never played pool before, and these games were an opportunity to practice the art of "it's not what you make that counts, but what you leave", as his good friend Buck Jackson taught him in the early days.

In his second year in Shelburne, the fire department had its annual pool tournament in winter. Buck took Hank as his partner, one of several two-man teams. After weeks of elimination games, Buck and Hank were one of two teams still standing. The other team was Buck's partner in boat building, 'Roll' Deschamp, and his partner Phil, who Buck and Hank ultimately beat for the trophy. Besides having their names inscribed on the club trophy, Chief

Ken presented both Buck and Hank with a 'keeper' trophy, and had their picture taken and published in the local newspaper 'The Coast Guard' the next week. That too, was a first ever trophy for Hank, and he still has it somewhere among his souvenirs. At the end of that social evening like many others, weather permitting, Hank walked the quiet city blocks of streets, home to the detachment, a wonderful time alone, simply to meditate and give thanks for the camaraderie of good friends, in a Town far away from home.

CHIEFS OF POLICE

When Hank first arrived in Shelburne Cst. Dunsford introduced him to Chief Vince Helpard and his Deputy George Aulenback. Vince had been chief for many years since Chief Mitchell retired, was a chain smoker and Hank noticed he tended to suppress his coughs. But then, most everyone smoked in those days including Hank. It was the 'macho' thing to do. He was a nice man who had a sense of humour, firm in his decisions when necessary and offered the continued support of his Police Force to Hank and his constable any hour of the day or night. Hank responded in kind. Vince had a wife and three daughters living home at that time and a furnace that burned sawdust, which was in ready supply from the mill at Shelburne Woodworkers. Hank happened to be there in the fall when a winter supply of sawdust was delivered and Vince was on his hands and knees in the bin of his basement spreading it around right up to the floor joists. Hank was in uniform or he would have helped him as they joked about the 'modern ' fuel supply similar to the monster bin of coal in the basement of the detachment which Hank was obliged to shovel into the hopper of the "iron fireman" every day and night. Hank later regretted not helping Vince especially when he was notified a few months later at his father-in-law's home in Cape Breton that Vince had suddenly passed away due to a heart attack. That same evening Hank had just arrived for a break after months on the job and seven hours on the road with his young family. Hank hastily decided not to go back to attend the funeral. He later regretted that decision too and apologized sincerely to the widow and family when he returned to Shelburne.

The Town Police Committee appointed Deputy Aulenback as Chief and hired Dave Roach from Sandy Point as Deputy. Hank congratulated George on his promotion at the same time extended his sympathy at the loss of his friend and chief and offered the same continued support from the R.C.M.P. in time of need. George and his wife Gail had three small children, lived a few blocks from the detachment, loved to hunt deer and sing country music. He could play the guitar and harmonica at the same time. He was small in stature but would back down from "nothing or nobody".

Retired Chief Mitchell would have been a giant of a man in his day but by now was a bit bent over, was an honorary member of the Fire Department and a community supporter and still loved to play pool. Because he had worked alone he was the subject of rumours that could not be proven, like how late at night, he was first on the scene of a fire of unknown origin behind a commercial business of the then chairman of the police committee. He would sound the alarm; the fire department responded and saved the premises from sure destruction, the Chief of Police receiving the desired recognition and assurance of continued employment. When the roof of his house started to sag, again late at night he was rumoured to have 'borrowed' a four hundred and some pound steel rail from the siding in town, carried it home on his back, where it mysteriously appeared in his backyard. Later friends and neighbours helped him install it in his basement and correct the sag in his roof. Sympathetic citizens quietly approved, due to Chief Mitchell's friendly attitude and paltry annual wage.

ICE SKATING

From the time Hank was seven or eight, he tried to skate on dull, second-hand skates with no ankle support and play hockey on an outdoor rink in the village where he was raised. It was always his dream if he had sons, he would give them every chance to learn how to skate and have the joy of it and playing hockey. The first winter Hank went to the city for high school, he wanted to try out for the college hockey team so he took what was left of his summer earnings picking berries and farm labour and went to Canadian Tire, bought his first ever shin pads, elbow pads, stick and hockey sweater to go with his too-small Red Horner skates his father had recovered from the Lost and Found bin at the CN Railway Station in the City. At the War Surplus store, he bought an old Army kit bag to put his 'stuff' in and walked alone to the Charlottetown Forum to the first night of tryouts for the college team. He was so out-classed in every skill; he was the laughing stock of his peers and never went back. But he kept the equipment and little by little over the years he honed his skills enough to be able to play shinny with his friends just for the fun of it.

His first winter in Shelburne, Hank and Mary Ann's twin boys turned four and Hank bought them each a pair of bob-skates held onto their boots by leather straps. Shelburne had no rink of any kind so Hank opened the window by the landing on the upstairs of the married quarters and put the two boys with new skates out onto a small patch of ice on the flat roof of the detachment. They stumbled and fell a few times but mastered the art of running on bob-skates, then falling and sliding to the edge of the ice but not off the roof. Before long they noticed the triangular tower for the police radio fastened to the rear of the detachment, sat down, took the skates off and proceeded to climb the tower. When Mom saw this, she cancelled the fun on the roof and ordered Hank to find a safer place for the boys to skate. So Hank got out the snow shovel, walked down across the back yard and cleaned the snow off the ice in the hole for neighbour Bill Dolliver's basement that was a 'work in progress' overtaken by the onset of winter. That became the boy's private rink, weather permitting, when Hank was there to prepare it for them. Bill had no children yet.

But that rink was too small for Mary Ann and Hank to skate on so on his winter days off, he would load the family including their one year old third son, shovels, toboggans, and sleighs into the family car and drove to Lake George about two miles east of town. They also packed wieners, hot dog buns, drinks and condiments for a picnic beside the lake, an axe to cut some dry wood for a bonfire and some newspaper to start it. Hank was still smoking cigarettes so there was always a light for the fire. Occasionally, another family from town would join them and that just made friends for the boys the more the merrier, so to speak. Hence, the long winter passed.

Should Hank and other jocks in town decide to have a game of shinney in a real rink, they would reserve 10:30 PM ice time for an hour on the indoor rink in the town of Bridgewater sixty some miles away. They would load up two or three cars or station wagons with men and equipment, drive the hour and twenty minutes there, one hour ice time and the same time to get back home weather and roads permitting and think they had a whale of a time. Hopefully some would be able to sleep in the next morning.

WEEKEND VISITS

To some members in the Force, Shelburne Detachment was considered an isolated post, but once they became established, it never felt that way to Mary Ann and Hank mostly because of visits from family and friends, but not all at once. One couple from Halifax was Mary Ann's life-long friend Kay, husband Bill and their sons approximately the same age as Mary Ann and Hank's three boys. The adults would eat, drink and be merry and the boys would play and get into mischief. This family would visit three or four times a year and when they could get away Hank and Mary Ann would visit Halifax and stay overnight with them.

Another couple from Dartmouth, Russ, Marion and two daughters visited once or twice in summer and on one occasion Hank decided to try out his newly acquired homemade boat called the Sea Sled. Hank borrowed two paddles from neighbour Mac, Russ and he loaded the boat onto the roof of his car and the two families went to Welshtown Lake for an afternoon picnic. That lake had a beach, and the water was warm in summer, not like the Atlantic which had nice beaches but if you tried to swim in it the ice-cold water would take your breath away. Russ and Hank took turns taking the children for rides in the boat and after a couple of bubblies, they both climbed in with their combined weight slightly below four hundred pounds. The water nearly came over the gunwales and after some hearty laughs from them and the ladies on shore, they managed to turn the thing around and paddle it back to shore. They loaded it back onto the car, the next week it was on the front lawn of the detachment with a 'For Sale' sign on it and sure enough, an unsuspecting customer bought it.

Closer by from the neighbouring detachment in Liverpool frequently came a member of the Highway Patrol to help Hank with his traffic law enforcement as required by headquarters in Halifax. A comical Newfoundlander named Derek who enjoyed shocking people with the frequent use of the four-letter word was like a breath of spring after he had written his 'quota' of tickets, mostly warnings. An avid Montreal Canadiens fan, he always had a barb ready for Hank, the Toronto Maple Leafs fan. When off duty Derek and his wife Bonna who had the heartiest laugh you ever heard, would come anytime they could even for an overnight. TV reception was almost non-existent so after the kids were in bed, the ladies might entertain the boys with a modeling display of some of their recent clothing acquisitions or exchanges.

From a bit farther away in Chester came Hank's best man Spud, his wife Beth and daughter Tracy as often as they could before Spud was transferred to Alberta as a Driving Instructor. Here Hank and Spud, both Maple Leaf fans could compare notes on recent successes, make excuses and lick their wounds over the losses. Instead of talking shop, the fellow policemen chose to discuss the welfare and whereabouts of members and friends they had left behind in Cape Breton, their first posting in the field. Beth, like Marion and Mary Ann hailed from Cape Breton so there was always something or somebody from home to talk about.

Welcome visits from both families were too numerous to mention, but the best was a surprise when Mary Ann heard a knock on her front door one afternoon and there stood her father, now in his seventies, had travelled eight hours alone by bus all the way from home just to come for a little visit and see the boys.

When Mary Ann's father finished his visit, Cst. Youden took him in his new car as far as Halifax on Jim's day off, so as to shorten the older man's bus ride home.

GUN CALLS

When Hank first arrived in Shelburne one of the 'men about town' that he met was Bill Fox, the lone roving reporter for the weekly newspaper The Coast Guard. Bill would call on the phone or drop in at the detachment if something newsworthy had happened in the county, to compare notes with Hank and get his approval before it went to press. Hank had asked for that favour from day one because he had had several instances of misquotes by reporters during previous postings and one that was a blatant misrepresentation of the facts. One morning in Hanks second or third year in Shelburne Bill dropped in while Hank was alone in the office. After some small talk about the weather and the affairs of the day, Bill asked Hank "Do you have any idea of how many gun calls you receive in the run of a month or even a year?"

"No, I hadn't really thought a lot about it, to tell the truth" Hank replied, "but I can look into it someday when I find the time and get back to you". "No hurry" said Bill "but I had done some research and I was really surprised at what I found" as he made his way to the door.

Reality in those days and probably still is in small communities in Canada when a accident or dispute occurs, someone will say "Call the Mounties" which was sometimes not an easy task because the caller had to first find a phone. Not all places had one. However, if a gun or even the threat of a gun reared its ugly head, for sure it was "Call the Mounties". When Hank finally got around to check his "Occurrence Ledger", he was surprised to find how many Gun Calls there really were in the past two years. Some were in town where the Town Police would call for back up, but the majority, twenty some in all were in the County. First of all, Hank had declared as Officer In Charge of Shelburne detachment that neither he nor his constable would answer a gun call alone, especially at night. Sometimes the town Chief or Constable would accompany the Mountie if it wasn't too far out of town. Otherwise, the Mountie could call an auxiliary policeman to go with him, or a forest ranger or anyone available as long as he wasn't alone answering the preliminary call. The two neighbouring R.C.M.P. detachments were at least fifty miles away and they had their own area to cover. The good news very often was, the threat was false of at least exaggerated, and by the time police arrived, cooler heads had prevailed and there was 'no gun' to be seen and no one wanted to lay charges, apologies all around.

By this time Hank had already observed that two factors came in to play involving gun calls. One was the instant availability of guns and ammunition in most homes because there was usually a gun rack with a selection of weapons for each hunting season. In some homes it was not in a closet or the back porch but on a finished wood gun rack on the living room wall, almost as a status symbol. The other factor, and this is just Hank's observation, some adults in those homes were not mentally stable due partially to generations of inbreeding between the white man and his slaves. So if you add to a family quarrel a little bit of liquor and convenience of weapons, the threat of violence is very real, so "call the Mounties." Perhaps a third factor was isolation in the early days when the only way in and out of Shelburne was by sea. The roads in and out of the county, even in Hank's time there, were narrow, poor-quality pavement and low shoulders that went around every cove and bay along the Atlantic shore.

NOTIFYING NEXT OF KIN

Hank now had over ten years service, had been promoted to Corporal, was in charge of Shelbourne detachment and thought he had just about seen it all. But one dark, rainy evening in the fall he was alone on duty when a call came in from the detachment in Prince Rupert, British Columbia. Cst. Underhill was trying to reach the mother of Arnold Chapman, who was one of the crewmembers on a halibut fishing dragger off the coast of Alaska in the Bering Sea. They had had a bountiful trip, too bountiful perhaps, when they encountered a severe storm enroute back to Canada. When he realized his ship was in trouble, the Captain called "Mayday" several times, but there were no other ships in the vicinity. Eventually the overloaded ship succumbed to the storm and all hands on board including Arnold Chapman was lost.

At the time, Hank couldn't recall a Chapman family living in Shelbourne, but he called his friend Father D. who lived just up the street, who had been in Shelburne longer than him and knew more families in Town. Father D. knew of Hilda Chapman, a widow who lived alone on Davis Street, a member of his church and a cleaning lady for some of the aristocrats in Town. When Father D. described her, Hank remembered her as a survivor who went quietly on foot minding her own business and didn't cause any stir.

"Would you like me to come with you?" asked Father D. "Sure, that would be great," replied Hank, "I'll pick you up, it shouldn't take too long if she's home." Hank mused that by this time in his service he probably had delivered between eight and ten such messages to next-of kin.

Hank put on his new Storm Coat and old Forage Cap, grabbed the car keys, locked the office door, ran to the police car in the cold, blowing rain, and drove the short distance up the hill to the back door of the Glebe House. Father D. appeared in the doorway, he too ran to the car and jumped in. They compared notes about Ms. Chapman enroute, and agreed she would be strong in the face of this kind of message. With Father D. as co-pilot, Hank pulled into the short driveway, they both got out of the car, dashed to the front veranda and Hank knocked on the door. The light came on in the hall inside and a middle-aged lady appeared at the door wearing a full-length winter coat.

"What brings you two gentlemen out on a night like this?" she greeted cheerfully. "We just had a call from the R.C.M.P. in Prince Rupert that the fishing boat Anthony was on was lost in a storm at sea today and there were no survivors." said Hank as softly as he could.

Without a sound Ms. Chapman reached for Hank, grabbed him by the front of his Storm Coat with such strength that Hank wondered if her fingernails penetrated the tough material in it, plunged her face between her hands into Hank's chest and sobbed like a baby. Father D. put his arm around her and tried to console her with appropriate words from the Bible at a time like this, and all three stood there in the blowing rain supporting each other for the longest time until the sobbing ended.

When she straightened up and looked Hank in the face, she asked

"What am I gonna do, what happened anyway?" Hank relayed to her the little information he had received and asked if she had a close friend to call at a time like this. When her reply was negative, Father D. offered to go back to the Glebe with Hank, retrieve his car and return, to call Prince Rupert with her from her home or come back to the Glebe and call from there. "Oh thank you Father, and you two Corporal, that would be nice." The next day Father D. advised Hank everything had been taken care of, and Prince Rupert detachment would notify him or Ms. Chapman if her son's body was recovered. In never was.

THE LINE SHACK

Along the South shore of Nova Scotia on the side of Highway #3 half-way between the towns of Liverpool, Queens County and Shelburne, Shelburne County the Department of Lands and Forests had erected a one-room building near the County Line as a meeting place\shelter, especially in bad weather. It was also convenient as a base station in case of a lost hunter or a forest fire. Over the years the building became affectionately known as the 'Line Shack'. It had electricity; telephone, a wood burning stove, table and chairs, some dishes, kitchen utensils and two bunk beds. The nearest home was at least ten miles either way. The area was named Granite Village probably due to the presence of giant granite boulders the size of a small house, scrub trees and swamp. During Hank's time in the area there were no other buildings in the 'village'.

It was also an excellent spot in the dark days of winter for forest rangers, law enforcement, J.P.s and friends to get away and have a break for an afternoon under the guise of the annual Rabbit Hunt. Not everyone chose to go rabbit hunting, rather, depending on the weather, go hiking, snow shoeing, skiing or just sit in the camp, read, chat, play cards and look at the fire. With invitations came suggested BYO food, favourite refreshments with a warning from the outdoor types, "Don't eat\drink it all before we get back, save some for us".

In earlier gatherings, men took turns staying behind to cook the main meal. In Hank's time, his senior constable Dennis Sutton cheerfully accepted that task after he transferred in from Liverpool. Due to the hunting skills of the participants, rabbits were never included on the menu. Rather, Dennis, a native son of rural Newfoundland made a delicious concoction in large frying pans of corned beef, large cans of whole tomatoes and a variety of fresh and canned vegetables. All due respects to Dennis' culinary skills, any hot food would have been a treat to someone tired and hungry coming in from a winter hike, empty handed or not.

If George or Doug were there with guitar, harmonica or mandolin, there would be music and a sing-a-long after supper, which would top off the evening. Hank usually went home after a reminder from Chief Ranger Art Smith to clean up and leave the place the way you found it. Those too tired or too much 'singing' might choose to stay and come home in the morning. During these gatherings that Hank attended, he was proud to say he never heard a discouraging word, display of anger or argument among the men present. The camaraderie developed by the men there would leave them with memories that would carry them through their working days ahead. All thanked Dennis for the food and looked forward to returning next year.

Three Cell Flashlight

THE BROWN BROTHERS

John Brown, the man who had shot a hole in the windshield of the Shelburne R.C.M.P. car before Hank got to Shelburne, early one frosty spring morning drove in to Jordan Falls with his windshield only partly scraped and promptly rear-ended another car on the bridge. The other motorist involved called Shelburne detachment and wanted Brown arrested. Hank, not a morning person, dug himself out, got dressed, scraped the windshield of the police car and drove to Jordan Falls six or seven miles east of town. Both drivers and vehicles were still there, the owners having moved them off the narrow bridge so as not to obstruct traffic. By this time the other driver Jim Bennett had cooled down, the ice on the windshield of the Brown car had melted and Hank could see there was minimal damage to both cars, which could still be driven.

Mr. Brown was uneasy but polite so Hank called him aside and told him this time would be a warning ticket and he would not be charged. Both cars were insured so Hank concluded the insurance adjuster could decide the liability of each driver. Hank collected their respective papers, went back to the police car and wrote out the accident report which he later typed and mailed into the Department of Motor Vehicles, Halifax. That was the last time Hank saw John Brown.

Later that year in the evening Martha, the wife of John's brother Harry who lived on the other side of the Jordan Falls bridge at the entrance to the Nine Mile Woods road called Shelburne detachment crying and screaming "Harry's drinking and acting crazy and HE'S GOTTA A GUN!" Hank knew Harry as a hard-working labourer\woodsman who had never been in trouble with the law during his time in Shelburne. Hank had no back-up so he took his time driving to Jordan Falls, over the bridge and cautiously parked the car on the gravel road with the passenger side towards the front of Harry's place about fifty yards back from the road. The house was long and narrow, parallel to the road with a sun-porch all across the front probably built with windows salvaged from a demolished building on the old Navy Base outside of town. The windows looked like they had a recent visit from a hurricane. By and by Harry, a small man, appeared in the front door holding what looked like a broken shovel handle by his side. Hank took his revolver out of the holster, held it low out of sight, stepped out of the police car and up onto the door sill with the car between he and Harry.

For a time Harry just stood there staring in Hank's direction. There was no sign of any other family members and no vehicles passed by on the road. "How are you doin Harry" Hank shouted. Harry quietly replied "Good". (Long Pause) Then Harry shouted back "She's mine ain't she". Hank didn't know if 'she' meant his wife or his house, it really didn't matter to Hank who now was extremely relieved that Harry hadn't taken a shot at him, replied "She sure is Harry, she sure is!" With that Hank stepped down onto the road, slipped in behind the wheel, dropped the car into gear, made a U-turn and headed back to town. Hank never heard from Harry or his wife again. Hank later learned that on the cusp of a family quarrel to vent his anger Harry had smashed the windows out of his sun-porch with the butt of his rifle, but never fired a shot.

SUICIDES

Early one cool, damp late winter or early spring morning, Hank was alone in the office when a mysterious call came in from a woman in Sable River stating only that something terrible had happened at her home and she really needed him to attend. Hank dropped what he was doing and headed out to Sable River some twenty miles away if he took the gravel Nine Mile Woods road instead of going all the way around the shore. When he arrived, the woman met him at the back door in tears, held the door open motioned and said "Come, see." She led Hank across the kitchen of the small bungalow, opened the bathroom door and there slumped on the floor with his upper body hanging over the bathtub was her father in a pool of blood, dead with a straight razor still grasped in his right hand. Hank bent down, caught his chin, lifted the man's head and could see he had cut his throat almost from ear to ear. As they retreated from the bathroom, closed the door, moved towards the kitchen table, she blurted out "I wasn't gone from the house two minutes to get some wood for the stove and when I came back in there was no sign of him, then I found him there."

She went on to say that he had been recently diagnosed with terminal cancer and just couldn't bear the thought of living with it. He was a seventy-four old widower who had come to live with her, his only daughter. "I never dreamed he'd go this far, but I guess he had his mind made up and the minute my back was turned" her voice trailed off and she began to sob deeply. Attempting to change the subject, Hank asked who else lived there she answered: "Just my husband Bob, he's away at work." Hank also enquired about close friends, relatives or neighbours she could call on during this time, she replied "Yes, but first I have to call the undertaker and get this mess cleaned up." Hank agreed and reminded her he'd have to notify the coroner and there may be an inquest, but that could come later. Hank asked "Do you mind if I take the razor as an exhibit?" "Yes!" she commanded. "Get it out of my sight!"

Hank returned to the office and called the coroner Dr. Angus in Yarmouth who advised he would be in Shelburne later the following morning and would like to visit the scene and see the remains. Hank made arrangements with the funeral home and with Mrs. Edwards to forewarn them of Dr. Angus' visit the next day. Dr. Angus arrived at the detachment mid-morning and Hank took him in the police car to both locations. On return to Shelburne Dr. Angus decided there was no need for an inquest as this was an obvious suicide, and little could be gained by more publicity. As it was close to Noon, Hank invited the doctor to lunch at the hotel and during conversation Hank asked Dr. Angus, a psychiatrist, about the suicidal mind.

After a brief pause, the doctor looked directly at Hank and replied,

"The pure suicidal mind is so foreign to those of us still walking around, we can't begin to comprehend such a severe state of mind." Up until now, Hank had seen results of several suicides and many attempted suicides (wrist slashers) looking for attention, sympathy or both, but had never seen one as gruesome and determined as this.

SUICIDES

When Police Chief Helpard passed away and Cst. George Aulenback was made Chief of police in Shelburne, the town hired Dave Roach as town constable. Dave was a quiet, polite, easy-going man in his early thirties, had little police experience, but was willing to learn. He was married to a woman whose parents lived in Sandy Point about four miles out of town. Late one morning Dave called Hank and asked him to meet at the town police station. When Hank arrived Dave told him that his father-in-law had just committed suicide outside his home in Sandy Point and was still there sitting on the ground. It was a beautiful sunny spring morning as Hank and Dave drove the short distance to the scene and as Hank turned into the driveway there slumped over on the winter 'banking' beside the house facing East towards the morning sun was this small man with a .22 rifle by his side. Dave had told Hank that his father-in-law was in his late seventies, had been widowed two years ago and asked his daughter and Dave to move in with him to keep him company. The old man was recently diagnosed with cancer of the mouth and had been quite despondent lately. So after his daughter and Dave both went to work that morning, Dave surmised that the father-in-law loaded his rifle, went outside, sat on the banking, put the barrel of the rifle into his mouth, reached down and pushed the trigger. A neighbour, Carl Hameon discovered him and called Dave.

Hank checked the jugular for a pulse, confirmed he was dead, opened the mouth and saw some bleeding from the roof and checked the exit point of the bullet high on the back of the head. There was no sign of a struggle and no visible bruises on the face or hands so Hank was inclined to agree with Dave's assumption. But just in case, Hank walked over to Hameon's next door, confirmed Dave's story with Carl and arranged to get his statement later. Back at the house Dave was calling his wife and the undertaker to have the body removed from its location, so conspicuous from the nearby highway. Hank suggested to Dave he not do anything more with the body until Hank had a chance to notify the coroner. Hank took possession of the rifle to have it checked later by Cpl. Cliff Follett from the Identification Section in Yarmouth.

As Hank drove back to the office, he couldn't help but reflect of the suicide at Sable River less than two months ago and compare the two events. Sable River had been so violent and bloody although the victim had the forethought to limit the mess his daughter had to clean up by bleeding over the bathtub. In contrast, this man quietly went outside, sat down in a peaceful setting facing the sun and left little that had to be cleaned up. When Hank contacted Dr. Angus, the coroner, he explained the situation at Sandy Point, gave his own opinion and that of Cst. Roach and the neighbour that no one suspected foul play, the coroner replied that he could see no benefit in his attendance at the scene or holding an inquest. Hank agreed, bid him farewell and proceeded to type up the necessary reports to conclude the case. Hank later notified Dave of the coroner's decision and he agreed.

THE ATLANTIC

Hank wasn't long in Shelburne before he realized how much influence the Atlantic Ocean had on the residents of the Town and the County of Shelburne, even though the ocean lie nine miles from town out at the entrance to the harbour. In the next four years Hank would learn how much influence the Ocean would also have on him and his work. Generations of jilted families, when given the opportunity, would tell you that the harbour was deep for shipping, never froze over in winter and that long before Halifax was made capital of the province that Shelburne had been first choice. Except, when the ship from England carrying the Envoy commissioned to make Shelburne the capital, got caught in a storm and took shelter in Halifax, those 'scoundrels' in Halifax wined and dined the Envoy and his entourage and persuaded them to forget Shelburne and make Halifax the capital.

The United Empire Loyalists who chose to remain loyal to the King of England when the U.S. broke away from the British Empire had founded the town in 1783. Already men were making their living from the sea catching and processing fish. Others were clearing land, farming, lumbering and ship building all the while reminding each other "Who needs Halifax?" Due to the rugged terrain, boulders as big as a small house, rivers and streams flowing towards the ocean that had to be crossed, roads were little more than wagon trails and most heavy traffic was by the sea in sailing ships.

By the time Hank arrived in the mid '60's, Shelburne was booming with shipyards, some building 'long liners' for fishing the 'banks', just an overnight trip from the harbour while others were building large deep sea trawlers and draggers that would go to sea for ten to fourteen days at a time. Shelburne fisheries owned several such trawlers and a large fish plant at the base of the government wharf to process the catches. All of this added up to jobs and low unemployment. At the mouth of the harbour was Canadian Forces Base Shelburne with at times a hundred or more personnel. Shelburne

Woodworkers through its divisions likely employed forty to fifty people in the busy seasons. Cox's General Store employed at times a couple of dozen men and women. Car dealerships, service stations, restaurants, motels and hotel needed a few dozen more workers. Roseway Hospital on the old navy base just outside of town also employed twenty or twenty-five people 24/7. Later on, Mary Ann worked there as a Nursing Supervisor part time.

Provincial government departments such as Highways and Lands and Forests also had offices there, the latter being managed by Art Smith with several employees like Ed Turner who loved to hunt down and catch poachers and other breakers of the law. Hank has dedicated a chapter to Ed elsewhere in this book. Ed didn't care for testifying in Court and when Hank first worked with him he, who like others in his generation told Hank he went to work as a boy and didn't finish school, would say "Myself personally, I always try to work towards a guilty plea." He was well connected in the County and knew the habits, routines and friends of most of the offenders who regularly broke the fishing and hunting laws. Ed would spend hours and days if necessary alone or with another officer trying to bring the offenders to justice.

THE ATLANTIC - COMMERCIAL FISHERMEN

Despite the nine-mile long Shelburne harbour, fishermen from both sides seldom missed an opportunity in good weather, to harvest fish from the mouth of the harbour all the way to Brown's Bank, fifty miles off the southeast coast of Nova Scotia. From inshore fishing boats with small engines to Long Liners out of Gunning Cove on overnight trips, to deep sea 'Draggers' with up to ten of a crew that stayed out on the Atlantic as many as fourteen days at a time, they all went to make a living.

The small, open air inshore boats with outboard motors sat idle on the shore, until the owner decided to go to the mouth of the harbour to jig for ground fish, or try with spinning gear and bait to catch a feed of mackerel in season, especially in the fall when they were bigger. The Long Liner fishermen, usually a two-man crew, would spend the afternoon making ready for a trip by fueling up, baiting tubs of 'trawl' or hiring school kids to do it, grab a bite of supper and set out for Brown's Bank in the early evening, weather permitting.

Three Cell Flashlight

The boat would usually be thirty to forty feet long with a wheelhouse and 'cud' including a bunk, where one man could sleep while the other steered.

With the two inboard V-8 car engines at full throttle, once they cleared the fairway buoy at the mouth of the harbour, they could cover the fifty miles to the bank long before sunrise. Usually the fuel tank was a full forty-five gallon drum of gasoline, that sat on the open stern providing fuel to the engines that ran wide open all night, conditions permitting, until they reached the bank at daybreak and set their first tub of trawl. Then if they wished, both men could crawl up forward and catch some sleep while the trawl line fished. Hauling and re-baiting the trawl would be repeated until the captain decided they had enough fish and headed for home, arriving sometime late morning or early afternoon. If the fishing was good and the boat didn't need servicing, weather permitting, the two men might do a turn-around and go back out that evening. The long liner was known as a very sea worthy vessel, and rumour had it, that some captains would allow, during the night trip for both men to sleep, for short periods with the throttles on both engines wired wide open, and no one at the helm. Whatever the practice, no accidents near miss or losses of life were reported to Hank, during his four years in Shelburne.

The deep sea draggers, some built in Shelburne, once a crew was rounded up, would sail when the company bosses directed, winter and summer in all kinds of weather. Those crew members, subject to sea sickness, would not be able to eat the first day at sea, and would spend most of the time in the bunk or throwing up over the rail saying to himself "never again no matter what"! After a day or two the sickness passed, they might be Okay the rest of the trip. If not, when the ship got back to shore two weeks later, he would try to find a job on land and forget about the sea. But as Hank had heard before, deep sea fishing is like going down in a mine or working on the railroad, it gets in your blood and you miss the camaraderie of your mates and the money, and some will try it again. Hank can't remember the details, but the captain and crew each received a percentage of the catch as pay, which sometimes was great but other trips not so good. When the catch was good, if the crewman had a friend or relative in the Force, Hank might find a small share of the catch, on his front doorstep when he went out in the morning. Such were the 'perks' of being posted in Shelburne at that time. Q. How much does a five-pound bag of scallops weigh? A. Not as much as a ten pound bag!

SHELBURN

THE ATLANTIC

To the people of Shelburne County, the Atlantic Ocean was not only a place to catch fish, but also a sports field where the men mostly could hunt shore birds, ducks and geese, in season or out, and sea ducks, during spring and fall migration. The intention of the Migratory Birds Convention Act, a Federal Statute in Canada, was to control the illegal harvest of this resource, and the enforcement was the responsibility of the R.C.M.P. Under the same statute, for example, loons and sea gulls are protected as are the eggs of all shore birds and sea birds, during the nesting season. But in some parts of Shelburne County, loons were considered a delicacy and some hunters would risk seizure of their guns, vehicles and boats, just to take that prize home to their ladies to cook. Some hunters would travel almost a hundred miles, two counties East of Shelburne to Cherry Hill, Lunenburg County to hunt sea ducks and loons out on the ocean using 'shadow decoys'. Before Shelburne, Hank had never heard of or seen 'shadow decoys'. Basically they are homemade, cut out of quarter-inch plywood, the silhouette of a duck five times the size of a real duck, to be visible to a flock of low flying sea ducks passing by, in spite of ocean-sized waves. They were usually painted black, with bills yellow and eyes white, attached to two wooden rails in sets of two so they would float upright on the water, attracting the real ducks and luring them into gunshot range. The boats the 'poachers' used on the open ocean were usually camouflaged, as they were to conceal the hunters and confuse law enforcement, until the real ducks landed.

Ranger Ed Turner, although not a federal enforcement officer, knew the habits and routines of most of the hunters in his part of the County, and welcomed any chance to join Hank or his constable searching and seizing from 'poachers' of any kind. A few of these same hunters not only broke the game laws, but a check of the gas tank of the vehicle might reveal 'marked' gas, yet another offence, this time against the provincial Gasoline Tax Act. Many a story had been told of hunter's encounters with the law in Shelburne County, long before Hank was posted there, and sometimes he thought Ed knew them all, or most of them. However Hank was there for this one. One clear, frosty fall night, Hank and Ed set up a roadblock at the eastern county line in an area appropriately called "Granite Village". There was no village and no homes in this isolated area, but there were granite boulders, half the size of a house, and no alternate route for a poacher to choose, only the highway number three that Hank and Ed had blocked. Using his three-cell flashlight, Ed with his single battery search light, and the flashing red light on the police car, they stopped and searched several vehicles in the first hour and found no game in any of them. By and by, along came this GM pickup of 1960's vintage, with the fleet side body and wide front fenders. It had an ocean-worthy dory and an out-board engine in the back, together with a tent and sleeping bags, empty fuel cans and supplies, and a dozen or more shadow decoys, coming back from a weekend trip, for the three hunters in the cab. Also in the cab were three state of the art shotguns, ammunition belts and jackets, rubber rain gear for three and everything they needed for 'the hunt'. When Ed asked, "How's yer trip me-sons?" all three were too quick to reply, "Not good, No luck" and such like. Ed quietly eased his way to the front of the truck, tripped the hood latch, and shone his light on not one but two burlap bags, one on either side of the six cylinder engine, full of sea ducks well beyond their legal limit. When Hank seized one bag and dumped it out on the side of the highway, low and behold, besides a dozen or more sea ducks of all shapes and sizes, there was a pair of loons, freshly killed.

With Ed's help, Hank seized the two bags of ducks, the three shotguns with cases, the remaining ammunition, wrote a ticket for each of the three hunters, listing the items seized and notifying them of a date to appear in court in Shelburne, to hear the charges against them. Hank did not seize the boat and motor or the vehicle, because all three offenders had mellowed by this time, and pleaded with Hank not to arrest them. Rather, allow them to keep the truck so they could get home to their families sixty some miles away, that night. Ed agreed and they went on their way. By this time, Hank was too weary to check the gas tank for marked gas, so he let that go. The following morning, Hank took the two burlap bags of ducks to Shelburne Fisheries, and placed them in a locker in cold storage, according to a previous arrangement for R.C.M.P. exhibits that were perishable. Then he returned to the office and typed up the paperwork related to the seizure and the charges, as well as a rough draft of the covering report. As good luck would have it, no other calls came in, and Hank was able to complete these tasks uninterrupted. Two weeks later the three men from Cape Sable Island appeared in court in

Shelburne before Provincial Magistrate C. Roger Rand, plead guilty to the charges under the Migratory Birds Convention Act, and were fined $100.00 each. The seized guns and equipment were ordered forfeited to the Crown for disposition. Ed Turner attended the trials, and happily didn't have to testify.

A year or more later, Cst. Jim Toner, the Migratory Bird enforcement specialist from R.C.M.P. Headquarters in Halifax, rented a helicopter and pilot. Early one morning he arrived, unannounced over Clark's Harbour on Cape Sable Island, in the Barrington Passage detachment area. The pilot flew over many presumed illegal hunters in their speed boats, taking photographs for identification purposes later. The boats scattered in all directions, but before the last one left, a hunter fired his shotgun at the helicopter, knocking out the rear rotor blade, forcing the copter to land unceremoniously in the water. Luckily the Marine Division boat Adversus was nearby and was able to perform the necessary rescue. No one was injured, but a strong message was sent to the Migratory Bird specialist and other law enforcement officers from Halifax. Hank was amused to listen to the commotion on the police radio and gave thanks that all this action was in the neighbouring detachment area, and not his.

As an aside, at times over many years, some of the inhabitants of Cape Sable Island were inclined to operate outside the law, especially when officers needed a car ferry to get there from the mainland. Before Hank's time on the South Shore, and while the causeway to the Island was under construction. The story is told that, one evening the then Cpl. Murray, N.C.O. in charge of Barrington Passage detachment, was standing on the deck of the ferry during the ten minute ride, surveying the construction of the causeway on his way to a call on the Island. A well meaning young man, trying to strike up a conversation with the Mountie, came up beside him and said "Just look at that Cpl. Murray, they're building a causeway to Cape Island, isn't that wonderful?" After a long pause and a disgusted glance, came the response "Harumph, they shudda put it on the other end!!!" Here, it should be noted that over the years many sons of Cape Sable Island families joined the R.C.M.P and had full, successful careers. Hank knew a few of them as fellow members and friends.

Three Cell Flashlight

BEAVER DAM SPORTS MEET

Each year on Labour Day Weekend, a Sportsman's Meet was held at Beaver dam Lake beside highway three, about half way between Barrington and Shelburne. Some years during Hank's time there, over twenty thousand people attended the three-day long weekend as contestants and spectators. Many took part in trap and skeet shooting, archery, races on land for all ages, two-man log rolling contests and dory races on water. Ladies also displayed their culinary and craft skills, and provided many good things to eat and drink, even alcohol. That's where the police came in, because no security was hired by the organizers. It was all well planned in advance, so Hank had plenty of time to invite the Police Boat 'Adversus' four-man crew to anchor in Shelburne for the weekend, to supplement his then two-man detachment to keep the peace, and direct traffic to and from the grounds onto the highway. Luckily, during Hank's four Beaverdam's, there were no accidents or injuries, including no drowning. Hank even met a senior lady from Cape Sable Island, who bragged she had never been out of Shelburne County, but attending Beaver dam every year was all she needed for travel and excitement.

One afternoon, Hank was able to inject some excitement into the day of Cst. Rollie Isnor, one of the crew members from the Adversus, when two young men in old cars chased each other out of the grounds, at high speed kicking up gravel and squealing tires when they hit the pavement, heading for Shelburne. Hank jumped into his nearby police car, invited Rollie to go with him, and followed in fresh pursuit. On the narrow, crooked, roughly paved highway, with granite boulders on both sides, the two vehicles alternated passing each other, sometimes in the face of oncoming traffic, at speeds in excess of seventy miles per hour.

Older than Hank, Cst. Isnor was not impressed, muttering words like "slow down you crazy b---ard or you'll get us both killed", but Hank was not to be deterred. On some curves, Hank could clearly see the bottom of one shock absorber-less car, and in the first five miles was able to overtake, pass, stop it and let the shaking Cst. Isnor out, to arrest and hold the young driver there. Hank continued after the other vehicle, overtaking it on the last downhill approaching Shelburne.

Hank arrested that driver and took him back to pick up Cst. Isnor and the other driver, and take both offenders to jail, ensuring along the way both vehicles were safely off the road. Hank later called the tow truck operator from Hipson's Garage to pick up the two cars, and take them back to town. Hank met with Crown Prosecutor Nat White, and on his advice, typed up two charges of Dangerous Driving under the Criminal Code. Hank had them held in jail to go Tuesday morning in front of J.P. Hobart Blades, where they were remanded in custody to appear before Magistrate Rand, when he came to town later that week. Both plead guilty to the charges and were sentenced to thirty days in the County Jail, for their displays of dangerous operation of a motor vehicle, with a stern reminder from the Magistrate to never do that again.

MEN ABOUT TOWNS

To the Courts and to the Police was a valuable and well-established man with whom Hank and others had frequent contact. He was Justice of the Peace Hobart Blades aka 'Hobie'. A quiet unassuming man with a no-nonsense air, conveniently available due to his office job and residence in town, his obliging nature made him priceless, to those who needed his experience and expertise. Whether signing documents for police or sentencing offenders for minor liquor or traffic offences, he projected authority. In extreme cases he was sometimes available on weekends, providing the police didn't abuse the privilege. In Hank's second year in Shelburne, due to the load Hobie carried, his job was made easier by the appointment of George Bruce, a neighbour at the top of the street from the detachment, as a second Justice of the Peace. George, a retired, jovial story-telling chap who loved to grow flowers, had some of the most beautiful beds of peony roses Hank had ever seen. George was also an amateur astronomer, and a reliable weather resource for all seasons.

Like Hank, he too was aware of the phenomenon of radio 'skip' in that part of the Province, during June and November, when on a clear night, one could clearly hear on the police car radio, voices of men on oil rigs in the Gulf of Mexico. This, in that part of the Province that was notorious for poor radio reception from anywhere else, believed due to the presence of thousands of huge granite boulders, on the surface of rural parts of the County.

Another senior, knowledgeable, valuable asset to the Police was Crown Prosecutor Nathaniel Whitworth White, who was to be consulted before charges were laid in all serious criminal cases. Affectionately known as 'Nat', he had P.E.I. roots, and readily developed an affinity for Hank, the farm boy, nick-naming him "the hay pitcher". Nat was the most disorganized, unpunctual man Hank ever knew, which was clearly evidenced by the stacks of files on the top his desk, on a nearby chair or on the floor beside it. Much to the chagrin of Magistrate Rand, he was often late for Court, hustling in while pulling on his cloak, as he entered the court room. When he took his place in front of Hank or another officer sitting behind him, the white tag on the inside of the collar of his cloak, would inevitably be sticking out. When the Magistrate wasn't looking, the officer would quietly reach forward and tuck the tag in. Consequently after that, Hank jokingly offered to any friend or fellow member, with a tag sticking out at the back of his or her neck "Here Nat let me help you finish getting dressed." In fact, Hank still does that to his wife Mary Ann, risking the chance of an elbow or a slap.

One warm spring afternoon, Chief Aulenback called Hank at the detachment and mysteriously asked if Hank had time to meet with him at the Town office. Hank met George outside his office where George slipped into the front seat of the police car, and related that a handicapped young man had just told him that he had been up at the Exhibition grounds picking up empty beer bottles. He had discovered Nat sitting in his car behind an abandoned building and "he thought he might be dead." Hank and Chief George drove directly to the Exhibition grounds, found Nat's car, with him slumped over in the front seat. George, now bolstered with Hank's presence, opened the front door of the car reached in, touched Nat on the shoulder and loudly called out his name. Nat stirred, slowly opened one eye towards George, hoisted himself up on an elbow and said in a slurred voice "Oh, Hi George, what are you doing here?" George replied jokingly "We thought you were dead". Sighs accompanied by laughs all around. There was little doubt in the officers minds that he had been 'high' on something, but had 'slept it off.' When the time was right, George, the charmer took his police cap off, and said "Shove over Nat and I'll drive you home". Nat reluctantly agreed, because he knew the welcome at home might need some explanation, but he complied.

Hank followed at a distance, through a couple of back streets to Nat's house where they left him in his car and departed. As Hank and George drove back to his office, they reflected on the situation, the very awkward position they had found themselves in, prayed no one noticed Nat being driven home by his new chauffeur, and swore each other to secrecy which remains to this day. Nat was too embarrassed to mention it later.

Fred Power, the keeper of the County Jail and his wife Elsie were a middle aged no-nonsense couple quite capable of receiving and handling prisoners. She cooked meals for prisoners and cleaned the cells when needed. He liked to garden in summer and ice fish in winter. Fred had recently acquired some seeds to grow giant pumpkins from Irwin Dill in the Annapolis Valley, and was diligently feeding mixed powered milk into the vines of two or three select pumpkins in his garden. He also told Hank, an amateur gardener, that he could leave parsnips in the ground all winter and dig them fresh as he needed them from his garden, only a few miles from the warmth of the Atlantic Gulf Stream.

MAGISTRATE RAND

During the four years Hank was in Shelburne and for some years before, the weekly Circuit Magistrate from Yarmouth was C. Roger Rand, a small but mighty man who ruled his Courtroom 'with an iron fist'. Unlike Nat, always prompt, dressed in his robe, Court was called to order Thursdays at 10:00 A.M. sharp, by the senior police officer present saying "Oh Yea, Oh Yea, all people draw near and pay heed. This Court is now in session." Having arrived the previous evening with his lady secretary from Yarmouth, at the Wildwood Motel, he was 'ready to go' the next day. Some Thursdays, he was serious and all business, others he was relaxed, noticeable by the smile on his face. One morning after Mary Ann had worked a night shift at the hospital, Cst. Alex Carter a quick-witted Newfoundlander, called the detachment to say that Court would be delayed a couple of hours. When Mary Ann, the 'second man' at the detachment, who was the Charge Nurse at the hospital the evening before, picked up the phone and answered "Roseway Hospital", 'quiet', then without hesitation Alex replied "the doctors will be delayed in the

O.R. for the next couple of hours" followed by a chuckle, then the retort "You brat, wait 'til I get my hands on you!"

LOCKPORT TOWN

Years before Hank came to Shelburne, and still the town of Lockport had its own two-man police force, now with Chief Bill Cooke and Cst. St. Clair Williams, one of many men in the area called after a favourite family doctor since passed, Richard St. Clair. Chief Cooke was a huge man, late in his career with limited mobility. On the other hand, Cst. Williams was young, strong, fit and usually available if Hank or his constable was alone in the area, and needed back-up. Hank and his constable reciprocated by returning the favour, duties permitting, when the Chief or Cst. Williams needed assistance with an unfamiliar or more serious case.

The town had two fish plants, Pearce's and Nickerson's. Both owned and operated ocean-going deep sea fishing vessels, some modern and some like the old dory fishing schooners. Both plants hired residents, men and women but sometimes the fishing vessels hired experienced fishermen like Bruce Moore from Prince Rupert, B.C. He, like some men from both coasts fished the Atlantic in summer and the Pacific in winter. Conveniently, some might be avoiding the law or bill collectors on the other coast, which required frequent exchange of information between R.C.M.P. detachments on both coasts. But some local criminals (poachers), were operating right under the noses of local authorities and never caught, like a fishing captain named Carl Roach. He was a notorious deer jacker but try as they might, Forest Rangers and R.C.M.P. alike were unable to catch him in the act. Roach, despite depending on the commercial fishery for a living, being Captain of his own long-liner and subject to the laws under the Federal Fisheries Act, was reported to have participated in the following offence:

One bright moonlit night, Roach in his long-liner and a buddy of his, also a captain of another long-liner, followed a large school of haddock into Jordan Bay, where the fish went to spawn. The fishermen dragged a large bag net between the two boats, scooping up enough fish to fill both boats to the guns. The following morning both boats unloaded their catch at Nickerson's fish plant. A confidential informant, who was one of the workers processing the fish in the plant that day, later told Hank that by the time the workers finished processing those two loads of fish, they were up to their ankles in roe (fish eggs). Hank passed this information over to the local Fisheries Officer, who shall remain unnamed, who told Hank he'd investigate it. That was the last Hank ever heard from him.

BOY CRUSHED UNDER OIL TANK

One weekday spring morning, Hank was typing a report when a frantic call came in from a distraught, young single mother in Jordan Falls. She sobbed as she told how her four-year-old son Ike had been playing with the dog outside in the yard, when the furnace oil tank fell over on him, and he was still lying there. "Come quick!" Hank drove as quickly as he could over the soggy dirt road, but by the time he arrived, some neighbour men had raised the tank off the boy, still lying on the ground lifeless. Visible on the ground nearby were the long poles and the blocks of wood, they had used as fulcrums to raise the barrel off the little boy. Close examination of the boy by Hank and a retired neighbour, Dr. Miller, who had arrived the same time as Hank, showed little sign of life. To appease the anxious mother, the doctor quietly suggested he and Hank take the boy to the Shelburne Hospital just to be sure. Hank knelt down and gently picked the boy up in his arms, with the image flashing through his head 'this could be one of our sons'. Hank carried him the few steps to the police car, and handed him to the doctor already sitting in the back seat of the car with arms outstretched. While the doctor continued artificial respiration Hank drove carefully back over the same, near impassable road to the hospital, entered and announced the arrival of the boy. Attending Dr. Michael Cooper came directly out to the police car, briefly examined the boy in Dr. Miller's lap, and asked if he could carry him inside for closer examination.

Just then a neighbour arrived with the mother, and Dr. Cooper asked her to wait outside. The mother, Beverly Hameon, still sobbing in an act of guilt and self-blame, explained to Hank that just the day before, she had the two hundred gallon oil tank filled. The extra weight may have caused it to topple because it was mounted on four long legs, and not fastened to the house. Seeing her despair, Dr. Miller offered that it was springtime, the frost coming out of the ground may have contributed to a block under one of the legs to shift, causing the tank to tip over. She seemed relieved and accepted that explanation.

Hank and Dr. Miller returned to the scene, examined the area where the tank had been, and could readily see where, the block under one of the outside legs had slid out of position. The tank was still on its side, with some oil weeping out of it, so Dr. Miller offered to call the oil man to come and pump the oil out of it, so it could be righted and re-filled. Hank thanked him for all his help and headed back to the office.

Hank called coroner, Dr. Angus in Yarmouth and outlined the tragedy to him. He offered to get in touch with Dr. Cooper whom he knew, and suggested that an autopsy or inquest would not likely be necessary in a case such as this. That in fact, was the ultimate conclusion of a very sad story!

U.F.O. BARRINGTON PASSAGE

In a predominantly rural part of the Province, especially along the Atlantic coast reports of a U.F.O. (Unidentified Flying Object) were not uncommon. In Hank's opinion, most such reports did not require an immediate response, if the object had already disappeared, but the name, address of the caller, and location of the sighting was recorded, and would be included as a visit on the next patrol to that area. But the call that did come in one night in the late summer, from the Barrington Passage detachment area, while the members there were out on patrol, was one that Hank decided deserved immediate response.

This U.F.O. had apparently fallen from the sky into the water beside the causeway to Cape Sable Island. On a clear night, Hank drove the forty some miles to the scene where he met a young couple at the Barrington end of the causeway. They both excitedly in their island lingo tried to explain what they had witnessed, so Hank suggested they lead the way onto the mile-long causeway to get a closer look. As they approached the scene, several vehicles had gathered, parked along the North guardrail, with the occupants standing outside, huddled against the northeast wind. As Hank exited his police car, he could easily see a half mile to the north a large, round, dark object floating on the water. Some witnesses present reported they had seen the object while still in the air, and followed it with their eyes until it splashed down into the water, and some had seen flashing lights coming from it. Others described a loud hissing sound as it hit the water, partially submerged, then bounced back up and rested on the surface. Everyone agreed it was not an airplane or helicopter, and some mused if there were "Marians" on board, but no one had heard voices coming from the mysterious object, and none wanted to go out in a boat late at night to check.

When Hank returned to his police car, he called the Barrington car on the police radio and Cpl. Vic Werbicki answered. He had been out of his car, up in the back country on a complaint of deer jacking, and never received the initial call. He agreed to meet Hank back at his detachment, but when Hank described the scene, Vic wanted to come there directly and see for himself. Hank, aware he was out of his own area and someone might be calling for him, gave Vic the names and telephone numbers of the people who had called him, and headed back to Shelburne.

Cpl. Werbicki later advised Hank that by the time he approached the scene, the object was barely visible on the surface, and by the next day it had sunk to the bottom of the bay, in water reported to be too deep to recover anything. Some local fishermen speculated that the neighbours to the South, namely the U.S.A. military, may have launched a test missile of some kind, and it got away on them. One seasoned fisherman in the group assembled, while Cpl. Werbicki was present was heard to mumble "It wouldn't be the first time", suggesting he had seen similar flying objects before in the area. Cpl. Werbicki told Hank he had typed a short report of the incident, placed it in a file and closed it.

MRS. MUNDY

Late one summer night, Hank was in the office typing a report when a frantic call came in from a very excited lady with a British accent. After Hank managed to calm her down, she told him she was calling from West Green Harbour, and two young men had just tried to rob her at gunpoint, but fled, when she threatened them. She gave Hank a description of the robbers and a vague one of their car, but it was too dark to get a license plate number. Hank loaded his revolver, dropped it into his holster, grabbed his three-cell

Three Cell Flashlight

flashlight and headed for West Green Harbour twenty some miles on a side road, towards Lockeport. Enroute Hank surmised, although it was a clear night, there was little chance he'd meet the culprits, coming out of the short dead-end road from the harbour. He was right, from the time he turned into the partly paved road, he never met another car. At the end of the pavement, he continued on according to Mrs. Mundy's directions, another half mile to the lone stately old farmhouse, on a point of land now serving as her summer place. There was no yard light, just a light over the back door.

When she opened the locked back door, she was still excited, but genuinely pleased and relieved to see Hank, and preceded to recite the information she had given him over the phone. She added that both young men were short in stature, wearing work clothes and the one holding the gun, which she could only describe as a small hand gun, was wearing a dark toque, and the other was bare headed. Both acted like they were 'high' on something. When she stood up to them and threatened to call the police, they fled. At first, Hank started to suspect her story, and chalk the whole thing up to a lonely, elderly woman wanting a bit of company. But as she continued talking, he was convinced by her words and body language that her story could be true. As an aside, she told Hank that her grandfather on her mother's side, was a member of the Royal Northwest Mounted Police, and although being a U.S. citizen, she always admired the Mounties.

Before Hank departed, she assured him she didn't mind staying alone, in spite of the events of the evening, and alluded to a personal arsenal of weapons, that she may have also mentioned to the culprits before their hasty departure. Outside in the gravel driveway, Hank checked with his three-cell flashlight for any unusual tire marks, but to no avail. Before returning to Shelburne, Hank drove the few miles in the opposite direction to the town of Lockeport, to check for vehicles with two male occupants, but all was quiet, and there was no one in the police station.

Early next morning Hank returned to Lockeport, dropped in to see Chief Cooke and Cst. Williams at the police station. They already knew about the attempted robbery, and St. Clair suggested a local lad Dave Welton and his sidekick Billy McIntyre from P.E.I. They were crew on one of Jim Reid's long liners, the 'Mary Jessie', which was currently tied up at the Government Wharf. Hank thanked St. Clair for his help and hurried to the wharf, to find the Mary Jessie near the outer end of the wharf. There didn't seem to be anyone around so Hank called out "Ahoy Mary Jessie is anybody on board? No answer.

Hank looked forward and noticed the door to the wheelhouse and the 'cud' was closed, he boarded the vessel and pounded on the door "Police open up." Quiet. Finally, a sleepy, scruffy McIntyre appeared in the doorway, followed shortly by another sleepy Williams. Hank invited them out onto the deck and asked them where they were the night before. In the answer to that simple question they both simultaneously contradicted each other. Hank told them they were both suspected of attempted robbery the night before, recited the police warning to them, arrested, cuffed them together and led them ashore and into the back seat of the police car. On the way to Shelburne, McIntyre asked "Are you takin us to jail?" "Not yet, you're coming to Shelburne detachment to discuss last night a bit more, and see if we can get to the bottom of things," Hank replied and called ahead on the police radio to tell Cst. Jim Youden that he was coming in with a couple of suspects.

At the detachment, Hank separated the two, and took one into his office and closed the door while the other stayed with Jim in the main office. Then after a short time, he switched the two suspects, and it soon became clear to Hank they had not rehearsed their stories very well. Cst. Youden confirmed Hank's suspicions. Williams, who owned the car, admitted being at Mrs. Mundy's, but just for a visit, the night before. When questioned further, he implicated McIntyre as the owner of the gun, and further that he had bought it from a U.S. fisherman, on George's Bank on their last trip out.

Hank took a written, signed statement from McIntyre, because he seemed to be the ring leader while Cst. Youden did the same with Williams. Hank told them both, they would likely be charged with attempted robbery with a weapon, McIntyre also with possession of an unregistered firearm.

Further, that they would be fingerprinted and as they had no fixed place of abode, they would be required to spend the night in jail. They would also have to appear before a Justice of the Peace the following day, for a bail hearing until next week, when the circuit Magistrate came to town. Before going to jail, Hank accompanied McIntyre to the Mary Jessie and retrieved the .22 calibre pistol which McIntyre willingly handed over, as evidence. Hank also contacted Crown Prosecutor Nat White who concurred with the charges to be laid. The next day, Hank laid the charges that Cst. Youden had typed, before Justice of the Peace Hobart Blades, who agreed to contact their Captain Reid, and arrange bail, because Blades knew and trusted him. Later that day, the two culprits were released on five hundred dollars bail each, backed by Captain Reid, who assured their attendance in Court the next Thursday before Provincial Magistrate C. Roger Rand from Yarmouth. Hank called Mrs. Mundy on the phone to advise her of the outcome of the investigation. Again she was pleased and asked if she could attend the hearing, to which Hank reminded her it was a public courtroom, where anyone could attend. She also announced she was inviting Hank and Mary Ann to her place for dinner, which they accepted later.

The following Thursday, both suspects appeared before Magistrate Rand and pled guilty to all three charges. Williams was sentenced to one month in the County Jail. McIntyre was sentenced to three months because of his involvement with the unregistered firearm, and a previous record of assault in his hometown on P.E.I.

NOVA SCOTIA SCHOOL FOR BOYS

Post World War II, the Province opened the Nova Scotia School for boys on the old Navy Base on the Sandy Point Road, about a mile outside the town limits, in the Shelburne R.C.M.P. detachment area. There were two buildings on the site, a smaller administration office and a much larger one as a residence for up to fifty boys, ages six to sixteen. They were deemed, by the authorities of the province, to be truants, unable to be managed at home or in 'foster' care, or perhaps even homeless. The school was staffed with "counselors" around the clock, mostly men from the area, and some specialists from other parts of the province. There were no fences around the residence outside, and very few locks on the inside, so any hour of the day or night, when no one was watching, a boy or two could simply walk away. When they were noticed missing, someone from the school would call the detachment with a name, description, approximate time of departure, and any other pertinent details.

The detachment member on duty would compile a message and send it to Halifax, requesting an 'all points bulletin' to detachments along the Atlantic shore, between Shelburne and Halifax. If duties permitted and the boy had a criminal record, Hank or the constable would drive the five miles to Jordan Falls, and set up a road block on the bridge, in the event that the boy was headed for Halifax or beyond. For some reason the boys rarely went in the westerly direction, towards Barrington or Yarmouth. Occasionally the Shelburne town police would discover a missing boy, and return him to the school. Or another detachment would call and report they had found him, and arrange a 'relay' back to Shelburne. Sometimes, the boy got tired of being out in the elements, alone, cold and hungry, and find his way back himself.

Under the administrator Ken Jones, when Hank first arrived in Shelburne, the resident psychologist John Conroy, according to some counselors, seemed to spend more time out of town on mystery trips, than he did on the job. Attempts by Hank to quietly determine his away activities, resulted in a number of phone calls from Conroy, telling Hank to mind his own business or he would report him to the R.C.M.P. headquarters in Halifax and complain harassment. As Hank had no real complaint, from anyone about Conroy's activities, he ceased his enquiries. Rumours of perceived physical or sexual abuse of the boys, by Conroy or other counselors, but no official complaint, proved to be just that "rumours".

During Hank's second year in Shelburne, Jerry MacIntyre, formerly from Cape Breton, replaced Jones as administrator of the school, and a few weeks later, Conroy left town and never returned. MacIntyre revived organized activities for the boys such as hiking, games, crafts, movies and age-friendly classroom teaching. He also sent out invitations for an informal guest night to the general public, clergy, police and firemen, with the offer to meet and greet the boys who chose to attend. To spend time with them, discuss their days, ask them what they wanted to be, when they grew up, and simply show interest in their replies. Hank, the father of three sons will never forget when he asked an eight-year-old boy "How do you like it here son?" The polite reply "I get three meals a day and a nice warm bed to sleep in, sir." followed by a happy grin.

In mid-afternoon of Hank's last year in Shelburne, a sixteen-year-old boy, big for his age, walked away from the school unnoticed, stole an old Chevy pick-up truck with the keys in it, from a neighbour's driveway, and went for a joy ride into town. Hank took the call at the office, radioed the police car in town enroute back from another call, with passenger Cst. Dennis Sutton and rookie Alex Carter driving.

Within minutes, they spotted the stolen truck and gave chase with siren and flashing red light activated. The lone young driver of the truck didn't stop, but accelerated out the Sandy Point Road passing and narrowly missing a car, with a woman driving, and children as passengers. She pulled over to the shoulder and stopped, as the police car continued the chase.

Here, we digress to Dennis in this situation. Dennis was brought up in a small out port on the coast of Newfoundland called Baie D'Espoir, and as a young man went to St. John's, the capital city and joined the Constabulary. To his chagrin, he soon learned that the officers of that Force didn't carry side arms, but 'Billy Sticks'. This situation was later compounded, when one night the lone Dennis encountered a group of drunken U.S. servicemen downtown, and attempted an arrest. He was beaten within an inch of his life, survived, but firmly with the belief that had he been armed, the beating never would not have happened. At the earliest opportunity he applied for, and was accepted into the R.C.M.P.

Now Dennis, a trusted senior constable by Hank who left him in charge when Hank was absent, finds himself in hot pursuit of a young fugitive in a stolen vehicle who has displayed carelessness behind the wheel of a stolen vehicle, and if allowed to continue, may well kill somebody. Dennis also has the luxury of a 'stick man', and doesn't even have to consider driving the car, and shooting with his left hand at the same time. He commands Cst. Carter to close in on the stolen truck, and position the police car so he can get a shot at that little bastard. Cst. Carter ensures there is no oncoming traffic, on a straight stretch of highway beside the harbour, with no dwellings or pedestrians, on the land side. He gives the 'all clear' to Dennis, who leans out the passenger window, and allegedly fires one shot at the back window of the truck. His aim was high and the bullet penetrated the upper cab of the truck, just above the rear window. The hand set for the police radio in the car must have jammed open, because Hank could hear every word of the two constables, back at the office.

The shot got the attention of the young fugitive, who abruptly pulled over, was arrested without incident, and returned to the school. The truck was towed to town for closer examination, and later that day returned to Mr. Hameon, who didn't seem to care about the bullet hole in the cab "I'm just happy to get my truck back with no scrapes and nobody hurt. I guess I better learn to take the keys in after this."

Due to a shot being fired by police, the Patrol Sergeant from Halifax was dispatched to Shelburne, obliged to investigate, and report back to the Commanding Officer of the Division, Chief Superintendent Fudge. He decreed that Constable Sutton be charged in 'Orderly Room', the R.C.M.P. in-service court for disciplinary matters.

The charge was careless use of an issue firearm and the trial was set for a later date, in Halifax with the Chief Superintendent presiding. Sgt. Murray was named as prosecutor, and there was no defense counsel made available. Hank's request to be a character witness on behalf of Cst. Sutton was granted, and the 'trial' was held in a meeting room adjacent to the Chief Superintendant's office in Halifax headquarters. The air in the room was heavy with a "guilty–until-proven-innocent" stigma, and when Hank was called to testify, he had to be careful not to bump into one of the many 'kangaroos', hopping around the Court Room. Cst. Sutton was found guilty, and Hank was so disappointed with his own testimony, he forgot how minor the sentence really was, maybe a delay in his next promotion. In Hank's opinion, selfishly, the main thing was that Cst. Sutton was allowed to continue with his service to the Force in Shelburne, without interruption.

As Hank reflected on those proceedings, he was reminded that the rank structure in the Force appeared to be alive and well. Here was the man in the field, Cst. Sutton on the front line, making snap decisions, maybe not always the best decisions, and maybe with the full 20-20 vision of the arm-chair lawyer, would have done something different. Yet here he was under the scrutiny of his superiors in Division Headquarters, Halifax, in the comfort of their armchairs, judging and punishing him. Hank couldn't help but remember Robbie Burns' poem, "The rank is but the guinea's stamp, A Man's A Man For Aw' That." And that is exactly how Hank felt about his Cst. Dennis Sutton, who had been his dependable 'senior man' for almost three years, mentoring several young recruits, holding down the fort in Hank's absence, loyal and trustworthy to the organization, that had just second-guessed and humiliated him. Hank also had a sense of futility, from his attempt to support Dennis in Orderly Room falling on deaf ears, even though there was little else he could do. After Hank was transferred out of Shelburne, Cst. Sutton, with more than ten years service, when he was transferred out to a supervisory position, was not promoted to Corporal, as was the custom of the day. He was obliged to wait until his next transfer.

LITTLE RIVER TOLLER

Neighbourhood friends to Mary Ann and Hank, also the Fina furnace oil delivery man Norman Hamilton, and his wife Elsie owned a special breed of dog, recently developed in Southwestern Nova Scotia called "the Little River Toller", this dog was named Sandy. He was average size, thirty-five to forty pounds with long light brown hair similar to a red fox, and a good-natured retriever.

When Norman told Hank he paid big money for this ordinary looking dog as a pup, because he could lure ducks ashore to within shotgun range, Hank thought he was joking. So Norman, sensing Hank's skepticism, invited him to come along on a duck hunting trip, when the season opened. Hank had hunted ducks since he was a teenager, without a dog or boat, by walking marches in hip waders or sat freezing in blinds, waiting for a lone duck to fly by, shooting it, and he or a friend retrieving it, if he was lucky.

One nice fall afternoon after work, Hank joined Norman and Sandy and headed for Norman's boyhood community of Gunning Cove on the shore of the Atlantic, twenty-three miles out of town. Hank had his recently acquired double-barrel shotgun, and Norman had his shiny nearly new Browning over-and-under, both twelve gauge. They parked the car on the roadside, and with Sandy walked along the beach of the cove until they came to a windrow of small granite beach rocks. There was also mixed driftwood which the hunters could lie down behind, out of sight, about fifteen yards from the water. From there they could see a 'raft' of twenty or more ducks bobbing on the water, at least one hundred yards out into the cove. The men crouched down behind the rocks and driftwood where they could still see the ducks and yet not be seen by them. After they got settled, Norman spoke to the dog and took some biscuits out of his jacket pocket. Then he'd throw the biscuits, one at a time, from his crouched position to different spots on the beach in front of him. Sandy responded by running back and forth after the biscuits, and for a time the ducks paid no attention. Hank was starting to doubt the logic of the exercise but said nothing. Gradually one by one, the ducks started flapping their wings and swimming, not flying, towards the shore, together in a pack. Norman kept tossing the biscuits and talking to Sandy so he'd stay out there. The closer the ducks got to shore, the more they'd flap their wings while almost running on top of the water, quacking loudly and even hissing.

It was obvious to Hank that the ducks saw the dog as the enemy, and they were on a mission to gang up and get him, which no doubt was the intention of the developers of the breed. Hank couldn't believe his eyes but he had to. When the ducks were almost ashore, Norman whispered "Now", and both men stood up and opened fire. They killed two and wounded one so it couldn't fly. Sandy retrieved all three, and the others naturally flew away. Norman gave Sandy more biscuits and patted him as a token of his service. Back home Hank, the believer, was on call that night, thanked Norman profusely, talked of going again, but never did. Norman and his wife Elsie plucked cleaned and froze the ducks. A few weeks later, when Mary Ann had to go home to Cape Breton, they invited Hank and three young sons over for a duck dinner, with apple pie for dessert.

The boys and the Hamilton children, although restless, were on their best behaviour, until Elsie set a piece of apple pie with cinnamon sprinkled on top in front of Hank's son Mark, age three, who quietly leaned over to his father and whispered, "I can't eat that, it's got rust on it." Elsie and those who heard him burst into understanding laughter, and the embarrassed Mark did eat the pie after Hank scraped the 'rust' off.

BEASTIALITY IN UPPER OHIO

One morning in late summer, Hank received a obscure call from a farmer in Upper Ohio named Maynard Jones, who preferred not to give details over the phone. He would only say he had a cow out on the island in the river that died under mysterious circumstances. Hank drove directly to Upper Ohio, twenty some miles of gravel road to the North of Shelburne and found the mailbox at the end of Jones' farm lane. Mr. Jones met him in the farmyard, and explained that he had some cattle pasturing that summer, on the island in the middle of the river in front of his place. Every other day, he rowed the short distance, over to the island in his boat, to check on his cattle.

Three Cell Flashlight

That morning he found one of his cows dead on the ground, with a half-inch nylon rope tied around her snout. He invited Hank to come with him in the boat to the island, and see for himself. As he untied the boat Mr. Jones commented "When I untied the boat this morning, I noticed it was not exactly the way I left it two days ago, but never thought anymore about it."

Once on the island, it was only a few steps to where the cow laid dead on her side, with the rope still attached to her snout. When Hank looked closer, he could see that the rope was so tight, that it had cut the air off from both her nostrils and mouth. He and Mr. Jones both agreed she probably died from asphyxiation. The ground around her showed signs of her struggle. To the rear of the cow was a large maple stump, less than a foot in height with traces of mud on it, but no clear boot prints, nor were there any on the ground around the cow, due to the natural debris on the forest floor. There were a couple of cigarettes butts with brown cork tips. Suspecting bestiality, both Hank and farmer Jones examined the vaginal area of the cow for signs of trauma, but there were none.

During ensuing conversation, Hank asked Mr. Jones if there were any neighbours who might be capable of such an act. He was reluctant to give a name but suggested "maybe a boy not too far from here." Hank knew that was his cue to conduct neighbourhood enquiries, which he planned to do anyway.

At the third farmhouse up the road, Mrs. Osborne answered the back door, when Hank knocked, and with a quizzical glance invited him in. Hank identified himself, enquired who lived there and she said, "just me and my son Howard, why what's wrong?"

Hank explained he was investigating the death of a cow on the island in the river, and he was checking with the neighbours for any information that might help to solve it. Now on the defensive she offered "I sure didn't have anything to do with it." Hank asked, "How about Howard, is he around today?" She replied, "I haven't seen him for awhile. He's supposed to be cleaning out the pig house."

Hank walked across the back yard, past the main barn and around the end to the pig house, where a tractor and trailer partly loaded with manure, were parked in front. The large young man was startled when, as he dumped another fork full of manure on the trailer, looked up and saw Hank standing there. He was wearing a tired ball cap, a torn checkered shirt and well-worn jeans, tucked into knee-high rubber boots. Hank verified he was Howard Osborne and when Hank asked where he was yesterday, the young man was nervously trying to light a cigarette, with a brown cork tip, and blurted out, "It wasn't me, I wasn't over to the island."

Even though Hank had 'farm-boy roots' the flies and the stink of pig manure was starting to get to him. In a partial bluff and an attempt to keep the conversation going, Hank lit a cigarette and invited Howard to accompany him over to a nearby empty hay wagon. Enroute, Hank asked Howard if he would mind removing one of his boots, so Hank could check the treads. Howard reluctantly complied, holding onto the side of the wagon. Taking the boot, Hank commented "You know there were some footprints around that dead cow on the island," watching for Howard's reaction. Examining the tread of the boot closely from every angle saying "Umhum, Ah ha" in an excited all-knowing tone, Hank could see Howard getting increasingly nervous.

Hank continued "I just might have to seize these boots and take them to our identification man for further examination." With that Howard looked directly at Hank, leaned back against the wagon and said, "no need, it was me, but……. I didn't mean to kill her, she just pulled back on the rope too hard and I couldn't stop her. Are you gonna arrest me?" Hank replied, "No, not if you come with me to the police car, sign a written statement to that effect, and promise me you'll stay with your mother until I come back to see you." He assured Hank he would, thanked him and went to the house to see his mother.

Hank returned to the Jones farm where he reported what he had learned. Mr. Jones was relieved but concerned about "making bad neighbours" and adding more stress to widow Osborne's situation.

He had also arranged with the 'dead-meat man' to come and pick up the cow. Hank replied "I'd have to discuss this with Crown Prosecutor White, and see what he says, also report to my headquarters, but I'll get back to you as soon as I can." It happened that Mr. White knew of the Osborne family, and was reluctant to prosecute the widow's only son, rather to ask the County to intervene, and obtain counsel and/or therapy for the son.

The next day Hank returned to Upper Ohio and reported Mr. White's decision to Mr. Jones and to Mrs. Osborne. Both agreed, seemed somewhat relieved, and thanked Hank for his help. Listening in the background, Howard also promised he'd "Never do that again."

NEW CAMP - LAKE JOHN

During Hank's second year in Shelburne, for several weeks Chief Aulenback spent his time off dismantling an old garage that a neighbour wanted removed, because he no longer had a car. George was able to salvage enough lumber from the building to build a hunting camp, on Crown land on an island in Lake John, some 15 miles West inland from Jordan falls, accessible only by air or an old logging road. In late summer George, Bill Acker and Junior Guy loaded the lumber onto a long homemade trailer fashioned from a steel truck frame and a front truck axle with two wheels, which Junior hauled with his truck to Jordan Falls. There they hooked it onto a borrowed Ford farm tractor for the trip to Lake John the next day.

Early next morning the trio and Hank headed for Lake John. Junior drove slowly for the first part of the trip, stopped for a break and asked Hank to drive next, which he gladly accepted, because he knew the model of the tractor from the farm back home. As they got started again, the sense of freedom and anticipation was mounting, George started singing and the rest joined in, while Hank opened the throttle just a little bit higher. George and Junior were sitting on top middle of the load, about six or seven feet off the ground, and Bill was sitting on the front of the load just behind Hank. As Hank drove through a swampy section with the mud flying, because he didn't want to get 'hung up', the tractor and trailer passed over a hidden tree root, the tractor lurched first, followed by the trailer which bounced violently, the front of the load catapulted Bill into the air. Luckily he did not fall between the tractor and trailer, but landed on his feet like a cat, off to the right hand side in a pile of brush. Hank stopped the tractor as quickly as he could, and all three ran back to check on Bill only to find he had sprained his right ankle. They all offered to turn around and go back so the ankle could be treated, but Bill wouldn't hear of it, hobbled over, climbed back up onto the load and shouted, "Let's go, it'll soon be dark." Hank apologized profusely for the accident, but Bill just laughed at him. They continued on to Lake John, where the others unloaded the lumber and made two rafts out of it, on the shallow water at the edge of the lake, while Bill sat on a log and watched.

George dug out of the bush the two-seater homemade boat which he and Hank had crafted, with plywood, glue and a few screws in the detachment garage the previous winter. Hank helped him drag it and the five horsepower outboard engine out to the shore of the lake. With perseverance and some good luck George and Hank got the outboard engine going, swung around in front of the first raft, hooked on and started very slowly across the half mile of smooth water to the island. Meanwhile, Junior stayed with Bill on the mainland. At the island, George unhooked the raft from the boat Hank tied it off to a boulder on the shore, and stayed on the island while George returned to retrieve the second raft and Bill. As he had with the first raft, Hank secured it and helped Bill ashore. George returned to pick up Junior and their supplies on the mainland.

After all four had a rest and something to eat and drink, Bill watched as the other three fashioned the floor and one wall of the camp, leveled and secured it on rocks before dark. Hank gathered wood, built a bonfire for Bill to attend, as they all dug out their sleeping bags, washed up and brushed their teeth in the lake, and bedded down on the new floor under the stars.

The next morning "all hands on deck" including Bill whose ankle had benefitted from the night's rest. After breakfast, all four worked on the next three walls and boarded them in, leaving space for the door and two windows. Bill was able to do most of the cutting, as long as the others brought the pieces to him, and took them away when he finished. George built a ladder to reach the rafters. With good weather and a break or two for lunch, by mid-afternoon, the small camp was starting to take shape, complete with the frames for four bunk beds, two on each side. The roof had yet to be boarded in. While others cleaned up the site, George made a list of supplies he still needed, got the boat ready to go, and with two trips to the mainland he retraced the exercise of the day before. Unlike the day before, the return trip by tractor and empty trailer was uneventful, arriving in Jordan shortly after dark.

In the weeks that followed George, Bill and Junior made several trips back to complete the camp which Hank didn't see until the second week of deer season, when all four returned to Lake John in a borrowed jeep. Bill's ankle was now fully recovered, he and Hank paired off the first morning walking quietly through the woods, when they came out on the edge of a clearing and stopped to check the area for sign. Minutes later a doe and her fawn, sensing their presence, darted across the clearing about fifty yards away. Before Hank could get the rifle to his shoulder, Bill fired one shot, the doe fell and the fawn ran off into the woods. Now the work began, gutting and dragging her back to the camp. When George and Junior returned to camp later in the day empty handed, they were impressed with Bill's deer. They were able to score a buck of their own the next morning. They hung it up beside the doe from the previous day. Following their hunting adventures, the animals were ferried across to the mainland and loaded onto the front fenders of the jeep for the return trip home. Junior was able to hang them in his shed for a couple of days to allow the meat to cure, then he and Bill skinned and quartered them and took them to a butcher to be cut and wrapped. All four hunters shared the cost of packaging the meat, Hank's part of which he was quite pleased to make room for, in his freezer in the basement.

Hank had two or three more trips to the camp that year but the next spring when George went in to Lake John alone, all he could see was ashes where the camp had once stood. The plywood boat he and Hank had built was still overturned, with a huge boulder dropped through the bottom in two places. The outboard motor was gone. When he brought the message back to Junior, Bill and Hank they all wracked their brains to try and come up with suspect(s), but they could only conclude perhaps a snowmobiler with an ' axe to grind' with one of them. But unless they got a tip from someone, considering the isolated location of the camp, the case remained unsolved. Hank learned after he was transferred out of Shelburne, that the other three had rebuilt the camp, but was also saddened to hear that Bill had died suddenly from a brain aneurism. Also, George had taken a job with another police force in P.E.I.

SAMMY SCOT

Sammy Scot was an ex-con who frequently terrorized his quiet little neighbourhood by telling people to their face, "You cross me, and you'll fry in your bed" or words to that effect, and most of them believed him. He had no car, to reinforce the threats, he walked the roads at all hours of the night, might appear anywhere without warning, adding to his overall mystery and cloak of fear. A few years earlier, he had been convicted of assault causing bodily harm, for leaving a neighbour man half dead on the side of the road. By the time Hank arrived in Shelburne, Sammy had done his time in Dorchester Penitentiary, and was now home with his young family in West Green Harbour. Hank's first encounter with him was when the small convenience store at the end of his road, was broken into overnight, and he was the prime suspect.

He had been questioned by the police many times before, and had a catalogue of evasive non-committing answers, plus whatever he had learned in the 'pen'. Hank called Cliff Follet, the Identification man from Yarmouth. He attended the scene later that day and found one fingerprint on a broken windowpane. Cliff retained the print in case a suspect was arrested sometime later.

During Hank's second full year in Shelburne, due to a variety of circumstances, he was unable to take any annual leave, so the following year he applied for and received six week's vacation. Hank and Mary Ann and three sons travelled by train to Alberta to visit his good friend, and fellow member "Spud" Mac Donald and his family. They later toured parts of Alberta, B.C. and Northwestern U.S. Meanwhile Halifax R.C.M.P. headquarters had temporarily transferred Cst. Gregory, who had five or more year's service, from Liverpool to Shelburne, to be in charge and to assist Cst. Simmonds, while Hank was away. Shortly before Hank departed, a charge of assault had been laid by a Lockeport fisherman against Scot.

Hank and Simmonds had tried unsuccessfully, to serve a summons for Scot to appear in court, so the Magistrate had issued a warrant for his arrest. The first week Hank was away, Gregory and Simmonds executed the warrant on Scot at his home, arrested him and momentarily left him unattended in the back seat of the four door, no-cage, police car. Scot escaped into the woods and was gone. Halifax headquarters immediately transferred Gregory back to Liverpool, and replaced him with Cst. Dennis Sutton, who did a great job 'holding the fort' until Hank returned. During this same time, Shelburne detachment was upgraded from two men to three and Sutton, to Hank's pleasant surprise, was made the permanent senior man. Sutton and Simmonds tried unsuccessfully to arrest Scot before Hank got back, so this was a number one priority when Hank returned.

Three Cell Flashlight

Due to the isolated location of Scot's house, surrounded by woods and not visible from another permanent residence, Hank decided on a middle-of-the-night raid with three other members of the Force. The plan was to quietly park the police car down the road, out of sight of the Scot house, walk to the small two storey house and surround it. Cst. Sutton, with his loud voice would knock on the front door and identify the police, Hank would cover the back door, and the other two would watch the ends of the house. When Sutton announced their presence, for at least a minute there was quiet. Then without warning, Scot jumped out the upstairs window to Hank's left, hit the ground running into the nearby woods, with Cst. Youden in hot pursuit and Hank not far behind, both with three-cell flashlights ablaze. In the dark, Youden tripped on a tree root and fell, Hank jumped over him, overtook the barefoot Scot in a short distance, tackled him and knocked him to the ground.

By the time the others arrived, Hank had Scot face down in the woods, straddling his back with one handcuff on and reaching for the other arm. Cst. Sutton nudged Hank away with a "Let me have him Corp." and dragged Scot kicking and squealing out of the woods, calling the officers every rotten, filthy name he could lay his tongue on. All four walked him down the road by the light of their flashlights put him in the middle of the back seat between Sutton and Youden, and Hank drove back to town. They had to arouse jailer Grant to open a cell, into which Sutton gladly deposited Scot, and returned Hank's handcuffs to him. The next week when Magistrate Rand came to town, Scot appeared before him, and was sentenced to two months in the county jail for escaping custody.

It was autumn, after Scot was released from jail, the moon was almost full, when he and his teenage son decided to' borrow' a neighbour's dory late at night, rowed across the harbour to a sandbar, to shoot ducks as they flew low over the bar. The next morning, the neighbour called to say he had found the Scot son's wallet in the dory, where it had probably fallen out of his pants pocket' while he sat on the seat. Hank retrieved the wallet with the boy's I.D. in it, and visited the Scot home alone where he found father, son, mother and three smaller children. Scot refused to let Hank interrogate the boy without him present (Jailhouse Lawyer), and launched into a tirade saying "Yes yer damn right that we was us, just tryin to get somethin for the family to eat. What's wrong with that? And what else do ya think the good lord put them ducks in the sky for? What?...(no chance for Hank to answer) I suppose you think it was for fat bastards like you, to stand there and look up at them go by and say "My aren't they purtey!!"

Hank was so amused at this hardened criminal standing up for his son and family that he smiled, returned the wallet to the boy, leaned over and whispered to him "Next time, let dad go alone, or leave the wallet home." Smiles all around as Hank walked out to the police car and drove back to the owner of the dory, who didn't want the matter, pursued any further.

This was not the last for Scot to be heard from by the police. The next spring when the snow was still on the ground, but the frost was mostly out, and some dirt roads were impassable by car. Hank got a call from a neighbour on the other side of Green Harbour one night that the vacant Mundy summer home was ablaze. He had also called the Lockeport Fire Department who dispatched a truck, but the last half mile of dirt road to the Mundy place was impassable. Hank decided not to attend the scene at night, called the Identification man in Yarmouth, Cliff Follett, who agreed to accompany Hank to the scene first thing in the morning. Cliff and Hank drove to the end of the pavement, parked the police car, put their rubber overshoes on and walked the last half mile to the site of the fire. All that was left of the large two-storey farm home was the chimney, a few smoldering embers in the basement, with remnants of appliances and plumbing equipment.

On their return to the car, both Cliff and Hank noted intermittent footprints of a common knee- high rubber boot, on the sides of the road going in both directions. Cliff took photographs of several footprints, but they lacked detail. Both suspected Sammy Scot who lived on a side road, less than a mile away. While in the area, they decided to check if he was home. To their surprise, he was home and invited them in. While they were standing inside the front door talking to Scot, both scanned the kitchen for any trace of similar boots. On a whim, Hank lifted the cover of the ringer-washer beside him, and there standing, surrounded by dirty clothes, were two rubber boots which Hank pulled out, turned over to reveal similar treads as those in the mud, on the road to Mrs. Mundy's house. Cliff glanced at the treads with recent traces of mud, and nodded silent agreement. Hank held the boots out towards Scot and asked, "Who owns these boots?"

Three Cell Flashlight

"Never seen them before in my life" was the instant response, and his wife quickly agreed. Hank knew he didn't have a warrant to search the place or seize anything, so he excused himself and Cliff to huddle outside. They both agreed Scot wasn't about to give a confession, and by the time they returned with a warrant, the boots would be long gone. They had also agreed earlier, while walking back to the car, that a plaster cast of one of the footprints on the road, would be impossible. So Hank stuck his head in the door, and before he could say anything Scot grinned and said "Better luck next time." Both officers knew in their minds they had found 'who done it' but wished they had taken a different approach.

Less than a year later Scot's wife Linda was fingerprinted, and Cliff positively identified her as being present during the break in at the convenience store near their home, four or five years previous. Hank took that report to Crown Prosecutor White, who considered the limitation of action, the lengthy exposure the mother of small children had had to the authorities, and recommended Hank not pursue it any further. Hank agreed.

LITTLE SISTER OVERBOARD

One morning around 9:00 AM in the early spring of Hank's third year in Shelburne he received a call from the Hopkins family in Birchtown that their youngest daughter Barbie had followed the two older children out to meet the school bus. As the children walked along the old road, they crossed a bridge with no railing, and while waiting for the bus, started throwing small stones into the rushing water of the brook fed by a spring freshet.

While imitating the older children, Barbie had gone too close to the edge, lost her balance, fell off the bridge into the water, and was washed away in an instant. The older children ran back home to tell their mother. When Hank arrived at the Hopkins home a short time later, the oldest boy Duncan, a ten year old with tears in his eyes, at his mother's request, went with Hank to the bridge a short distance away and demonstrated where and how his little sister had fallen in. He spoke of how Barbie had tagged along some days to say goodbye, while he and his sister Stella waited for the bus. Hank sensed that the boy more or less blamed himself, being the big brother and all, should have known better, and tried unsuccessfully to console him. He told Hank that Barbie had made only a small cry as she fell face first into the water and was gone. She was wearing long pants, rubber boots, a pink bonnet and a rose colored jacket.

Because of the accident, Duncan and his sister had been excused from school to stay home and keep their grieving mother company. Their father Harold worked in the quarry at Dauphnie Granite Works just up the road. Hank had watched him and his young team of oxen competing in the 'Ox Pull' at the Shelburne Exhibition the previous September. Harold had raised the oxen and trained them to pull heavy loads by hauling large boulders of granite, on the overturned engine hood of an old car, around a pasture field on his farm. The team had won first prize in their division, and received a blue ribbon which Harold, a short but rugged man, proudly displayed on the kitchen wall.

Hank returned to town, contacted fire chief Ken Morton, who rounded up several volunteer firemen, with dories or small boats, to commence a search of the eight mile river that the brook emptied into before it reached the ocean. Hank also called headquarters in Halifax and requested the police boat Adversus, with Captain Bill Vance to search the river mouth for the missing little girl. For the next two days, Hank and others took turns plying up and down the small river, without success. When fire chief Morton consulted Hank on behalf of the volunteers who had to go back to work Hank reluctantly called off the search. By the middle of the third day, Hank received a call from Cpl. Vic Werbicki of Barrington Passage detachment, some forty miles to the west, that a deep sea fisherman Clayton Swim from Cape Sable Island, had found the body of what he believed to be that of the missing little girl, floating on a calm sea amongst his lobster buoys, almost thirty miles out into the Atlantic. She had apparently been kept afloat by a bubble of air, trapped inside the back of her jacket when she fell into the water. Captain Swim estimated with the wind and the tides she would have travelled over fifty miles.

She had been first noticed by his crew, because the color of her jacket didn't match any of the lobster buoys around her. In the distance, at first they wondered if another fisherman might be poaching in their territory.

Hank drove out to the Hopkins home in Birchtown with the good news that Barbie's body had likely been found, and a brief description of where and by whom. They were overjoyed, but didn't know what to do next, because they weren't aware of where to go, and they didn't have a car or the money to hire one. Hank could sense their bewilderment, and offered to drive the fifty some miles to Cape Sable Island to retrieve the body. As he drove along the highway alone, he had time to reflect on the past three days, the terrible loss to the Hopkins family, their grief and resignation that they might never see their little girl again. The devoted efforts of the volunteers in the search party, and their reluctance to abandon the search without finding her were encouraging. Like the others, Hank could not avoid thinking that this could have been one of his three adventurous young sons. Now, in steep contrast for everyone and almost magical, the lost had been found, and through Captain Swim and Hank, she would be returned to the home she had left three short days ago. With the cooperation of members at Barrington Passage detachment and the citizens of Cape Sable Island, by early afternoon Hank located the Swim residence and the man who had found her. There on a work bench in his boathouse, wrapped in a baby blanket, was the body of the missing little girl. After a brief discussion on the odds on anyone finding a body floating that far out in the Atlantic Ocean, they concluded the Gods must have been smiling on Captain Swim and his helper to find her so far from home.

On behalf of the family Hank gave Captain Swim a hearty handshake for his kindness, bundled the little girl's body into his arms, and while Swim held the police car door open, laid her gently onto the back seat. It was late in the afternoon when Hank arrived at the Hopkins home. Tears of gratitude flowed like a river from both sides, as Hank handed the mother the body of their little girl. They explained they couldn't afford a regular funeral, so had made plans with neighbours and the local clergy for a funeral and burial in the community cemetery.

By now, Hank was almost cross-eyed with fatigue, but he stopped in at the old school yard, which they had set up as a temporary search headquarters. He spotted Chief Mitchell's aluminum boat and five horsepower motor inside, sitting on his trailer. To save someone else a trip out to get it, Hank remembered his police car had a trailer hitch on the back, so swung around and backed up to the trailer. It had no crash chains and Hank had never used the hitch before, but he did the best he could to hook it up and started slowly back to town four miles away.

Hank drove slowly, kept a close eye on the rear view mirrors, and was doing fine until he topped the last hill into town. There was a dip in the pavement and as the rear of the car crossed it, the pole of the trailer disconnected from the hitch. To Hank's amazement, the trailer proceeded to pass his car on the left, Hank thanked God there was no oncoming traffic, pulled over and stopped on the right shoulder. Glancing to his left, to his horror the trailer was now entering the left hand ditch headed for a bungalow, but just then the pole of the trailer dug into the side of the ditch, the trailer and boat did a graceful pirouette and landed upside down on the front lawn of a bungalow. As an embarrassed but thankful Hank walked across the road, and through the ditch, the lady of the house came out the front door, asked Hank if he was okay, and she said "Don't worry about the boat, it will be okay there until tomorrow." Hank was tempted to hug her but thanked her profusely instead, went back to his car and drove home. Chief Aulenback and a friend with a truck and the proper hitch retrieved the undamaged boat, motor and trailer the next day. Chief Mitchell was pleased to have his boat, motor and trailer returned to him unscathed.

BANGEY'S LEDGE

In the late fall or early winter of Hank's last year in Shelburne, he bought a used double barrel twelve-guage Steven's Savage shotgun, for seventy dollars from Les Morash, Ed Turner's sidekick at the Department of Lands and Forests. On a raw winter morning two weeks later, Hank had a chance to try out his new shotgun, when Ed and his seasoned black lab 'Scout' led the trio in hip waders, at low tide, through deep mud out to Bangey's Ledge, one of Ed's favourite goose hunting spots on the Atlantic Coast. The Ledge turned out to be a wedge-shaped island that jutted out of the water, at low tide a hundred yards from shore, in a small unnamed cove off the Atlantic Ocean. Hank was tempted to quit half-way out, with the shotgun raised above his head, when he was reminded of punishment drills in training, with .303 Army rifles, but didn't say a word, for fear of the teasing he'd get from the other two. On the ocean side, the Ledge rose gradually twenty some feet above the mud, with a sheer cliff on the front side facing the ocean. The top was grass covered, now receiving large flakes of snow, making the grass wet when it came time for the hunters to settle in, prostrate, so as to not alert the low flying geese, when they arrived. At low tide some geese would fly around the ledge, and some would elevate just enough to clear it, as Ed described, "So low you could knock them out of the sky with a broom." He added the warning, "But we don't stay out here til the tide starts comin in."

From the time they arrived at the cove, they could hear geese calling back and forth on the water and in the sky, as the trio gained the top of the ledge; they became clearly visible to the geese in the air. During the first twenty minutes, as the men prepared themselves, either kneeling or lying on the ground several yards apart, with Les and Hank facing the ocean and Ed facing the shore, two small flocks flew by, out of shotgun range to the South. Within the hour, a large flock of geese approached from the ocean, flying into the wind at eye level towards the Ledge. As they drew near, too late the lead gander flared up over the ledge, with the three hunters now standing ready and waiting to open fire. They struck four geese, one was able to keep going and fell into the trees on shore. Another crashed into the mud behind the Ledge. The men were later able to retrieve it on the way back to shore. Two geese veered off to the North, and landed dead in the water, fifty or sixty yards in front of the Ledge. They no sooner hit the water when Scout, without a command, jumped the twenty feet off the front of the ledge into the water, and headed for the nearest goose. The white caps on the surface concealed the dog's head, as he got behind the goose and steered it towards the shore side of the ledge. He dropped the first goose at the base of the ledge, and swam back out to retrieve the other one.

By this time, the men were starting to pack up and head for shore, as the next tide was on its way in, and no one wanted to be wading through mud half way up to their knees, and water too. Les and Hank each picked up a goose that Scout had retrieved, giving Scout a pat on the head for a job well done. Enroute, Ed picked up the one that fell into the mud, and a brief search of the woods on shore, failed to find the goose that probably hid in some brush or low ferns. The trio remarked they hoped it was fit to fly, before a four-legged predator came calling. Back at Ed's home, Hank gave his goose to Ed to pluck, clean and freeze, so he could donate it to a needy neighbour for Christmas. After a hot cup of tea, thanks to Ed's wife Edith, and reflections on their successful hunt, Les and Hank departed to their respective homes.

SAILOR B.J.

In the fifties and sixties, most small towns and villages in the Maritimes had a garage or service station where young men with wheels would gather to "talk car." Shelburne was no exception. Some of them were local and some were stationed at the naval base at the mouth of the harbour, 'Canadian Forces Base' Shelburne. In Hank's time there the most notorious driver of all was known by "B.J." He was a handsome young sailor, driving a nearly new Dodge Charger, 'loaded'.

The talk of some young ladies about town was also the subject of several complaints of erratic driving, from citizens both in town and along the Sandy Point Road leading to the base. Try as they might, neither the Town Police, or the R.C.M.P. managed to 'catch him in the act.' Sooner or later the talk at Ferretti's garage of horsepower, driving skills and speed would lead to a challenge between two combatants. Their favourite spot, a 'straight stretch' of highway number three, west of town named the Birchtown Strip. It was a straight piece of uninhabited highway surrounded by boulders, approximately a mile in length, designed for two-way traffic only, which ended in a sharp right hand curve at the East end.

One evening in late fall, just before dusk, at Ferretti's, Gordie Rayfuse a local boy with a souped-up Chevy Camaro challenged B.J. to a race on the Strip and offered to take his buddy Mickey Deschamp as combined lookout and flagman. When no other traffic appeared on the 'Strip', the two cars lined up side by side at the West end, Mickey dropped the flag, two cars took off with tires squealing, rear ends Zigzagging and smoke flying. Later it was reported that the two vehicles changed the lead at least once during the race, and Gordie was in the lead heading for the curve. Too late B.J. tried to overtake him on the left, lost control on the curve and went straight into the roadside of small trees and big boulders. The Charger struck the first boulder with such force that it popped the engine clear out of the car, leaving the engine lying in its wake, while the car became airborne. It spiraled and twisted sideways, before coming down into consecutive rolls, finally coming to rest on its top in some bushes, over two hundred yards from where it left the highway. B.J. was ejected somewhere in flight and left lying on his back unconscious,

Three Cell Flashlight

on a clear patch of ground. The Camaro made the curve and disappeared into town. No one seemed to know where Mickey went.

Hank took the call while visiting Chief Aulenback at the town police office, and both rushed out to the scene as fresh snow began to fall. Not one spectator, if there was any, was present when the police arrived, just B.J. lying there on his back, alone and unconscious, still breathing, wearing only a T-shirt, pants, and no shoes, in nearly freezing temperatures. He had no outward signs of injury. After a couple of uncomplimentary remarks about the victim, were exchanged between the two officers with no witnesses, Hank removed his storm coat and spread it over B.J., tucking the collar up under his chin. Before long the ambulance arrived, B.J. was quickly loaded onto a stretcher and taken to the hospital at the other end of town, where he survived but didn't regain consciousness. Billy Keeping, came with the tow truck from Huskilsons, and George and Hank helped with their three-cell flashlights picking up the scattered pieces of the car. The only recognizable piece, was the rear view mirror with adjustment cable dangling from the driver's side, but still intact. The Naval Base was notified, and set about arranging transport of the casualty to the Victoria General Hospital in Halifax.

At the Roseway Hospital the following afternoon, Dr. Jeffery and staff were doing everything possible to keep the unconscious B.J. comfortable, while the Navy personnel were making arrangements to have a 'Sea King' rescue helicopter make the two-hour flight to Shelburne, to retrieve their injured sailor. Mary Ann was the nurse in charge helping to prepare the patient for the trip, while Hank was patiently waiting for word of the arrival time of the helicopter. He had already given the Navy the location of the hospital, and the surrounding area suitable for the helicopter to safely land, without trees or overhanging wires. By the time Hank was notified of the arrival time of the helicopter, an early winter storm was brewing. When the helicopter came into view, darkness had settled in, and the wind had picked up considerably. The pilot had asked for all the light that could possibly be provided, at the temporary landing pad, and someone to guide him in. Hank had already recruited Chief Aulenback with his police car, with its lights flashing and headlights on high beam, facing from one side of the landing area, and Hank positioned his police car facing from the opposite side, with the same equipment engaged. When the helicopter came into view with its powerful headlight, in spite of the blowing snow, the area was lit up just like the daytime.

In the middle, waving two three-cell flashlights, complete with red wands, over his head, was Hank walking backwards, guiding the aircraft to a safe landing. It was just like he had watched the ground crews guide a passenger aircraft in to a commercial airport.

In a matter of minutes, the hospital staff wheeled B.J. on a stretcher, out into the blowing snow, and helped to load him onto the aircraft, which closed the doors, fired up the idling engines, lifted off and disappeared into the night. With sighs of relief, George and Hank high-fived each other, and did likewise with the hospital staff who invited them in out of the storm to have a coffee and cookies. Days later the Commander of the Shelburne Navy Base notified Hank that B.J. had regained consciousness and was scheduled to return to active duty at another base, hopefully to drive a car again, a bit wiser due to his near-death experience.

BIRCHTOWN SHOOTING

When Shelburne was founded by the United Empire Loyalists in the 1770's, some of them brought their slaves with them from the U.S.A. Years later when the slaves were freed, some of them moved four or five miles West of town along highway number three and settled in the small rural community of Birchtown.

There, some men developed small farms, some worked in the woods cutting lumber, pulp and timber, and some worked in the Dauphinee marble quarry nearby. By the time Hank arrived in Shelburne, their community was well established, known to the Police as a group of law-abiding citizens, who could take care of themselves. One of the patriarchs, a descendant from the slaves, was a tall, stately 80-year-old black man named Otis Jackson. He lived with his daughter Matilda and her teenage daughter Amanda.

One summer evening, during Hank's last few weeks in Shelburne, Cst. Sutton received a call from Jackson, advising that he had just shot a young white man from Birchtown, who was drunk and pursuing his granddaughter, in spite of her objections. Csts Sutton and Carter responded directly, and found the suitor whom they knew, Danny Guthro, lying dead on the ground at the highway end of the Jackson driveway, with a fresh bullet hole through his neck. Cst. Sutton had called the ambulance before proceeding to the Jackson house, where Jackson was standing outside, and readily admitted that he had shot Guthro after he had ordered him off his property, for assaulting and threatening his granddaughter. Guthro had walked down to the end of the driveway onto the highway, and stood there calling Jackson "every foul, racist name he could lay his tongue on". Finally Jackson had enough, went into the back porch of his house, loaded a round of ball shot into his forty caliber buffalo rifle with a hexagon barrel, came out, rested the rifle on top of a fence post, took aim at Guthro and shot him.

In spite of protests from the daughter and granddaughter, the constables arrested Jackson, walked him down to the police car, and brought him and his rifle to the detachment office. Hank assisted in taking a statement from Jackson, and explained to him that he would have to be charged, and spend the night in jail before appearing before the Justice of the Peace to arrange bail. Jailer Fred Power and his wife knew Mr. Jackson, were compassionate, and assured him they would take good care of him during his stay.

Consultation with Crown Prosecutor White the next day resulted in a charge of second-degree murder, to remain in jail awaiting bail hearing before Magistrate Rand the next week. No neighbours had witnessed the shooting, but the consensus was that Jackson had done the community a service, as this wasn't the first confrontation Guthro had with the black citizens of Birchtown, due to his penchant to become obnoxious when drunk. A neighbour of Guthro notified his family who arranged with the funeral home in Shelburne to retrieve the body.

Jackson was released on his own recognizance awaiting trial, where he plead guilty to the charge of second degree murder, and was sentenced to two years less one day in the County Jail, to avoid time in the Penitentiary. By now, Hank had been transferred to New Glasgow and did not have to return to testify at the trial.

NEW GLASGOW

MOVING TO NEW GLASGOW

Each of the last two years in Shelburne, Hank had a staffing interview with Staffing Officer Insp. Rammage. When the transfer topic came up, Hank asked for a transfer to a larger detachment anywhere in mainland Nova Scotia, where he could learn from a senior N.C.O. how to operate a larger operation. The Inspector ultimately recommended a transfer to New Glasgow, one of the largest detachments in Truro Sub-Division. By that time Mary Ann was pregnant with their fourth child, due in mid-August. With the confirmed transfer, the couple travelled to New Glasgow in the spring on a house-hunting trip. There they met 'Little Henry' McNeil, a real estate agent who toured them around the area, stopping in a small, new sub-division of three-bedroom bungalows. As they stepped from the car Mary Ann remarked "Ooooh, what's that awful smell?" Indicating the direction of the wind from the nearly new pulp mill. Henry replied "My dear, around here we've learned to call that 'the sweet smell of success." Everyone chuckled. The couple chose one of the not-yet finished bungalows, and returned to Shelburne.

When the transfer date of July 31st.was confirmed weeks later, Hank realized that was only a week before Mary's Ann's scheduled Caesarean Section. He was tempted to ask for a later date to allow for the delivery in the Shelburne hospital, where it was already arranged with Dr. Marcus, in whom Mary Ann had great trust, but Hank didn't ask. They had both been pleased with New Glasgow as a destination, because it was much closer to both Mary Ann's and Hank's aging parents, and the unborn child was to be an addition to Mary Ann's parent's first grandchildren. They discussed this dilemma long and hard before staying with the transfer, rather than risk the wrath of the powers that be in Halifax. In hindsight this was mistake, which was vividly obvious in the weeks that followed. Hank, Mary Ann and family completed the five and one half hour transfer by private car, got partially settled in their new home and Hank's job, arranged for their three sons to go to Mary Ann's parent's home in Cape Breton for a week or more, and returned the next week to Shelburne.

In that time Hank learned after he arrived at New Glasgow detachment, that the previous N.C.O. in charge had already transferred out, AND his replacement had not yet arrived. So Hank was by default, temporarily in charge with no remuneration. Talk about stress!! The only saving grace was the lone plain clothes man, Cpl. Tom Barlow, who was a friend of Hank's from Sydney, and who had been at New Glasgow detachment two years before Hank's arrival. Tom was also well-acquainted with the area and the twenty-one other members stationed there. He and Hank had several brief, private meetings, some of which were attended by Cpl. Ed Byrne, in charge of the four-man Highway Patrol, to plan some interim strategy, until the next unknown Sgt.- in- charge arrived.

New Glasgow detachment area encompassed all of Pictou County except for five towns, all within a fifteen-mile radius of each other. Four towns had their own police force of different size and capability. The other town Pictou was, by contract, policed by a five-man R.C.M.P. team, with a Sgt. in charge. They were close-by in the event New Glasgow needed assistance in an emergency, as were members of New Glasgow detachment available to Pictou detachment, if needed. Hank soon learned that a major problem was, some of the Independent police forces, did not share their information on activities of local criminals with the R.C.M.P., or with the other three Town Forces. In other words, a paradise for criminals.

AT NEW GLASGOW

At the end of Hank's first whirl-wind week in his new posting it was time to drive Mary Ann the five hour trip back to Shelburne for the birth of their fourth son. After Mary Ann got settled in the hospital, Hank stayed overnight as a welcome guest of Glenna and Mac Oxner next-door neighbours for his four years in Shelburne. Next morning Hank visited the hospital, waited until their new son was born, spent a couple of hours with mother and son and headed back to work the next day in New Glasgow. He had agreed to allow a few days for Mary Ann to heal before he returned to Shelburne to bring mother and son to his new home. That week Tom, Ed and Hank, all graduates of the R.C.M.P six week in-service Advanced Training Course, planned and held a meeting of all available personnel upstairs in the recreation room of the detachment. With no agenda but to allow the men to discuss concerns and offer solutions, to speak their minds. This was to be Hank's first and largest meeting he had chaired in fourteen years of service. The meeting seemed to clear the air and set a precedent for when the Sergeant in charge arrived should he wish to follow suit.

In a few weeks Sgt. Ron Pettit arrived from Halifax, barely got his feet wet when Insp. Walling O.C. Truro Sub-Division chose him to go to Canso, Guysborough County in charge of a team of members policing a Fisherman's Strike.

Guess who returned to Temporary in charge of New Glasgow? Once again it was Hank at the helm. By now Mary Ann's sister had returned their three other sons from the grandparents home and Mary Ann and Hank had their family intact again. At work, it was business as usual for Hank, five and a half days a week including his first experience with shift work, two eight hour shifts covering the detachment area from 8:00 AM to 12:00 AM the following day. Trying to massage a schedule to suit everyone's needs given sick days, court days, training courses, days off, annual leave and other surprises was a challenge indeed. When Sgt. Pettit arrived back four weeks later he told Tom and Hank he was pleased with what he found commenting in jest "That's just great, you guys know more about running this place than I do." In the weeks that followed Tom and Hank never said it, but concluded perhaps that was the case. It didn't much matter because in less than a year Sgt. Pettit was commissioned and transferred out.

Tom and Hank were pleased with Sgt. Pettit's replacement; Sgt. Avery Stairs from Sydney Sub-Division who they both knew well and respected his knowledge and experience. In fact a few years earlier when he was still single Hank had relieved at his detachment in St. Peters while Avery and his family went on annual vacation. Avery was laid back, easy-going and with a few exceptions was inclined to let Tom, Ed and Hank continue as they had before he arrived. The following summer Tom, Ed and Avery were still at New Glasgow detachment when Hank transferred in to Halifax as a C.I.B. reader, reading report from the field, and if necessary writing replies for the C.I.B. Officer's signature, in other words driving a desk. Although it was Hank's first tour out of the field, it became a welcome change once he adjusted to the routine, including new friends, weekends and Statutory holidays off and a lot more civilized time with his young family.

During his service on Cape Breton Island Hank had worked on three separate Mi'kmaq Reserves none of which had a population of a hundred residents. The reserve at Governor's landing in Pictou County on the Northumberland Strait twenty some miles from town had a population of two hundred or more. The driver of the police car responding to a call from the reserve, of which there were many, was obliged to navigate through the towns of New Glasgow and Trenton needed almost thirty minutes to arrive there safely.

Unlike Hank's experience of earlier years, he found the people on this reserve had learned all about their human rights and most were prepared to challenge the police on their issue of choice. In addition, the officers would find upon arrival sometimes the nature of and the origin of the call could not clearly be determined which led to the conclusion that the call was false, only a waste of their time. Some officers suspected such calls were simply entertainment to relieve the boredom or a set-up to see how a young officer might react in certain circumstances, or both. Should the false call lead to an arrest or two then that was icing on the cake and a source of a later complaint of harassment, discrimination, even police brutality.

Adjacent to the reserve along the shore of the strait to the east were private summer cottages owned by town residents most of which were vacant fall, winter and spring and not visible from an occupied residence. Some cottages had liquor left over from the summer. A young Mi'kmaq lad and his lady companion seeking privacy with refreshment, need only walk or ride a skidoo, undetected, less than a mile even in inclement weather day or night, break a window pane, turn an inside door knob or window latch and enter. Once inside, especially if the electric power was still connected, turn up the heat, spend an hour or two, even stay overnight, then close the door and leave. The Break and Enter might not be reported or even noticed until the owner arrived to open-up in late spring or early summer. Perhaps a good neighbour or passer-by discovered the break and called the owner. Some owners might not bother to call the police and charge it up to location.

When an owner did call the police and arranged to meet at the scene, both might suspect a visitor from the reserve, but it could have been a lost or nosey hunter, someone on a skidoo or someone walking along the shore on the ice. Either way, the investigating officer would have very little tangible evidence to go on.

On the other side of the reserve, nestled in the trees at least two hundred yards from the harbour and more than two hundred feet from the highway stood the Pictou County Yacht Club with full bar year round. It too was not visible from an occupied residence, easily accessible from the highway on foot and only a five minute walk through the woods from the back of the reserve. Hank knew first-hand because he investigated one of the break-ins his first spring in New Glasgow, searched the perimeter for footprints, tire tracks or other outside evidence, and walked the footpath through the woods to the reserve. He did not see anyone outside the nearby homes and chose not to visit one in case the resident would take offence and claim discrimination. Captain Brian Perry reported only three or four part bottles of liquor stolen from behind the bar and no damage other than the back door point of entry. Hank strongly recommended they cease keeping liquor on the premises when vacant, AND make that fact known in the community and on the reserve.

During Hank's first winter in New Glasgow, after the first heavy snowfall one Saturday morning, a call came in from Joe Butler at the department of highways garage. He sounded excited because a fight was breaking out between several of last winter's snowplough operators and this year's operators appointed by the recently- elected government.

"Somebody better do something about this or we're gonna have a riot on our hands" he warned. 'Gentle' George Batt and Hank were the only members available, so they proceeded to the highway garage three or four miles east of town. Mr. Butler, one of last year's operators, one of forty men assembled pointed out Harvey Matheson the new Superintendent of Highways for that region. He seemed bewildered, not really prepared to deal with this situation and thanked the officers for their prompt attention. The presence of the police seemed to quell the notion of fisticuffs. Perhaps 'Gentle' George's reputation preceded him. He knew some of the men present and firmly asked them to 'stand down' until they and the superintendent could iron things out. One of the seasoned operators quoted the new Premier saying publically "There would be no indiscriminate firing of government employees."

Reluctant to make a decision, the superintendent called the head office in Halifax only to find his boss was away for the weekend and the supervisor there had less experience than he did. But the supervisor did offer to call the Minister of Highways at home.

Until now, Hank's exposure to Government Ministers was slim to none but sure enough when Minister Smith called, Morrison handed the phone to Hank. The Minister first thanked Hank for their attendance, empathized with them and offered to contact his senior deputy and friend in Truro forty some miles away. He would instruct his deputy to attend on his behalf, ask the new operators to be patient until head office in Halifax could resolve the problem early next week. Meanwhile in the interest of safety, allow the seasoned operators to proceed and clear the highways of this snowfall. The Minister also asked that Cst. Batt and Hank remain at the scene until his deputy arrived, during which time they circulated amongst the new operators pointing out the advantages to a peaceful settlement versus continuing the dispute and someone getting hurt.

HANK HOWARD

As complicated as some things seemed to be during and after Hank's transfer to New Glasgow, the brightest spot of all were the next-door neighbours to the South, Hank and Rose Howard and their family. They had three boys and one girl, some still at home, some grown up and gone. (For this chapter, the new Hank will be known as Hank H and the old one Hank J.) Hank H, the semi-retired woodsman from the paper mill in Abercrombie on the outskirts of town and his wife Rose simply could not do enough for the new couple next door with three small boys and a baby.

When the baby became old enough, their teenage daughter Jan would baby sit for a short time to give Mary Ann a break if Hank J was on duty. Hank H was always there with the right tool if something in the new house needed fixing and Rose shared almost every item of home cooking with the new neighbours. The entire yard around the new house was not landscaped, so

Hank J undertook to grade and seed it by hand. But before he could attempt it he needed to build a twenty some foot long two foot high retaining wall on Hank H's side of the front lawn. Instantly Hank H offered to take him to an abandoned pit on Mt. Thom twenty-five miles away where he could get some natural flat stone to build the wall. One fall morning Hank J borrowed a used pick up from Harold Lockheed, salesman at the G.M. dealer in town, the two Hank's headed for Mt. Thom and loaded enough stone to build the wall. In the next few days, duties permitting, both Hanks completed the wall, and Hank J. was able to seed his lawn. That night, a 'monsoon' rain came and washed most of the new front lawn into the roadside ditch and some of the back lawn down over the embankment into another neighbour's back yard. Don was very understanding, saying, "Don't worry about it, that just filled in some of the holes in my yard." An ophthalmologist, he and his wife Georgie later became good friends of Mary Ann and Hank J visited back and forth and the children played together.

On their earlier house-hunting trip Hank J and Mary Ann bought that new, small three-bedroom bungalow, their first-ever home, in a small subdivision near the end of Kennedy Court. The builder J.R. MacDonald was new to the trade, carefree and inclined to take short-cuts. For example, both front and back doors were hollow-core bedroom doors modified by inserting three small panes of glass at eye level with no insulation. They were covered with two low-grade outside aluminum doors that barely repelled the rain let alone the howling winter winds. There was a wood-burning fireplace in the living room that proved to steal more heat from the baseboard hot water heaters than it generated. When first occupied the concrete foundation in the basement was so green it caused items stored there to absorb moisture and eventually turn moldy. Before winter, Hank bought a small cast iron radiator from a scrap dealer and Sonny's friend from work Donnie MacIsaac, a plumber, installed it. What a vast improvement in that basement including drying snow suits, mitts, boots and hockey gear. The whole experience turned out to be the epitome of buyers beware.

At the same time Hank J was getting to know his new neighbor, Hank H had a sixteen-foot clapboard, soon to-be-canvass-covered canoe under construction in his carport. If Hank H was working in his carport when Hank J was coming home from work, Hank J would stop by to chat and check on the progress of the project.

A native of Plaster Rock in northern New Brunswick Hank had worked in forestry all his adult life, loved the outdoors and even took up prospecting when he was fully retired. Eventually the canoe was completed, a definite work of art in Hank J's opinion. The second winter they were neighbours, the two Hanks, some members from New Glasgow detachment and some Rangers from the Lands and Forests department met in Hank H's living room to discuss a possible canoe trip down the Liscombe River in Guysborough County, fifty miles south and east of New Glasgow. Throughout the winter there were more meetings and the final count was eight would-be voyageurs, in four canoes committed to the trip. Then one fine spring morning the eight men and four canoes were dropped off at the head of the river, loaded up and set out on their three day, sixty-some mile trip. All had agreed earlier not to pack overland at portages, rather to leave the canoes in the water and walk beside them with one man on a short bow line and the other with a longer line at the stern.

The first day was uneventful with the two Hanks in Hank H's canoe third in line behind two canoes and one canoe following. Each canoe had two close friends of choice paddling and exchanging the lead as they went along. After a bonfire and mug-up on the bank beside a placid stretch of the river in mild temperatures before dark, all hands turned in early for a good night's sleep and were up, rearing to go the next morning. Tom and Billy re-kindled the fire, boiled some hot drinks, all agreed to munch sandwiches along the way and started out. The weather was clear and all was going well until they came upon a lengthy stretch of the roughest rapids they had seen so far.

The two Hanks disembarked as they had the day before, Hank H on the bow line and Hank J on the stern. Part way down the stretch, Hank J was not sure what happened whether he lost his balance, stumbled, and allowed the stern of the canoe to drift out from the bank a bit. In a 'flash' the fast moving water yanked the stern line from Hank's hands, grabbed the canoe, turned it broadside in the river and jammed it between two boulders, one near the shore in front of Hank H and one fourteen feet out. In an instant the river filled the canoe, cleared out everything not lashed down like sleeping bags, paddles and other belongings and sent them down the river where the front canoes had a shot at retrieving them. The canoe now became the precipice of a small waterfall where the river had a fierce grip on it, not about to let it go without a struggle. The two Hanks yelled out a number of expletives, not cognizant of what they were saying nor could they remember. The commotion alerted the two teams ahead who went ashore, tied up, hurried back while the crew behind gingerly caught up, secured their canoe and came down to help.

All six gathered round as a show of support and Tom Lowe said, "We can't leave her here, the river will rip her to pieces." One by one all eight waded into the water, some knee-deep above the canoe and some up to their waist below. They all soon learned the river was not going to give up its latest victim without a fight and there was nowhere or way to reroute the water at that location.

The relentless force of the water against the upside of the canoe and the weight of the water in the canoe was too much for eight men to consider a straight lift. Neither the bow nor stern of the canoe would come free of the boulder with four men lifting. Finally, Tom Lowe went ashore into the woods and a short time later came back with a six-foot pole three or four inches in diameter at the butt end and handed it to the men at the stern of the canoe to use as a pry. Hank H was with them and in spite of his caution to "go easy"; the first attempt cracked two of the wooden ribs. On the second try of the pole combined with manual lifting slowly the stern began to climb up the boulder to allow some water to pass under the canoe and to spill some out over the bow. Eventually the men below the canoe vacated their positions allowing the canoe to be completely tipped over, drained and pulled ashore. Close examination on shore by a relieved Hank H followed by a trial dip in the river with two or three men hanging on, revealed no leaks. After a brief break on shore by all including a snack, ringing water out of pants and socks, then putting them back on wet, the voyage resumed almost two hours after the mishap. The two Hanks breathed a sigh of relief when both paddles were returned by mates and the canoe was able to carry them onward in their journey. They each quietly shuddered at the alternative.

Below the rapids, Tom and Billy found Hank J's sleeping bag snagged in a deadfall, still rolled up and tied but soaked right through. Another crew picked up Hank H's knapsack in similar condition but intact. That night the weather was cool and damp and so were most of the travellers.

A short-lived bonfire was welcome but did little to dry all the wet clothes. The first crew chose a clear grassy area below a small waterfall. Someone offered Hank J a small metallic survival blanket, he tried to lay on the damp ground under it but couldn't sleep, so he stayed up all night finding dry wood, tending the fire and hanging wet clothes on nearby branches to dry. Early next morning the sun came up lifting the spirits of all combined with thoughts of going home that night to a soft, warm, dry bed. After an hour or so of paddling, the river slowed down and opened into a ten-mile-long lake. No more single file as the entourage spread out into the face of a strong southeast wind that met them head on, but they all persevered without anyone having to go ashore. After almost three hours, the lake emptied into the river again and those who had been wearing wet clothing joyfully realized that due to the effort required crossing the lake and the heat from the sun, their clothing was now dry.

As prearranged, at a landing near the mouth of the river two drivers waited, one with a van for most of the adventurers and the other with a truck to carry the canoes and maybe one or two friends of the driver. Thanks to those drivers all hands made it back home before dark with a boatload of fond memories, tired but happy and uninjured in spite of the struggle with the trapped canoe. The two broken ribs were replaced in Hank H's canoe before the next week was out.

MURDER IN EAST NEW GLASGOW

During Hank's last month in New Glasgow just as the R.C.M.P two-man night patrol was coming to an end a call came in from a motorist on the eastern outskirts of the town. He had stopped to gas up at the Petro Can 24-hour service station on his way to work and found the attendant sitting in a chair with a fatal gunshot wound to his torso. Constable Dale King phoned Hank at home and told him what they had found and said he'd send a car to pick Hank up and bring him to the scene. He would also call Cpl. Pat Dornan the Indent man in Truro and ask him to attend. Robbery appeared to be the motive. When Hank arrived, the body had been removed by the ambulance, but blood was spattered on the inside of the windows, the office showcase and pooled on the floor. Cst. King described the victim as a middle-aged man

Three Cell Flashlight

"just sitting there in the chair with his insides in his lap." He had checked the body for I.D. and found none, but was trying to reach the owner of the service station to determine who he was.

Constable King and his partner had guarded the gruesome scene since they arrived, now it was time for them to go home and get some rest. Hank summoned three other constables, one to continue finding the name of the victim and notify next of kin, and the other two to conduct enquiries door to door along the road on both sides in an easterly direction from the service station while Hank took the road leading back into town on foot. Not all homes were occupied at that time of the morning but at the seventh or eighth home Hank checked, a surprised middle-aged lady named Emma Dunphy answered the door. When Hank asked who else lived there she answered "My son Donnie is upstairs asleep, why is anything wrong?" Hank told her about the robbery at the service station and asked what time Donnie got home last night. "I'm not sure, I think it was late" she replied.

Hank asked her to wake the son up so he could talk to him meanwhile Hank sat on a kitchen chair and waited. When the son came down, he was half asleep and noticeably nervous.

Hank asked him where he was last night he said, "out with Kevin". Hank asked him for Kevin's last name and where he lived Donnie replied "MacPherson from Westville". When Donnie refused to answer a question about the time he got home last night Hank arrested him and took him to the detachment for further questioning by his friend Cpl. Tom Barlow. Meanwhile Hank assigned Cst. Egan to obtain a search warrant from the town magistrate for the Dunphy residence and Cst. Batt to go to the Town Police in Westville to help find MacPherson and bring him to the detachment for questioning.

When Batt returned with MacPherson, he placed him in a separate room alone to let him 'think' for a while, then went in and interrogated him about the robbery. Later Batt reported to Hank that MacPherson confessed he willingly went with Donnie to rob the service station and that Donnie took a shotgun along as a threat. During the robbery the attendant Dan Matheson balked at giving them anything even with the shotgun pointed at him. The argument became heated, Kevin begged Donnie "Don't Shoot!" but without warning Donnie pulled the trigger and "his guts spilled out into his lap." Cpl. Barlow fingerprinted Dunphy and Cpl. Dornan found a fingerprint on the cash register in the service station that matched Donnie's right middle finger. Hank and Egan executed the search warrant at the Dunphy residence and found Donnie's blood-spattered shoes under a pile of dirty clothes at the back of his bedroom closet.

Both Dunphy and MacPherson were charged with First Degree Murder and elected Trial by Magistrate. Both were convicted. Hank was included in the list of witnesses, but was never called to testify. Dunphy was sentenced to ten years in Penitentiary without parole and MacPherson was sentenced to two years less a day with conditions.

THE ART OF SERVICE

As Hank reflects on his 'service' to the R.C.M.P. throughout his career, he also recalls those people who provided good service to him and his family along the way. Be it his early days in Glace Bay when he would gas up a police car, have the oil changed or a tire repaired, there was a person, usually a man to do the job. For Hank who had an inherent fear of dentists, he received great service from a recommended dentist and his lovely female assistant who helped allay most of Hank's fears. In fact, Hank drove back to Glace Bay from Inverness the hundred plus miles at least once a year to get his teeth 'serviced'. In Inverness when Hank got to know the Service Station proprietors when they were often busy, Hank might pump the gas himself as a favour to a friend.

Dry Cleaning and Laundry Service came all the way from Antigonish once a week with a jovial lad everyone called 'Silver'. The same held true for Baddeck, service was alive and well, from the restaurants to the hotel, to the Post Office, to the Drug Store, to the County Jail, to the Hardware Store, to the Government Offices, to the Car Ferries (Hank held a pass to five of them around the Bras D'or Lakes) NO SELF-SERVE.

Three Cell Flashlight

In the City of Sydney wearing plain clothes, the service was still there from doctors, dentists, Service Stations, Furniture and Appliance Stores, Banks, Clothiers like Jack Yazer with a tailor named Eddie on the second floor, small Food Markets like Morrison's IGA on a residential street not far from where Hank and Mary Ann rented their first small bungalow. With the exception of the refrigerator, they got a deal on, they outfitted their new home with six hundred dollars worth of furniture from Bonnell's Furnishings on Charlotte Street. Up until then they used the Coin-a-matic Laundry, but when Mary Ann learned she was having twins, the young couple splurged and bought an automatic washing machine. By now Hank had befriended a lady banker who was born and raised in the same community as Mary Ann, recommended he take out a loan instead of paying cash and pay it off in monthly installments to establish a credit rating. Hank listened and silently thanked Ena many times ever since throughout his adult life for her service.

In Shelburne, for the N.C.O. in charge of the R.C.MP. detachment Hank and Mary Ann received service from people too numerous to mention in all walks of life. Of course, Mary Ann as a nurse in the local hospital had many opportunities to offer her excellent service in medical matters and Hank delivered his service, whether appreciated or not, to the citizens in his part of the County.

Examples of services received by Hank and Mary Ann included a large truck load of coal delivered for Hank to shovel into the furnace in their first winter there, later converted to oil. A food market that would receive a grocery order from Mary Ann by telephone, placed on tab until Hank came in to pay for it, delivered to the married quarters, in a cardboard box on the shoulder of Auxiliary policeman Ralph Buchanan and even placed in the refrigerator and cupboards if no one was home. A friend named Bob MacKay who worked in the liquor store, upon receipt of a coded message would deliver to the kitchen a dozen warm lager beer on his way home from work, collect the money and even stay and have one if he had time. And Freddie Farmer, a single, black man who lived alone would come and clean the office one morning a week for fifteen dollars paid by the men who worked there, and the married quarters for another ten dollars if he stayed and had supper, which he sometimes helped to cook, with Hank's family. How about that for service!! Mary Ann and Hank knew "knew they had it good."

NEW GLASGOW
TO HALIFAX

AFTER 17 YEARS IN THE FIELD HANK WAS TRANSFERRED TO HALIFAX ONTARIO THE FINAL CHAPTER

During Hanks service in the force, he had regular interviews with the Staffing Officer. In the later part of his second year in New Glasgow inspector Beaudrow advised due to his field experience he was – recommending Hank for a transfer to head quarters in Halifax. CIV – Criminal Investigation Branch, as a Reader. Hank and Mary-Anne didn't need a house-hunting trip, because Hank found out that corporal Dave Smith was transferring to New Glasgow and vacating a rented bungalow in Lower Sackville, which was just outside of Halifax.

Once there, Hank joined a car pool to Halifax five days a week and learned the ropes of his new job. Hanks boss Sargent Don Burges happened to be from PEI. Don and three others helped Hank get adjusted to his new position as CVI.

(Al Palmer, now Staff Sargent, with whom Hank for two weeks, wore his first plain clothes in Glace Bay, was working just down the hall.)

The great thing about this new job was, Hank now had a job that was five days per week, all weekends off, which meant more time for family. Before long Hank found that he personally knew thirty-seven out of forty-two detachment commanders in the Province. Sometimes if a routine case needed more investigating Hank could call the commanders to get the details for his report, because he knew them and it would be faster to have a conversation.

During the winter of early 1973, the centennial year of the RCMP, Hank was chosen to wear one of the period uniforms to commemorate this milestone. This uniform was identified by the Pith helmet. Corporal Stan

Ferguson assumed the role wearing the "pillbox" hat. Both men were expected to represent the force wearing these uniforms on special occasions, any where in Nova Scotia. On social events Mary-Anne and Stan's wife Beth, wore period gowns and hats and attended with their husbands. Stan and his wife had no children, while Mary-Anne and Hank were obliged to hire a babysitter for these special events.

These representations on behalf of the RCMP, where an honour that neither Stan, Hank nor their wives ever dreamed the would be a part of. The formal events have always been fondly remembered over the years.

During his time in CIV, Hank was qualified to be a Sargent, while his colleague Bergious was a bashful man, and he was very nervous about a promotion. While in Halifax Hank had the opportunity to attend two in service courses. One course was about people management and the other learning instructional techniques, enabling Hank to a teacher the junior RCMP. Both courses boasted Hanks confidence when he received an invitation to address any group, including a class of student lawyers, at Dalhousie University.

After two years in Halifax Hank was transferred to Ottawa, where he preformed the same job of reading crime reports. This time the reports were from all across Canada. Two years later, Hank transferred to the Commissioners Secretariat Planning Branch, where he was with a group of senior members called the Operational Audit Team. During those two years Hank visited seven out of ten provinces for a week to ten days at a time, working with other RCMP officers, learning and sharing in experiences of policing.

The fall promotions arrived, Staff Sargent was commissioned, and the shy Sargent Bergious inherited his rank. Hank received Don's Sargent Rank, and spent the rest of his year working as a Sargent for the RCMP.

At the end of twenty-four and a half years of service Hank was proud he had so many opportunities to service his country. It was now time for him to retire and move onto other endeavours. Hank and Mary-Ann now had four young sons and it was a perfect opportunity to transition into this new chapter with the family. His final move was to Ontario, relieved the worry of another transfer!

Printed in Canada